INSPIRE / PLAN / DISCOVER / EXPERIENCE

ENGLAND'S SOUTH COAST

DK EYEWITNESS

ENGLAND'S SOUTH COAST

CONTENTS

DISCOVER 6

EXPERIENCE 52

NEED TO KNOW 204

Left: Telephone box on a rainy day
Previous page: Beach huts in Kent
Front cover: St Agnes Head, Cornwall

DISCOVER

The city of Bath veiled in a hazy light

WELCOME TO
ENGLAND'S
SOUTH COAST

Towering, windswept cliffs and tranquil sandy bays. Iconic historic monuments and forward-thinking cities. Picture-perfect countryside and chocolate-box villages. Whatever your dream trip to England's south coast entails, this DK Eyewitness travel guide is the perfect companion.

1 Lounging on deck chairs at Brighton Beach.

2 The bright lights of London's Leicester Square.

3 Wandering through woodland in East Sussex.

4 The scenic cliffs of Dorset's Jurassic Coast.

Sitting pretty beside the sea and bursting with bucolic bliss, the south coast offers scenery and sun in abundance. From the chalky cliffs of Kent and wild crags of Cornwall to the fossil-filled beaches of Devon and golden shores of Dorset, this region has an epic coastline, and a patchwork of paths to explore it. Cocooned within are the pastoral pockets of Wiltshire, Hampshire, Somerset and Sussex, where welcoming villages are dotted across an unspoiled landscape of wild flowers and farmland. Locals still celebrate ancient traditions here and observe the rich history of the land – which is evident in the area's many ancient monuments and stately homes.

The cities of the south coast are just as enticing. London, the region's pulsing metropolis, has something for everyone: lively street markets lure foodies in, swathes of parkland please outdoor enthusiasts, and art aficionados are never short of galleries and pop-up events. Hot on the capital's heels, the quirky cultural hubs of Bristol and Brighton beckon with cutting-edge museums, alternative vintage shops and enviable culinary scenes; while history-laden Bath, Winchester and Exeter thrive as ancient treasure troves.

We've broken England's south coast down into easily navigable chapters, with detailed itineraries, expert local knowledge and colourful, comprehensive maps to help you plan the perfect trip. Whether you're here for a flying visit or a grand tour, this Eyewitness guide will ensure that you see the very best England's south coast has to offer.

REASONS TO LOVE
ENGLAND'S
SOUTH COAST

Spectacular sandy beaches, postcard-pretty villages, a foodie scene to savour and adventures around every corner - there are so many reasons to visit England's south coast. Here are some of our favourites.

1 SEASIDE FUN
The tangy aroma of vinegar-drenched chips, herring gulls screeching overhead and a walk along the prom, prom, prom – you simply can't beat a day beside the seaside.

A PINT IN THE PUB 2
Whether for a swift pint of Somerset cider, a sunny afternoon in a beer garden or a leisurely Sunday lunch, a visit to a pub is an essential part of any trip to the south coast.

3 ARTISTIC LEGACY
From Jane Austen to Daphne du Maurier, Barbara Hepworth to J M W Turner, authors and artists have long found inspiration in the landscapes and towns of the south.

PICTURESQUE VILLAGES 4

The south coast's villages are often little more than a church, a pub and a handful of cottages with lovingly tended gardens. Head to the sticks to appreciate the slow pace of life.

MARITIME HERITAGE 5

Surrounded as it is by water, the region is inextricably linked to the sea. Learn of naval battles, wartime vessels and contentious voyages in Portsmouth *(p122)* and Plymouth *(p174)*.

QUIRKY FESTIVALS 6

Dancing hobby horses, burning effigies, an all-you-can-eat stinging nettle competition: these are just some of the region's weird and wonderful local festivals.

GREAT CITIES 7

London aside, England's second cities thrum with an irresistible energy. Travel to Brighton (*p90*) or Bristol (*p134*) for a forward-thinking cultural scene and alternative spirit.

OUTDOOR ADVENTURES 8

Surf the waves in Newquay (*p192*), set off on a hike along the South West Coast Path, cycle around the Isle of Wight: (*p125*): the list of outdoor activities on offer is endless.

9 GLORIOUS GARDENS

Whether you're after classical landscapes, exotic greenhouses or a foliage-packed flower show, England's south coast offers plenty of inspiration for the green-fingered.

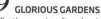

10 ANCIENT HISTORY

England's countryside is littered with the debris of its ancient past. Ponder the mysteries of ancient stone circles and hillside chalk figures in Wiltshire, Dorset and Somerset.

11 LONDON'S WORLD-CLASS MUSEUMS

Spend an afternoon with the Old Masters at the National Gallery *(p73)* or meet a roaring dinosaur at the Natural History Museum *(p78)* – all without spending a penny.

12 FOODIE RIVALRIES

Cream first or jam? Who invented the pasty? Where will you find the tastiest seafood? Every county has its answer. Sample your way around each area to decide for yourself.

EXPLORE
ENGLAND'S
SOUTH COAST

This guide divides England's south coast into six colour-coded
sightseeing areas, as shown on the map below. Find out more
about each area on the following pages.

Shrewsbury

Worcester

Gloucester

Swansea

Newport

Bridgend   Cardiff

Weston-
super-Mare   Bristol

Bath

Lundy
Island

Minehead

Warminster

Barnstaple

Bridgwater

**DORSET AND
SOMERSET**
p130

Bideford

Taunton

Tiverton

Yeovil

Bude

DEVON
p158

Okehampton

Exeter

Dorchester

Tavistock

Weymouth

CORNWALL
p182

Bodmin

Torquay

St Ives

Truro

St Austell

Plymouth

Penzance   Falmouth

English Channel

0 kilometres   50

0 miles   50

N ↑

LONDON
p54

HAMPSHIRE
AND WILTSHIRE
p108

KENT AND SUSSEX
p84

EUROPE

ENGLAND'S
SOUTH COAST

GETTING TO KNOW
ENGLAND'S
SOUTH COAST

Skirted by the sea, the counties that make up England's south coast - Kent, East Sussex, West Sussex, Hampshire, Wiltshire, Somerset, Dorset, Devon and Cornwall - all have their own stories to tell.

PAGE 54

LONDON

A truly global city, the UK's cosmopolitan capital has it all: mind-blowing museums and forward-thinking theatre; opulent royal palaces and incredible religious architecture; cosy neighbourhood pubs and world-class restaurants; street art, street food and bags of street chic. If culture fatigue or big-city ennui set in, there are also countless swathes of green in which to relax and reboot – from royal parks to huge commons – it's not the world's first National Park City for nothing, after all.

Best for
World-class museums and live entertainment

Home to
Buckingham Palace, Westminster Abbey, British Museum, St Paul's Cathedral, Victoria and Albert Museum

Experience
A stroll along the South Bank, past Shakespeare's Globe

KENT AND SUSSEX

PAGE 84

With London's sprawl confined by a vast Green Belt, the populous and – by and large – moneyed counties of England's southeast remain remarkably unspoiled, encompassing the sweeping chalk uplands of the North and South Downs and the tranquil sunken lanes of the Weald. Along the coast – most famed for its towering white cliffs – there's plenty of buzz at bohemian Brighton and up-and-coming Margate, while inland, in the so-called Garden of England, you'll find handsome market towns, mighty castles and an array of beautifully manicured gardens to explore.

Best for
Buzzy seaside towns and gorgeous gardens

Home to
Canterbury, Brighton

Experience
Browsing the independent shops of Brighton's North Laine

HAMPSHIRE AND WILTSHIRE

PAGE 108

Ancient history and intriguing legends are writ large in these two leafy counties. First, there's Stonehenge – the enigmatic stone circle that has evaded explanation for millennia – then there's Winchester, the capital of the Anglo-Saxon kingdom of Wessex, which claims to have King Arthur's round table. Add Salisbury, with its magnificent cathedral, and the maritime city of Portsmouth, and there's plenty to keep history buffs entertained. But that's not all – this is also a land of outdoor adventures, from sailing the Solent to cycling the flat grassland of Salisbury Plain.

Best for
Ancient monuments and skyscraping cathedrals

Home to
Winchester, Stourhead, Stonehenge, Salisbury Cathedral

Experience
The legacy of King Alfred in Winchester

→

PAGE 130

DORSET AND SOMERSET

From the plunging ravine of Cheddar Gorge to the drama and majesty of the Dorset coast, this varied region makes for a thrilling introduction to England's Westcountry. Explore the street art and cutting-edge cultural and culinary scenes of Bristol, one of Britain's most dynamic cities, or relax in Bath, a classy place that retains the elegance of its Georgian heyday. Cities aside, don't miss the evocative ruins of Glastonbury Abbey, seaside life in Poole and Bournemouth, and the exquisite sandy bays of the Isle of Purbeck.

Best for
Alternative city life and a craggy, fossil-studded coastline

Home to
Bristol, Bath

Experience
A steam and sauna in Bath's thermal spa

PAGE 158

DEVON

With a stretch of sea to the north and south, and a huge expanse of wild moorland in its centre, Devon welcomes outdoor enthusiasts and adrenaline junkies with open arms. Rock-climbing, rambling, rafting: all this and more keep visitors active on Dartmoor and Exmoor. In the south, the sparkling English Riviera, with its palm trees and seaside resorts, transports holidaymakers to the Continent, while the cities – maritime Plymouth, rebuilt after World War II, and Exeter, with its Roman and medieval heritage – have tales of the past in abundance.

Best for
Wild moorland and a rich maritime history

Home to
Dartmoor National Park, Exmoor National Park, Exeter

Experience
Hiking across Dartmoor and Exmoor on the Two Moors Way

CORNWALL

Sea-battered cliffs, hidden coves and windswept moorland: opportunities for the romance of the wild have long attracted writers and artists to England's myth-steeped corner. Beyond the fantasies and legends, Cornwall lives up to its reputation as a holiday haven, luring lovers of the great outdoors to the pounding surf, coastal paths and golden sands. Foodie fans, meanwhile, are in for a treat, with exquisite seafood on offer in practically every picturesque fishing village in the land.

Best for
Surfing, sandy beaches and succulent seafood

Home to
Eden Project, St Ives

Experience
Surfing the waves in Newquay

←

1 Looking towards iconic Tower Bridge.

2 The historic street of Shad Thames in Bermondsey.

3 St Paul's Cathedral.

4 The London Eye.

With so much to see and do when exploring England's south coast, it can be difficult to know where to start. Here we suggest a few itineraries to help you get the most out of your visit.

1 DAY
in London

▌ *Morning*

By following the river you can fit an awful lot into one day without having to travel too far or rely on public transport. Begin at Butler's Wharf; located close to Tower Bridge (*p77*) and lined with decent river-facing restaurants, it's a great spot for breakfast. From there, walk across the iconic bridge to the Tower of London (*p76*) and immerse yourself for a few hours in a thousand years of royal history and scandal. Ready for lunch? Follow the river to London Bridge and cross back over to the south side, where you can pick up tasty street food or a gourmet picnic from Borough Market (*8 Southwark Street*).

▌ *Afternoon*

Wander through the streets of Southwark past the *Golden Hinde* and along Clink Street. Soon you'll pass by the circular Shakespeare's Globe (*p76*) and the striking Tate Modern (*p74*). Stop at the Millennium Bridge to enjoy a picture-perfect view of St Paul's Cathedral (*p66*), sitting elegantly across the river. Then head into the gigantic former power station that now houses the Tate Modern to admire – or puzzle over – modern art. Check out the views from the top floor of the Blavatnik Building before having a coffee in the gallery's café (the view from here isn't bad, either). Revitalized, continue along the Thames Path, around a bend in the river, to the South Bank. Pause to watch skateboarders and browse the popular second-hand book stall under Waterloo Bridge before joining the queues for the London Eye (*p74*), which is open until at least 6pm on most days of the year.

▌ *Evening*

It's a pleasant half-hour walk back along the river to reach Southwark again. Have a spot of dinner at one of the many restaurants in the area – there are some terrific independent ones on the streets around Borough Market – before ending the day with a pint at London's only remaining galleried pub, the 17th-century George Inn (*75–77 Borough High Street*).

7 DAYS
in Southeast England

Day 1

Start in the delightful city of Canterbury *(p88)*. Wander its narrow lanes and visit the magnificent cathedral. After lunch at Tiny Tim's Tearoom *(34 St Margaret's Street)*, with its outstanding range of sandwiches, teas and cakes, head to the nearby Canterbury Roman Museum, where you can discover more about the city's ancient past. Afterwards catch the train (35 mins) to the seaside resort of Margate *(p94)*, home of the Turner Contemporary art gallery. Stroll the beach before returning to Canterbury, where you could catch a show at the Marlowe Theatre *(www. marlowetheatre.com)*. For dinner and a hotel, head for ABode *(30–33 High Street)*.

Day 2

Hire a car and drive southeast to Dover *(p95)* to explore its splendid castle. After taking a peek at Dover's famous white cliffs, drive to Rye *(p98)* and wander around its medieval cobbled streets. Carry on inland, traversing some of Kent's finest scenery to reach enchanting Leeds Castle *(p94)*, surrounded by its reedy moat. After visiting the castle, return to the coast to

Hastings *(p99)*, and grab a dinner of fish and chips on the beach at Maggie's *(www. maggiesfishandchips.co.uk)*. Stay the night at boutique B&B The Laindons *(23 High St)*.

Day 3

It's a short drive from Hastings to Battle Abbey *(p99)*. Here you can walk around the site of the Battle of Hastings. Then continue to Eastbourne *(p100)* – stroll along the pier and relax on the beach. Have lunch at the Lamb Inn *(36 High Street)*, then continue to Brighton *(p90)*. Explore the exuberant Royal Pavilion and then browse the independent shops in the Lanes. In the evening, enjoy some live music at the Brighton Music Hall *(www. brightonmusichall.co.uk)*. Stay overnight at the classy MyHotel *(17 Jubilee Street)*.

Day 4

Spend the morning in Brighton, soaking up the atmosphere and strolling out along the Victorian pier. Take lunch at Food for Friends *(p92)*, Brighton's foremost vegetarian restaurant, and then drive to the imposing ramparts

1 Medieval cobbled street in Rye.

2 Royal Pavilion in Brighton.

3 Nave of Winchester Cathedral.

4 HMS *Victory*, the star attraction in Portsmouth Historic Dockyard.

5 Prince Albert's dressing room at Osborne House on the Isle of Wight.

and immaculate gardens of Arundel Castle *(p102)*. Afterwards, it's a short scenic drive to Chichester *(p103)*, which is famous for its cathedral and the remarkable Fishbourne Roman Palace. Eat at the Field & Fork *(4 Guildhall Street)*, where the trout is particularly delicious, and bed down at Musgrove House *(63 Oving Road)*.

Day 5

Drive to Winchester *(p112)*, where you can wander the city centre and pop into 8 College Street, where Jane Austen spent the last few weeks of her life. Take lunch at Kyoto Kitchen *(70 Parchment Street)*, one of southern England's finest Japanese restaurants, before visiting the splendid cathedral *(p114)*. From here, you can follow the River Walk, which leads you up St Catherine's Hill for breathtaking city views. Have dinner at the cosy Wykeham Arms *(p113)* and stay at Hotel du Vin *(14 Southgate Street)*.

Day 6

Head to Portsmouth *(p122)* and make the Charles Dickens Birthplace Museum,

which occupies the house where the author was born, your first stop. Afterwards, wander over to Gunwharf Quays and hit up one of the waterside restaurants for lunch. You'll need most of the afternoon to explore Portsmouth Historic Dockyard – many of the city's maritime sights can be found here, including warships and the D-Day Story. Once you've covered the naval attractions, dine at nearby abarbistro *(58 White Hart Road)*, then spend the night at The Wellington *(62 High Street)*.

Day 7

In the morning, set off for Portsmouth harbour to catch the ferry to the Isle of Wight *(p124)* – it usually takes less than an hour to cross. Start your island tour at Osborne House, a grand palace which was the holiday home of Queen Victoria and Prince Albert – you can also have lunch here. Push on to Carisbrooke Castle, another of the island's main sights. After sightseeing, splurge on your final meal at Thompsons *(11 Town Lane)*, in Newport, before heading to your coastal hotel, the Wight Mouse Inn *(Church Place, Chale)*.

$\longrightarrow$

1 Lyme Regis harbour, Dorset.

2 The Rainforest Biome in the Eden Project.

3 The Great Bath in the Roman Baths complex, Bath.

4 Salisbury Cathedral cloister.

5 DAYS

in Southwest England

Day 1

Start your tour in Salisbury. Explore the Market Square and visit the cathedral *(p120)*, admiring its spire, the highest in England. Lunch at Fisherton Mill *(108 Fisherton Street)*, a combined art gallery and café. In the afternoon, explore the world-famous prehistoric standing stones at Stonehenge *(p118)* and the stone circle and ancient earthworks at Avebury *(p126)*. In the evening, head to the charming city of Bath *(p136)*. Dine at Sotto Sotto *(p137)* before turning in for the night at the cosy Harrington's City Hotel *(8–10 Queen Street)*.

Day 2

Start your exploration of Bath by visiting the Roman Baths and the Royal Crescent before having lunch at the hipster Wild Café *(10a Queen Street)*. In the afternoon, drive south to Lyme Regis *(p147)* and take a stroll around the centre of this picture-perfect resort with a well-protected harbour. Continue to Torquay *(p168)*, a classic English seaside resort where you can dine on excellent seafood at the appealing Number 7 Fish Bistro *(7 Beacon Hill)* and bed down at the imaginatively decorated The 25 Boutique B&B *(25 Avenue Road)*.

Day 3

Drive to the enchanting fishing village of Fowey *(p197)*, where you can stroll the streets before visiting the Eden Project *(p186)*, a garden lover's paradise. Eat here, and then drive to St Michael's Mount *(p199)*, a granite islet that rises steeply

from the ocean. Tour the mount before journeying on to beguiling St Ives *(p188)*. In the evening, enjoy a tasty dinner at the town's informal Cornish Deli *(3 Chapel Street)* and settle down for the night at the Primrose House B&B *(Primrose Valley)*.

Day 4

Begin by visiting St Ives' splendid art galleries Tate St Ives and the Barbara Hepworth Museum and Sculpture Garden. Then journey on to Padstow *(p191)*, a bustling fishing port with a string of outstanding seafood restaurants – try lunch at the smart Prawn on the Lawn *(p191)*. Suitably refreshed, carry on to Tintagel *(p190)* to visit its ruined castle. In the early evening, head to scenic Boscastle *(p191)* for a pub dinner at the Napoleon Inn on the High Street and book a bed at The Old Rectory B&B in nearby St Juliot.

Day 5

In the morning, cut inland from Boscastle to travel across the windswept landscapes of Dartmoor National Park *(p162)*. Pause to stretch your legs in minuscule Princetown at the heart of Dartmoor, and grab lunch at the Fox Tor Café *(2 Two Bridges Road)*. In the afternoon, continue to Glastonbury *(p152)*, home to one of the world's most famous contemporary music festivals. Visit Glastonbury Abbey and take the 30-minute hike up to the summit of Glastonbury Tor to enjoy the views. Eat at the Hundred Monkeys Café *(52 High Street)* and spend the night at the family-run Magdalene House on Magdalene Street.

Sun, Sea and Shingle

Shingle beaches aren't everyone's cup of tea but if you want to avoid finding sand in mysterious places they're your best bet. Stretching some 29 km (18 miles), Chesil Beach (p146) in Dorset is as famous for its shingle as it is for its starring role in Ian McEwan's novel. Talking of famous: Brighton's pebble front (p90), flanked by its promenade and pier, is simply iconic. In Devon, Beer (p168) and Budleigh Salterton lead the pack, while in Kent, Dungeness (p98) and Deal offer atmosphere in spades.

→

The shingle sweep of Chesil Beach, stretching to the Isle of Portland

ENGLAND'S SOUTH COAST FOR
BEACH LIFE

When the sun shines (and even when it doesn't), there's only one place you'll want to be: beside the sea. Luckily, this part of the UK has beaches to spare. The only problem? Choosing which one to visit.

Sandy Shores

Building sandcastles, digging a pit, rolling down dunes: these are the activities that make up a great day at the beach. Pick a long stretch of sand for maximum space to run wild - Woolacombe (p180), in Devon, has 5 km (3 miles) of uninterrupted golden sand; Perranporth has one of Cornwall's largest beaches (and claims the UK's only true beach bar). Over in East Sussex, Camber Sands (p98) seems to go on for miles and miles - brace yourself for a long trek to the sea when the tide is out.

←

Digging in the sand on Perranporth beach, on Cornwall's north coast

TOP 3 BEACHES NEAR LONDON

Botany Bay
🅰️G1 🚇Broadstairs, Kent 🚆
Much-photographed beach, 90 minutes from London St Pancras.

Camber Sands
🅰️F2 🚇Rye, East Sussex 🚆Then taxi
Miles and miles of sand, 75 minutes from London.

Sunny Sands
🅰️F2 🚇Folkestone, Kent 🚆
Home to an annual sandcastle-building competition, this beach is a 55-minute train ride from St Pancras.

Cute Coves

Nestled in the nooks and crannies of the coast are countless coves. Kynance Cove, on the Lizard Peninsula (p193), is stunningly scenic and Cornwall's worst-kept secret - arrive early to get it to yourself. Skirt the coast west of Salcombe (p172) and you'll hit upon pretty Soar Mill Cove and Hope Cove. In the east, trace the path from Margate (p94) to Broadstairs and you'll find peaceful coves.

→

Soar Mill Cove, a tiny inlet near Salcombe that is accessible only on foot

Canines on the Coast

There are few sights more joyous than seeing your four-legged friend sprint to the sea. From November to March, you can pretty much take your pick of the sands; come April, restrictions mean you need to do your homework. Open year-round, Porthkidney Sands near St Ives (p188) and Saunton Sands near Westward Ho! (p179) are perfect for a dog's day out.

←

An excited labrador retriever frolicking in the sandy shallows

Skirt the Coast

Fancy a bit of sea air and a fine view? You've come to the right place. For white cliffs, extraordinary geology and stunning beaches, amble the 4 km (2.5 miles) from Lulworth Cove to Durdle Door *(p145)*. Rugged Cornish scenery more your thing? Venture 16 km (10 miles) from Marazion to Porthleven, spotting secluded coves and rocky inlets as you go. The 8-km (5-mile) walk to Tintagel from Boscastle *(p190)* offers myth and mystery aplenty, plus the chance to spot seals.

←

Tracing the banks of the River Valency in the village of Boscastle

ENGLAND'S SOUTH COAST FOR
WALKS AND HIKES

From the wild expanse of Dartmoor to the landscaped gardens of Stourhead, the south of England is certainly scenic. Hundreds of walking routes – both short footpaths and epic trails – traverse the land, so lace up your boots and head out on a hike worth writing home about.

Going the Distance

Hardy hikers are spoiled for choice. Doable in about 7–10 days, the Two Moors Way *(p163)* takes in the dramatic landscapes of the Westcountry moors, while the South Downs Way *(p106)* features a walker's favourite, the undulating Seven Sisters. For a truly epic challenge, the 1,014-km (630-miles) South West Coast Path *(p165)* begins in Somerset and wends its way around the coast to Dorset. Love hiking but don't have weeks to spare? Pick a section of any of these for a wonderful day's walk.

→

Walking along the South West Coast Path, past Durdle Door

A Walk in the Woods

It's easy to think that this region is all about the sea, but stay inland and you'll be well rewarded. The New Forest *(p125)* has 225 km (140 miles) of tracks and footpaths: find easy woodland walks around Bolderwood and Brockenhurst. In Kent, the Sevenoaks Circular (15 km/9.5 miles) features rural farmland, fragrant lavender fields and bluebell-studded woodland – plus the opportunity for a pub lunch. Perfect for a Sunday jaunt.

↑ Tramping through woodland in the New Forest National Park

Stately Home Strolls

The era of the grand country house reached its zenith in the 18th and 19th centuries. And one of the best things about these stately homes? Their vast grounds are perfect for a stroll. Walk around the stunning gardens at Stourhead *(p116)*, admire the unspoiled estate of Kingston Lacy *(p142)* or take in the sights that inspired J M W Turner at Petworth House *(p102)*.

← The façade of Kingston Lacy, one of Dorset's many stately homes

ENGLAND COAST PATH

In 2012, Wales became the first country in the world to have a dedicated footpath the full length of its coastline. Work is well underway for England to go one step further: knitting together new stretches with long-established trails – such as the South West Coast Path – the England Coast Path will, once complete, become the longest continuous coastal trail in the world. For news on progress see *www.nationaltrail.co.uk*.

Britain at War

As World War II passes out of living memory, the region's wartime monuments and museums deserve a visit. Explore the nerve centre of the wartime government at the Churchill War Rooms *(King Charles St, London)*, then find out more about the man himself at his former home, Chartwell *(p97)* in Kent. Learn about the 1944 Allied landing in Normandy, France, at Portsmouth's D-Day Story *(p122)* and at Nothe Fort in Weymouth *(p144)*.

The Churchill War Rooms, the base of wartime government ↑

ENGLAND'S SOUTH COAST FOR
HISTORY BUFFS

Everywhere you turn there are reminders of England's long history: Iron Age hillforts and Roman ruins, grand castles and stately homes, wartime memorials and historic sailing vessels. Head to world-class museums to find out more or simply stumble across signs of the past as you tour the region.

Invaders in the East

The southeast of England has seen a conveyor belt of new arrivals over the centuries. Landing in Kent in the 1st century AD, the Romans quickly made themselves at home, building towns and making the most of the rich landscape. Visit Fishbourne Roman Palace in Chichester *(p103)*, the largest Roman villa in Britain; find old Roman walls in London; and discover the impressively sophisticated Roman Baths in Bath *(p136)*. Fast-forward several hundred years and William of Normandy and his fleet have invaded England, taking on King Harold II at the Battle of Hastings; walk around the battlefield at Battle *(p99)* or time your visit for the annual re-enactment of the fight in October.

→

Re-enactment of the Battle of Hastings on the site of the original battle at Battle Abbey

Off to Sea

From the Tudor Age of Exploration to Olympic mastery of water-based sports, Britons have long pushed the boundaries of possibility on the ocean. Learn the stories of these seafarers, and see some of the most famous ships in history, in the maritime museums and dockyards that protect the country's naval heritage. Find out about Francis Drake's legacy in Plymouth *(p174)*, board Nelson's HMS *Victory* in Portsmouth *(p122)* or explore Brunel's masterpiece the SS *Great Britain* in Bristol *(p134)*.

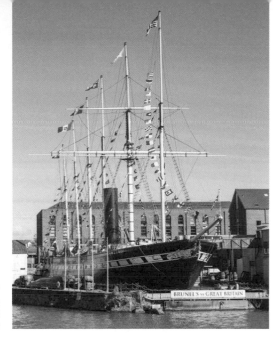

$\rightarrow$

The world's first ocean liner, Brunel's SS *Great Britain* at Bristol Docks

Ancient Beginnings

England's south coast is rich in ancient relics. World-famous Stonehenge *(p118)* is a remarkable record of the prehistoric era; seek out another stone circle in Avebury *(p126)* for fewer crowds. Heading out on a road trip? Keep your eyes peeled for chalk figures carved into the hills; the Cerne Abbas giant *(p149)* in Dorset will have you pondering the mysteries of the past.

$\leftarrow$

Neolithic monuments near the village of Avebury in Wiltshire

Taste the World

Ever since medieval merchants first brought spices to these shores, the English have absorbed culinary influences from across the globe – and nowadays are as likely to tuck into a *banh mi* as bangers and mash. Stick to the cities to sample global flavours though; the more rural you go, the more traditional the menu tends to be. London's markets offer an irresistible buffet of options, while Brighton's restaurants import international ideas to create plant-based menus.

→

A stall selling fragrant Moroccan food on London's historic Brick Lane

ENGLAND'S SOUTH COAST FOR
FOODIES

With a strong focus on locally grown produce, the food on the south coast is always fresh and full of flavour. There's little need to seek out fine-dining restaurants to get a good meal; bakeries, farmers' markets and fish shacks offer some of the best-tasting food around.

Room for Dessert

The south coast's mild climate is ideal for the cultivation of fruit, so it's little wonder desserts here tend to be on the fruity side. Puddings made with apples or summer berries are popular: tuck into apple crumble in the winter, and summer pudding (soft fruits encased in bread) or Eton mess (meringue, strawberries and cream) in the warmer months. All that soft fruit means delicious jams, too, best enjoyed with cream and scones during afternoon tea.

Pasties and Pies

When hunger strikes, you need something quick, filling and, preferably, delicious. Enter the humble pasty. A simple pastry pocket traditionally filled with seasoned meat and vegetables, these hearty handheld meals are found in practically every bakery in the Westcountry (just don't ask who invented it - the answer remains a contentious issue). Definitely invented in Cornwall is the truly unique Stargazy Pie: picture a dish of baked pilchards, heads breaking through the pastry top. Kent is home to Lamb's Tail pie, made from docked tails and not for the faint-hearted.

← Pilchards' heads poking out of a traditional Stargazy Pie

TOP 5 SOUTH COAST CHEESES

Cheddar
Firm and nutty, with a sting on the finish depending on maturity.

Cornish Yarg
Creamy, semi-hard cow's milk cheese with a mouldy nettle rind.

Dorset Blue Vinny
Light and crumbly skimmed-milk cheese with fine blue veins.

Golden Cross
Soft, raw Sussex goat's-milk cheese, log-shaped and covered in a velvety white rind.

Old Winchester
Firm, dry and tasty with a washed rind, nicknamed "Old Smales".

↑ Traditional English fish and chips, complete with mushy peas

↑ Enjoying a traditional afternoon tea in the sun in Torquay, Devon

Catch of the Day

Firm, flaky cod, freshly caught and crisply battered; fat, juicy scallops, tossed in butter; delicate oysters, slurped from the shell. With the ocean on its doorstep, it's little wonder that seafood in this region is such a treat. Fish and chips, of course, is a firm favourite – you'll find a chippy in almost every town - but there's plenty of variety here. Look out for oysters and Dover sole in Kent, and mussels, crab and lobster in Devon and Cornwall.

Paddle Power

The stand-up paddleboarding craze has given its fans cores of steel and a unique way of seeing the sights of England. The lazy, winding river of Cuckmere Haven in Sussex is an ideal place to start if you're a beginner; alternatively, book some lessons with SUP in a Bag *(www.supinabag.co.uk)*, which has locations across Cornwall. Once you've found your groove, why not combine a city visit with an SUP? Learn about Georgian history as you paddle through Bath *(p136)* or do your bit and pick up litter while cruising along London's urban waterways.

→

Paddleboarding in the sun around Porthminster Point, Cornwall

ENGLAND'S SOUTH COAST
ON THE WATER

On a hot summer's day, there's nothing more enticing than getting into the cool water. Whether you want to dive straight in for a refreshing swim, catch some wild waves or paddle gently along the shore, there's a river, lake or scenic sliver of sea just around the corner.

Alfresco Swims

Britons' love affair with wild swimming doesn't seem to be waning; fortunately, there are hundreds of rivers, lakes and pools in the south perfect for a delicious dip. Favourites for experienced swimmers include the River Stour in Kent and River Dart in Devon. In the capital? Head for Hampstead Heath, where segregated and mixed ponds offer a taste of the wild. If you're nervous about going it alone, the lidos in Plymouth and Penzance are a great alternative.

←

Relaxing in the quiet shallows of a river in Somerset

Surf the Waves

With wind and waves buffeting the coast, it's little wonder the Westcountry has such a superb surfing scene. One of the best spots for beginners is Newquay *(p192)*; check out Westcountry Surf School *(www.surfingschool.co.uk)* for lessons. Croyde Bay *(p180)* and Saunton Sands in Devon and Porthleven and Praa Sands in Cornwall also have great surfs for all abilities.

$\longrightarrow$

A surfer riding a wave on Fistral Beach, near the surfing hub of Newquay

Catch the Breeze

Fancy yourself as the next Helena Lucas or Ellen MacArthur? Get your sea legs with a sailing lesson in Weymouth *(p144)*, home to the sailing competitions during the 2012 Olympic Games, or in Falmouth *(p194)*, whose sheltered harbour is ideal for novices. If you'd rather watch the action, pencil in the Isle of Wight's Cowes Week *(p125)*, one of the world's largest sailing regattas.

$\longleftarrow$

Sailing boats bobbing around in Falmouth's picturesque marina, in Cornwall

Written in the West
From tales of smugglers to murders most horrid, many a story has been penned in the Westcountry. Head to Fowey (p197), stopping off at the real Jamaica Inn on Bodmin Moor, to see the places that inspired Daphne du Maurier, or to Torquay to celebrate crime writer Agatha Christie *(p168)* on the dedicated literary trail.

←

Visitors relaxing outside at the famous Jamaica Inn in Cornwall

ENGLAND'S SOUTH COAST FOR
ARTISTS AND AUTHORS

Literary classics, page-turning murder mysteries, iconic pieces of art: all these and more have been created by artists and authors while on the south coast. Venture to the places they lived, worked and visited, and be inspired to pen, or paint, your own masterpiece.

The picture-perfect town of St Ives, and *(inset)* the Tate St Ives modern art gallery ↑

On the Trail of Jane Austen

Capturing the people of Georgian England with wit, Jane Austen remains a firm favourite among book lovers. Begin any Austen tour in Hampshire: the author was born in Steventon, penned most of her major novels in Chawton (p123) – Jane Austen's House is a must-visit here – and spent her final years in Winchester (p112). It was in Bath (p136) that she found more inspiration; head to the Jane Austen Centre to learn about her time here.

💬 INSIDER TIP
Walk with Keats

In 1819 John Keats spent a few months in Winchester, walking daily from the city centre to nearby St Cross. Follow in his footsteps to see the scenery that inspired his famous seasonal ode "To Autumn".

↑ Tour guides outside Jane Austen's House in Chawton

Artist Enclaves

With spectacular landscapes as far as the eye can see, it's no surprise countless artists have sought inspiration in the south. St Ives (p188), with its enchanting light, has drawn artists for centuries; visit the Barbara Hepworth Museum and Sculpture Garden or Tate St Ives to see works by St Ives School artists. In 1916, Vanessa Bell and Duncan Grant, members of London's Bloomsbury Group, decamped to a Sussex farmhouse, Charleston (p101), decorating the house with their incredible paintings and ceramics. The result? A truly unique and powerful piece of artistic history.

Go the Distance

A multi-day cycle is a great way to experience the diverse beauty of England's south coast at your own pace. The epic 160-km (99-mile) Devon Coast to Coast from Ilfracombe to Plymouth follows three converted railway paths and encompasses spectacular coastal scenery, patchwork fields and the wild, desolate landscapes of Dartmoor. Another favourite is the Great Western Way, a long-distance cycle route connecting Bristol and the Westcountry with the capital. For a ride of awesome proportions, National Cycle Network 2 from Exeter to Brighton covers 350 km (217 miles) and crosses an impressive five counties – Devon, Dorset, Hampshire, West Sussex and East Sussex.

→

Road cyclists whizzing by
Clearbrook in Dartmoor
National Park, Devon

ENGLAND'S SOUTH COAST FOR
CYCLISTS

A vast network of traffic-free cycle paths, quiet country lanes and long-distance waymarked routes makes England's south coast the perfect destination for two-wheeled adventures, while cycle-friendly cities offer ample opportunity for sightseeing from the comfort of your saddle.

On the Trail of History

The latest addition to the country's list of scenic cycles is drenched in history. The King Alfred Way is a 350-km (217-mile) loop that connects some of the country's most ancient sights, including Stonehenge *(p118)*, Avebury stone circle *(p126)* and Winchester Cathedral *(p114)*.

INSIDER TIP
Sustrans

The UK's National Cycle Network has thousands of miles of waymarked routes, many of which are traffic-free. For route information, check out the Sustrans website *(sustrans.org.uk)*.

Cycling past Stonehenge
on the long-distance ↑
King Alfred Way

Family Friendly
Disused railway lines that once ran up and down the country now offer great family-friendly cycle trails. The Tarka Trail *(p179)* is a terrific traffic-free tour of the North Devon countryside, while the Two Tunnels Circuit takes in Bath's historic centre. In Cornwall, the Camel Trail follows the River Camel from Wenford Bridge to Padstow, weaving its way through wooded countryside which opens out at the picturesque Camel Estuary.

← Kids riding bikes on the traffic-free Tarka Trail in North Devon

Capital Cycles
While a tandem tour of Piccadilly Circus is not recommended, London shouldn't be overlooked as a cycle-friendly destination. Dedicated cycle superhighways make cycling in the city less daunting, or avoid the roads by picking up a Santander Bike *(p208)* and making a beeline for one of the city's many parks.

↑ Cyclists travelling along a London cycle super-highway below Big Ben

39

Great Gardens

There are gardens and then there are gardens. Cornwall's Eden Project *(p186)*, with its vast biomes and extraordinary range of plant life, attracts big numbers for good reason. Over in Wiltshire, Stourhead *(p116)* is one of the best examples of 18th-century landscape gardening in Britain; in Kent, Sissinghurst *(p96)* arranges plants by colour, texture or season to spectacular effect.

→

Sissinghurst Castle, famed for Vita Sackville-West's unconventional gardens

ENGLAND'S SOUTH COAST FOR
GREEN SPACES

Wander through the grand gardens that surround many a stately home, explore a platoon of art gardens that combine magnificent scenery with modern sculpture, or enjoy scores of leafy city parks. Those with green fingers are spoiled for choice in each and every part of England's south.

Celebrate the Seasons

From spring's blooms to autumn's golden foliage, England's gardens offer a splendid show all year round. The quintessential English rose is best enjoyed in June: visit Lady Churchill's romantic walled garden at Chartwell *(p97)* or discover over 500 varieties at Mottisfont Abbey *(p124)*. In spring, daffodils and crocuses fill Rosemoor's meadows *(p179)*. Sheffield Park in East Sussex is the best place to see autumn colours.

←

Red leaves framing one of the lakes at Sheffield Park in East Sussex

City Parks

With its eight million trees and 3,000 parks, London is one of the greenest capitals in Europe – in fact in 2019 it became the world's first National Park City. Linking a lot of the city's green spaces together, along rivers, canals, old train tracks and park paths, is the Capital Ring, a 126-km (78-mile) circular walking route. It's well signposted but you can download the routes to your phone for free with the Go Jauntly app.

Enjoying a leisurely stroll through Hyde Park in early spring ↑

Sculpture Gardens

A range of glorious natural settings host striking works of art all over the region. The garden of Barbara Hepworth's former home *(p189)* has beautiful displays of her work, while 300 sculptures are found throughout Broomhill Sculpture Gardens *(p181)*. For a more unusual experience, seek out the hidden sculptures in eerie Tout Quarry on the Isle of Portland *(p144)*.

→

One of Carol Peace's sculptures at Broomhill Sculpture Gardens

South Spirit

From mother's ruin to a trendy treat, gin has undergone a renaissance in the UK. Traditionally, it divides into two main types: juniper-led, slightly citrussy London Dry, which covers many of the best-known brands, and the earthier Plymouth Gin. To learn more, join a tour at gin-making stalwarts Plymouth Gin or London Sipsmith.

← Plymouth Gin, made by the oldest British gin distillery

ENGLAND'S SOUTH COAST
BY THE GLASS

Celebration, commiseration or just a good old chinwag: the English accompany practically every occasion with a drop of their favourite tipple. Pint of ale, refreshing gin and tonic, flagon of Somerset scrumpy or a reassuring cup of tea – what's it to be?

Mine's a Pint

Draught bitter, drunk at cellar temperature, is the most traditional British beer. Brewed from malted barley, hops, yeast and water, and usually matured in a wooden cask, it comes in a variety of flavours and hues, from straw-coloured pale and golden ales to malty stouts and porters. Pop into your nearest pub and ask to taste a few varieties before you buy.

↑ Celebrating with beer, one of Britain's most popular drinks

Sparkling Success

British wine production – helped in no small measure by ever-warmer summers - is growing and many wines have gained plaudits from all over the world. Almost 300 vineyards, producing red, white, rosé and sparkling wine, are planted along the south coast. On the sunny, south-facing slopes of Kent, Sussex and Cornwall, sparkling wines dominate the scene; sample some of the best on a vineyard tour, such as those at Cornwall's award-winning Camel Valley.

←

Grapes in a vineyard in East Sussex, where Britain's wine industry is booming

PUT THE KETTLE ON

In the UK, there's nothing that a good cup of tea won't solve and so it's little wonder that Britons consume some 60 billion cups a year. Popularized in Britain in the 1660s, tea today is drunk with an essential splash of milk – anathema to the rest of the world but, to Brits, tea without milk is quite simply not a proper cuppa.

Scrumptious Scrumpy

The south of England's orchards, buoyed by a mild, southern climate and plenty of sun, provide apples by the bushel, making for delicious desserts, yes, but also everyone's favourite summer thirst-quencher: cider. Hands down, Somerset rules the cider-making scene, using fermented apples to create scrumpy, a particularly potent beverage. Distilled cider brandy, matured for 20 years, is even stronger. Want to avoid a sore head? In Kent, producers use sweeter dessert apples, which results in a slightly lighter tipple.

↑ Cider apples being harvested in Somerset and (inset) pickers gathering apples in Devon

A YEAR IN
ENGLAND'S
SOUTH COAST

There's no bad time to visit England's south coast. Summer may be the busiest season, but spring, autumn and winter offer a wealth of events, from flower fairs to Christmas markets, fêtes to literary festivals.

Spring

Prestigious flower shows and traditional May Day celebrations signal the start of spring. In the countryside, woodlands are carpeted in wild flowers, while the cities kick off their annual cultural programmes. London also sees a flurry of sporting events, including the Boat Race and the London Marathon.

1. One of the garden displays at the Chelsea Flower Show, London

Summer

Locals flock to the coast as the weather warms to surf, sunbathe and mill around seafood festivals. Music events fill the calendar, with Glastonbury stealing the show. LGBT+

THE HARVEST FESTIVAL

Farming communities have been giving thanks for good crops since pagan times but it has since been given a Christian spin. On a Sunday in autumn, produce is placed on altars and harvest hymns are sung.

1 | 2

Pride events take over big cities, such as London and Brighton, while in the countryside, village fêtes – which feature old-fashioned games and local stalls – bring communities together.

2. Strolling along Porthmeor Beach in St Ives, Cornwall

Autumn

September marks the start of the harvest season. The corn-fields turn golden and orchards are heavy with apples, which Kent and Somerset celebrate with cider-drinking events. Book fans make for festivals commemorating the works of Agatha Christie (Torquay) and Jane Austen (Bath). The season ends with a bang on Guy Fawkes Night, when bonfires and fireworks draw crowds outside on 5 November.

3. An autumnal display of pumpkins and gourds

Winter

From December, Christmas markets pop up throughout the region. Notable festivals include Rochester's Dickensian Christmas, which sees costumed processions through the Kentish town, and Brighton's Burning of the Clocks, where the Winter Solstice is celebrated with parades and fireworks. Temperatures continue to drop but that doesn't stop some hardy swimmers from braving the sea for a Boxing Day dip.

4. Canterbury's festive lights and (inset) a snowman on Brighton Beach

TOP 5 **TRADITIONAL EVENTS**

Beltain
To kick-start summer, a wicker man is burned on Butser Ancient Farm, Hampshire in May.

Obby Oss Festival
Crowds in Padstow dance with hobby horses on May Day.

Battle of Hastings Re-enactment
The battle is performed at Battle Abbey, East Sussex, in October.

Apple Wassailing
The ancient custom of singing to apple trees to ensure a good harvest takes place in December.

Hurling the Silver Ball
This ancient game happens in Cornwall around Shrove Tuesday.

3

4

A BRIEF
HISTORY

A mere 32 km (20 miles) from France at its closest point, the south coast has acted as England's defensive bulwark ever since the last successful invasion in 1066. Skirted as it is by the sea, the region developed shipbuilding and maritime expertise that were crucial in advancing the country.

Ancient Britain

Great Britain has been inhabited for roughly half a million years. The earliest archaeological remains include bones and flint tools. The Bronze Age, which began around 2,500 BC, witnessed the evolution of farming and livestock-rearing and the construction of stone and timber circles – most famously at Stonehenge. With the advent of the Iron Age around 800 BC scores of hillforts were erected across the south of England – such as those on the South Downs – and archaeological finds from this time have included splendid jewellery.

1. A 17th-century map of Great Britain. ↑
2. A 19th-century engraving of druids at Stonehenge.
3. Mosaic at Fishbourne Roman Palace.
4. King Alfred's galleys in battle with the Vikings.

Timeline of events

c 2500 BC
Beginning of the Bronze Age.

c 800 BC
Iron Age begins, with construction of hillforts.

c 500,000 BC
First evidence of human habitation in Great Britain.

AD 43
The Roman Emperor Claudius invades Britain.

The Romans

Julius Caesar (100–44 BC) and his Roman legionnaires first landed in Kent in 55 BC, but it wasn't until AD 43 that the Romans invaded Great Britain, conquering southeast England, and then pushed north, building roads and establishing military outposts. The Romans could be brutal: they persecuted the Celtic Druids to extinction. By the beginning of the 3rd century, all inhabitants of Britain were granted Roman citizenship. Roman Britain lasted for 400 years. Trade flourished and peace prevailed – but Roman power ultimately waned.

The Saxons and Vikings

In the 4th century AD, Saxons and Angles from northern Germany regularly raided Roman Britain. By AD 700, England had been invaded and parcelled up into a series of Anglo-Saxon kingdoms, with Wessex in the south predominating under Alfred the Great (848–99). However, the power of Wessex was subject to another threat. Sailing across the ocean in their mighty longships, the Vikings of Scandinavia were bent on settlement, resulting in endemic warfare into the 11th century.

Did You Know?

The Romans introduced Christianity to England in the 3rd century AD.

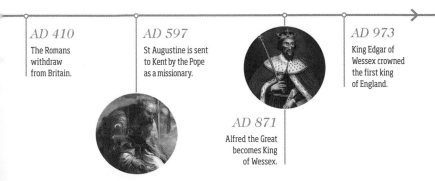

AD 410
The Romans withdraw from Britain.

AD 597
St Augustine is sent to Kent by the Pope as a missionary.

AD 973
King Edgar of Wessex crowned the first king of England.

AD 871
Alfred the Great becomes King of Wessex.

The Middle Ages

In 1066, William the Conqueror (1028–87) sailed from France and defeated the Saxons at the Battle of Hastings. He was then crowned king and both he and his successors ruled a feudal kingdom with local barons exercising regional control. The tension between royal and regional authority plagued England and led to both the curtailing of royal power in the signing of the Magna Carta in 1215 and, much later, to a prolonged period of civil war – the Wars of the Roses. Only in 1485, with the defeat of Richard III (1452–85) and the accession of the first Tudor king, Henry VII (1457–1509), was order restored.

Tudor Renaissance

Under the Tudors (1485–1603), England blossomed into a major European power. Henry VIII (1491–1547) broke ties with Papal Rome to establish an independent Church of England – and to divorce his wife Catherine of Aragon to marry Anne Boleyn. So commenced the Reformation, which included the Dissolution of the Monasteries, whereby Henry closed down all monasteries and appropriated their assets. His daughter Mary I (1516–58) tried

1 *The Battle of Hastings in 1066,* painted by François-Hypolite Debon. ↑

2 An old naval print of the Defeat of the Spanish Armada in 1588.

3 Portrait of Charles II by Peter Lely.

Did You Know?

The Union rose, the floral emblem of England today, was created by Henry VII.

Timeline of events

1066
Battle of Hastings; William the Conqueror becomes king of England.

1170
Thomas Becket is murdered in Canterbury.

1215
Signing of the Magna Carta at Runnymede.

1349
The first case of Black Death (bubonic plague) appears in Dorset.

1485
Richard III dies at the Battle of Bosworth Field; accession of Henry VII.

to re-establish Catholicism but the country was returned to Protestantism by her sister Elizabeth I (1533–1603). In 1588, England faced a Spanish invasion force; after engaging with the Royal Navy off Plymouth, the Spanish Armada was defeated.

The Stuarts

Elizabeth I died childless and her throne passed to James Stuart (1566–1625), the king of Scotland. Two years later, a group of dissident Catholics planned but failed to blow up Parliament and kill the king. There were deep divisions over religion: some Protestants wished to reform the Church of England, while many other worshippers remained devout Catholics. Eventually the antagonism of Protestant Parliament was too much; a nine-year Civil War broke out, with Oliver Cromwell's Parliamentarians crushing the Royalists. Charles I (1600–49), James's successor, was executed and Cromwell (1599–1658) became the Lord Protector of a republican Commonwealth. The Stuarts returned to the throne (a period known as the Restoration) under Charles II (1630–85) and the dynasty staggered on until the death of Queen Anne (1665–1714), who was succeeded by George I.

DEFEAT OF THE SPANISH ARMADA

Spain was England's main rival for supremacy on the seas. In 1588 Philip II sent 100 powerfully armed galleons towards England, bent on invasion. The English fleet - under Lord Howard, Francis Drake, John Hawkins and Martin Frobisher - sailed from Plymouth and destroyed the Spanish navy in a famous victory.

1538

The Pope excommunicates Henry VIII for his break with Rome.

1603

James VI of Scotland becomes James I of England, uniting the two kingdoms.

1639

Outbreak of the British Civil Wars, also known as the Wars of the Three Kingdoms.

1714

Death of Queen Anne, the last of the Stuarts.

Georgian Britain

The reigns of George I (1660–1727) and George II (1683–1760) were lacklustre, with royal power leaching into the hands of a series of prime ministers. The expansion of the British Empire meant increased trade, much of it facilitated by slavery, but also several expensive wars. The resultant high taxation, especially on imported luxuries, led to smuggling along the entire length of the south coast. As wealth increased, so leisure became more sophisticated; spa towns and seaside resorts became fashionable. The threat of French invasion loomed throughout the era and, following the French Revolution, Britain was at war with France from 1792. Eventually British pre-eminence in Europe was secured by the defeat of Napoleon's France at the Battle of Waterloo in 1815.

The Victorians

During the long reign of Queen Victoria (1819–1901), Britain became the most powerful country in the world, its economy buoyed by the success of its manufacturing industry, its railway boom and the exploitation of its ever-expanding empire. The

↑ Isambard Kingdom Brunel, a prolific figure in the Industrial Revolution

Timeline of events

1783

Britain is defeated by its American colonists in the Revolutionary War.

1805

Nelson wins the Battle of Trafalgar; British maritime supremacy is secured.

1836–8

London is linked to the south coast by railway.

1914–18

World War I; Britain declares war on Germany and her allies.

great figures of Victorian Britain – such as Charles Darwin and Charles Dickens – cut an international profile, while a Methodist-led religious revival resulted in the ban on slavery across the Empire in 1833. The era's most successful engineer, Isambard Kingdom Brunel was the chief designer behind the Great Western Railway and created the world's first iron-hulled steamship, SS *Great Britain*, launched from Bristol in 1843.

The Modern Era

In the 1900s, Britain's supremacy faded. After staggering through the Great Depression of the 1930s it took an economic and military pounding during World War II. After the war, a reforming Labour government established the much-admired National Health Service and, despite the slump of traditional industries such as fishing and agriculture, the country began to recover, enjoying an economic boom, predominantly led by leisure and tourism. The opening of the Channel Tunnel in 1994 provided a physical link to mainland Europe, but Britain's close ties to the Continent suffered a setback in 2016 when the electorate voted for withdrawal from the European Union following 43 years of membership.

1 Portrait of George II by Thomas Hudson.

2 The launch of SS *Great Britain* in Bristol.

3 Men receiving free coffee during the Great Depression in 1933.

4 A pro-EU march in 2016.

Did You Know?

Sir Robert Walpole was Britain's longest serving prime minister, from 1721 to 1742.

1939–45

World War II; for a second time, Britain declares war against Germany and her allies.

1967

Abortion (April) and homosexuality (July) are legalized in Britain.

2012

The Queen's Diamond Jubilee celebrations mark the 60th year of her reign.

2016–20

Referendum vote to leave the EU, followed by protracted negotiations and bitter debates in parliament.

EXPERIENCE

Sunset over Brighton's West Pier ruins

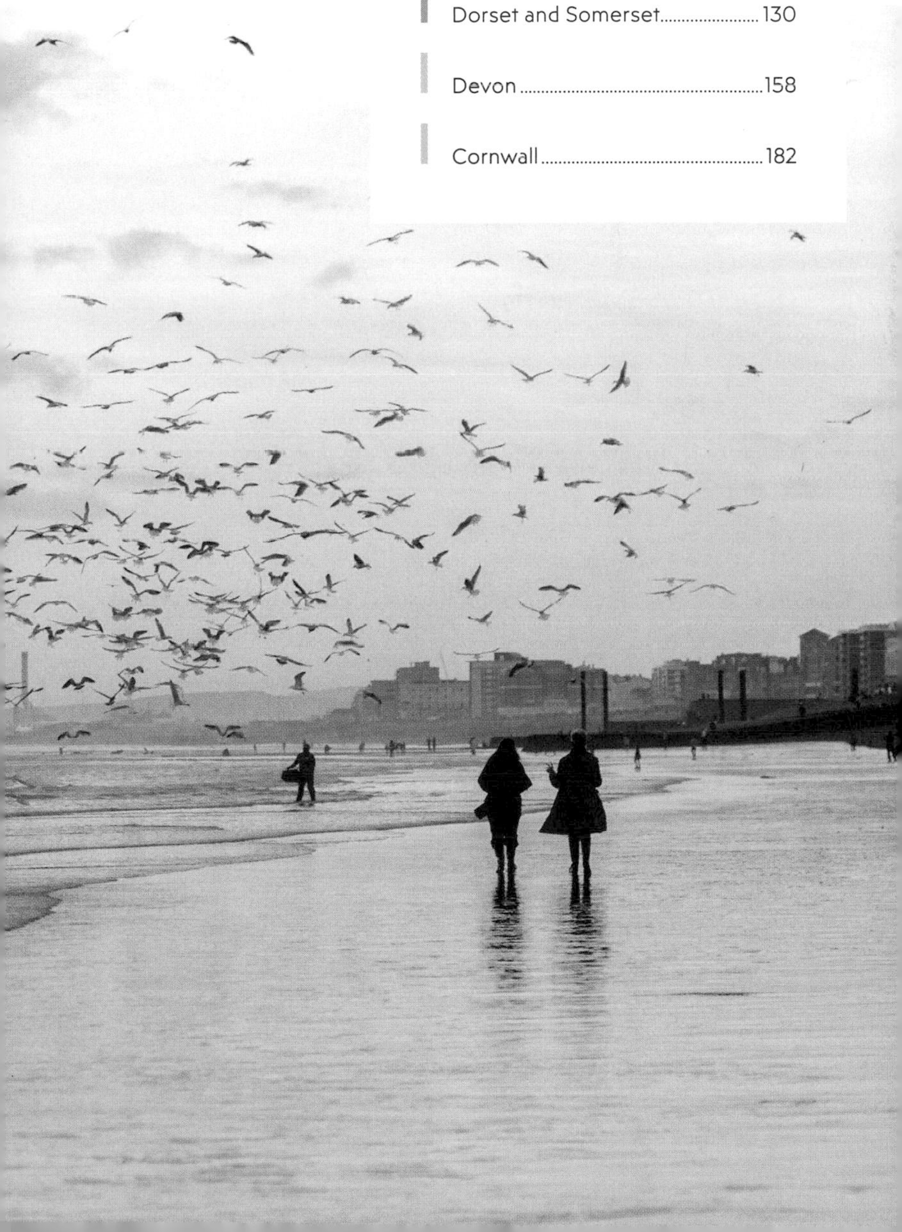

LONDON

London has changed hands time and again over the course of history. The city's beginnings can be traced back to the ancient settlement of Londinium, founded by the Romans around AD 43. It was later occupied by the Anglo-Saxons, attacked by Vikings, invaded and conquered by the Danes and ruled over by the Normans.

From the 16th to mid-17th century, medieval London grew rich through England's expansion in maritime trade, headed up by the Tudors and continued by monarchs to come. Gracious Georgian estates sprang up around the city, and under Queen Victoria many of London's iconic buildings and structures took shape – the Houses of Parliament, Tower Bridge, St Pancras station and the London Underground were built. Fuelled by the wheels of industry and financed by its unsavoury role in the transatlantic slave trade, London soon became the epicentre of the largest and most powerful empire in history.

Having risen from the rubble of two world wars, the city saw in the new millennium with a swathe of grand building projects – the London Eye, Tate Modern and the Millennium Dome – and cranes continue to dominate the skyline in this city that is constantly reinventing itself.

LONDON

Must Sees
1. Buckingham Palace
2. Westminster Abbey
3. British Museum
4. St Paul's Cathedral
5. Victoria and Albert Museum

Experience More
6. Houses of Parliament
7. Downing Street
8. The Mall
9. Tate Britain
10. Royal Academy of Arts
11. Leicester Square
12. Trafalgar Square
13. National Gallery
14. Covent Garden Piazza and Central Market
15. Bloomsbury
16. London Eye
17. Tate Modern
18. Southbank Centre
19. The Shard
20. Shakespeare's Globe
21. Tower of London
22. Tower Bridge
23. Natural History Museum
24. Science Museum
25. Royal Albert Hall

Eat
1. Daquise
2. Hawksmoor
3. Medlar

Drink
4. Queen Elizabeth Hall Roof Garden
5. BFI Riverfront

Shop
6. Fortnum & Mason

State guests are presented and royal christenings take place in the Music Room.

The Victorian Ballroom is used for state banquets and ceremonies.

② (160 m/ 525 ft)

①

→ Buckingham Palace, official home of the British monarch

BUCKINGHAM PALACE

C3 **SW1** **St James's Park, Victoria** **Victoria** **State Rooms and Garden: Jul–Oct: 9:30am–6:30pm daily (last adm: 4:15pm); selected dates Dec–May, check website rct.uk**

The Queen's official London residence is one of the capital's best recognized landmarks. Visit its opulent state rooms for a glimpse of how the royals live.

Both administrative office and family home, Buckingham Palace is the official London residence of the British monarch. The palace is used for ceremonial occasions for visiting heads of state as well as the weekly meeting between the Queen and the Prime Minister. John Nash converted the original Buckingham House into a palace for George IV (r 1820–30). Both he and his brother, William IV (r 1830–37), died before work was completed, and Queen Victoria was the first monarch to live at the palace. She added a fourth wing to incorporate more bedrooms and guest rooms.

THE CHANGING OF THE GUARD

Palace guards, dressed in traditional red tunics and tall furry hats, march from Wellington Barracks to Buckingham Palace, parading for 45 minutes while the palace keys are handed over by the old guard to the new at this colourful and musical military ceremony. Crowds gather to watch this striking show of pageantry (*www.changing-guard.com*).

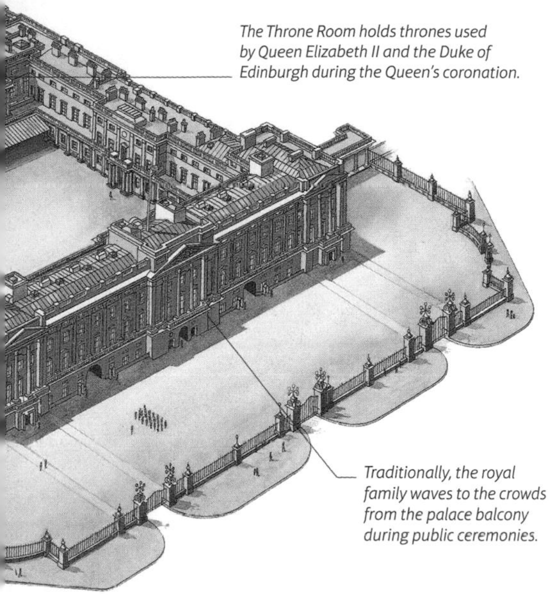

The Throne Room holds thrones used by Queen Elizabeth II and the Duke of Edinburgh during the Queen's coronation.

Traditionally, the royal family waves to the crowds from the palace balcony during public ceremonies.

① 🗺 🏛
The Queen's Gallery

🏠 Buckingham Palace Rd SW1 ⏰ 10am–5:30pm daily (late Jul–Sep: 9:30am–5:30pm; last adm: 4:15pm) 🔒 Between exhibitions, check website

Britain's royal family possesses one of the finest and most valuable art collections in the world, rich in the work of Old Masters such as Johannes Vermeer and Leonardo da Vinci. The Queen's Gallery hosts a rolling programme of the Royal Collection's most impressive masterpieces, with temporary exhibitions featuring fine art, porcelain, jewels, furniture and manuscripts.

→ Soldiers taking part in the Trooping the Colour ceremony

② 🗺 Ⓜ 🏛
Royal Mews

🏠 Buckingham Palace Rd SW1 ⏰ Apr–Oct: 10am–5pm daily; Nov, Feb–Mar: 10am–4pm Mon–Sat 🔒 Subject to closure at short notice, check website; Dec–Jan

Head to the Royal Mews to discover plenty of royal pomp. Stables and coach houses, designed by Nash in 1825, accommodate the horses and coaches used by the royal family on state occasions. The Mews' extensive collection of coaches, motorcars and carriages includes the Irish State Coach, bought by Queen Victoria for the State Opening of Parliament; the open-topped 1902 Royal Landau, used to give the crowds the best view of newlywed royal couples; and the Glass Coach, also used for royal weddings. The newest coach is the Diamond Jubilee State Coach, built in 2012. The star exhibit is the Gold State Coach: built for George III in 1761, with panels by Giovanni Cipriani, it has been used at every coronation since 1821.

↑ Dusk falling over the east façade, which was added to the palace in 1913

② ⬡ ⬡ ⬡ ⬡

WESTMINSTER ABBEY

The West Front towers were designed by Nicholas Hawksmoor.

📍C4 🏛Broad Sanctuary SW1 🚇St James's Park, Westminster 🚉Victoria, Waterloo 🕐Check website for specific parts of the church 🌐westminster-abbey.org

The glorious Gothic Westminster Abbey has some of the best examples of medieval architecture in London and one of the most impressive collections of tombs and monuments in the world.

Westminster Abbey is the stunning setting for coronations, royal marriages and Christian worship and is the final resting place of 17 of Britain's monarchs. The first abbey church was established in the 10th century by St Dunstan and a group of Benedictine monks. The present structure dates largely from the 13th century; the new French-influenced design was begun in 1245 at the behest of Henry III. The abbey has been the fittingly sumptuous setting for all royal coronations since 1066.

The interior presents a diverse array of architectural and sculptural styles, from the austere French Gothic of the nave, through Henry VII's stunning Tudor chapel, to the riotous 18th-century monuments. The latest addition is the 2018 Weston Tower, which provides access to the triforium and its Queen's Diamond Jubilee Galleries, packed with historical treasures.

← The stalls in the quire where the Westminster Abbey choir sing

Timeline

1050
△ New Benedictine abbey church begun by Edward the Confessor.

1245
New church begun to the designs of Henry of Reyns.

1269
△ Body of Edward the Confessor is moved to a new shrine in the abbey.

1540
△ Monastery dissolved on the orders of King Henry VIII.

The stonework here is Victorian.

The north transept's three chapels contain some of the abbey's finest monuments.

St Edward's chapel houses the shrine of Edward the Confessor.

The south transept contains Poets' Corner, where famous literary figures are commemorated.

The Queen's Diamond Jubilee Galleries offer superb views.

The Lady Chapel has a superb vaulted ceiling.

The octagonal Chapter House contains 13th-century tiles.

↑ Cross-section of Westminster Abbey, revealing the interior

The cloisters were built mainly in the 13th and 14th centuries.

Massive flying buttresses help spread the weight of the nave.

The nave – 31 m (102 ft) tall – is the highest in England.

> 💬 **INSIDER TIP**
> **Evensong**
>
> Attend evensong to hear spellbinding choral music and get a glimpse of the abbey's interior free of charge. The service, which includes prayer and readings, is held daily, except for Wednesday, at 5pm (3pm on Sunday).

1745
△ West Front towers completed.

1838
△ Queen Victoria's coronation.

1953
Elizabeth II's coronation is beamed to televisions across the nation.

2011
△ Prince William and Catherine Middleton marry in the abbey.

③ 🛇 🍴 🖵 🛍

BRITISH MUSEUM

📍 C2 **🏠 Great Russell St WC1** **🚇 Tottenham Court Rd, Holborn, Russell Sq** **🚉 Euston**
🕐 10am–5:30pm daily (to 8:30pm Fri) **🌐 britishmuseum.org**

The British Museum holds one of the world's greatest collections of historical and cultural artifacts. This immense hoard of treasure comprises over eight million objects spanning the history of mankind, from prehistoric times to today.

💬 **INSIDER TIP**
Eye Openers

The museum offers an excellent set of free tours. There are over a dozen daily "eye-opener tours" of individual rooms, while on Friday evenings the "spotlight tours" focus on specific exhibits such as the Rosetta Stone. There's no need to book, simply check the website for where and when to meet.

One of the oldest national public museums in the world, the British Museum was established in 1753 to house the books, antiquities and plant and animal specimens of the physician Sir Hans Sloane (1660–1753). The collection expanded rapidly and during the 19th century the museum acquired a mass of Classical and Middle Eastern antiquities, some of which still make up the top attractions here, such as the Rosetta Stone and the Parthenon sculptures. You can now see items drawn from a dizzying number of cultures and civilizations, from Stone Age Europe and Ancient Egypt to modern Japan and contemporary North America. There are sculptures and statues, mummies and murals, coins and medals, ceramics, gold and silver, prints, drawings and innumerable other man-made objects from every corner of the globe and every period of history.

In addition to the vast permanent collection, one of the largest in the world, the British Museum hosts regular special exhibitions, talks and events.

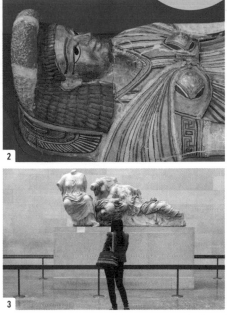

⓵ The Rosetta Stone was the key to interpreting Egyptian hieroglyphs.

⓶ The museum holds the largest collection of Egyptian mummies outside of Egypt.

⓷ Beautiful statues from the Parthenon in Ancient Greece.

The Greek Revival-style main entrance to the British Museum on Great Russell Street

A World of Treasures

There are 95 galleries covering 4 km (2.5 miles) over three floors of the museum, though the majority of exhibits are on the ground and upper floors. Ancient Egyptian artifacts are on the upper floor in Rooms 61 to 66 and in Room 4, beside the Great Court. The Greece, Rome and Middle East collections are also spread across the two main floors, though major items such as the Parthenon sculptures are in the large rooms of the ground floor to the west of the Great Court. The Africa collection is on the lower floor, while Asia exhibits are on the ground and upper floors on the north side. The Americas collection is located in the north-east corner of the main floor. The Sainsbury Gallery hosts major temporary exhibitions. of the ground floor.

← The world-famous Reading Room, designed by Norman Foster, at the centre of the museum's Great Court

Did You Know?

The Portland Vase, made before the birth of Christ, was reassembled after it was smashed by a visitor in 1845.

Inside the Enlightenment gallery, formerly the library of King George III ↑

GREAT COURT AND READING ROOM

The architectural highlight of the building is the Great Court, a breathtaking conversion of the original 19th-century inner courtyard. Opened in 2000, the court is now covered by a tessellated glass roof, creating Europe's largest indoor public square. At the centre of the Great Court is the glorious dome-roofed Reading Room of the former British Library, completed in 1857, where figures such as Mahatma Gandhi and Karl Marx studied.

Top Collections

Prehistoric and Roman Britain

▶ Highlights among the relics of ancient Britain on display include the gold "Mold Cape", a ceremonial Bronze Age cape found in Wales; an antlered headdress worn by hunter gatherers 9,000 years ago; and "Lindow Man", a 1st-century AD victim of sacrifice who was preserved in a bog until 1984.

Europe

Sutton Hoo's treasure, the burial hoard of a 7th-century Anglo-Saxon king, is in Room 41. The artifacts include a helmet and shield, Celtic bowls, and gold and garnet jewellery. Exquisite timepieces include a 400-year-old clock from Germany, designed as a model galleon; in its day it pitched, played music and even fired a cannon. Nearby are the famous 12th-century Lewis chessmen. Baron Ferdinand Rothschild's (1839–98) Renaissance treasures are in Room 2a.

Middle East

Galleries devoted to the Middle East collections cover 7,000 years of history, with famous items such as 7th-century BC Assyrian reliefs from King Ashurbanipal's palace at Nineveh, two large human-headed bulls from 7th-century BC Khorsabad and the Black Obelisk of Shalmaneser III, an Assyrian king. The upper floors contain pieces from ancient Sumeria, part of the Oxus Treasure (which lay buried for over 2,000 years) and the diverse new Islamic World galleries.

Egypt

Egyptian sculptures in Room 4 include a fine red granite head of a king, thought to be Amenhotep III, and a huge statue of King Rameses II. Here too is the Rosetta Stone, used as a key for deciphering Egyptian hieroglyphs. An array of mummies, jewellery and Coptic art is upstairs.

Greece and Rome

◀ The Greek and Roman collections include the controversial Parthenon sculptures. These 5th-century BC reliefs decorated the temple to Athena on the Acropolis, Athens. Much of the temple was ruined, and what survived was removed by the British diplomat Lord Elgin. There is also the Nereid Monument and sculptures from the Mausoleum at Halicarnassus.

Asia

Fine porcelain, Shang bronzes (c 1500–1050 BC) and ceremonial bronze vessels are in the Chinese collection. In the Sir Percival David gallery the Chinese ceramics date from the 10th to early 20th centuries. There is a fine collection of sculpture from the Indian subcontinent, including sculpted reliefs that once covered the walls of the Buddhist temple at Amaravati. A Korean section contains works of Buddhist art, and there is a traditional Japanese teahouse in Room 92.

Africa

African sculptures, textiles and graphic art are in Room 25. Famous bronzes from the Kingdom of Benin, set in due course to return to Nigeria, stand alongside modern African prints, paintings, drawings and colourful fabrics.

④ 🔨 Ⓜ 🖥 🛍

ST PAUL'S CATHEDRAL

📍E2 🚇Ludgate Hill EC4 🚇St Paul's, Mansion House
🚆City Thameslink, Blackfriars 🕐Cathedral:
8:30am–4:30pm Mon–Sat (also 7–9pm Thu); Galleries:
9:30am–4:15pm Mon–Sat 🌐stpauls.co.uk

Built between 1675 and 1710, Sir Christopher Wren's Baroque masterpiece has one of the largest cathedral domes in the world, standing 111 m (365 ft) high and weighing 65,000 tonnes. The splendid cathedral has formed the lavish setting for many state ceremonies.

Following the Great Fire of London in 1666, the medieval cathedral of St Paul's was left in ruins. The authorities turned to Christopher Wren to rebuild it, but his ideas met with strong resistance from the conservative Dean and Chapter. Wren's 1672 Great Model plan was rejected and a watered-down plan was finally agreed in 1675. Despite the compromises, Wren created a magnificent Baroque cathedral. It has a strong choral tradition and is famed for its music, with regular concerts and organ recitals.

Did You Know?

A whisper against the wall in the Dome's Whispering Gallery can be heard clearly on the opposite side.

The balustrade, was added against Wren's wishes.

Carvings on the pediment depict the Conversion of St Paul.

↑ Illustration of the exterior of St Paul's Cathedral

↑ The mighty dome of St Paul's, viewed from the Millennium Bridge

The main entrance is through the West Portico, approached from Ludgate Hill.

Wren intended a single colonnade along the West Portico, but it now has two tiers of columns.

CHRISTOPHER WREN

Sir Christopher Wren (1632–1723) was a leading figure in the rebuilding of London after the Great Fire of 1666. He built 52 churches, 31 of which have survived. Nearly as splendid as St Paul's is St Stephen Walbrook, his domed church of 1672–7. Other landmarks are St Bride's, off Fleet Street, said to have inspired the traditional shape of wedding cakes, and St Mary-le-Bow in Cheapside.

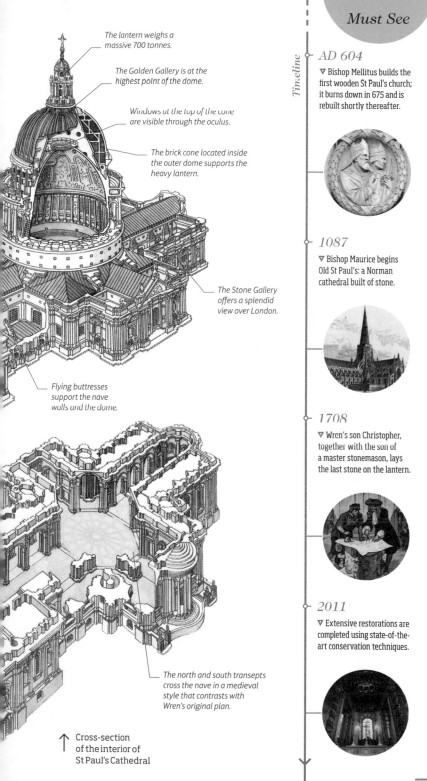

The lantern weighs a massive 700 tonnes.

The Golden Gallery is at the highest point of the dome.

Windows at the top of the cone are visible through the oculus.

The brick cone located inside the outer dome supports the heavy lantern.

The Stone Gallery offers a splendid view over London.

Flying buttresses support the nave walls and the dome.

The north and south transepts cross the nave in a medieval style that contrasts with Wren's original plan.

↑ Cross-section of the interior of St Paul's Cathedral

Timeline

AD 604

▽ Bishop Mellitus builds the first wooden St Paul's church; it burns down in 675 and is rebuilt shortly thereafter.

1087

▽ Bishop Maurice begins Old St Paul's: a Norman cathedral built of stone.

1708

▽ Wren's son Christopher, together with the son of a master stonemason, lays the last stone on the lantern.

2011

▽ Extensive restorations are completed using state-of-the-art conservation techniques.

⑤ 🅜 🍴 🖥 🛍

VICTORIA AND ALBERT MUSEUM

📍A4 🏠Cromwell Rd SW7 🚇South Kensington 🕐10am–5:45pm daily (to 10pm Fri) 📅24–26 Dec 🌐vam.ac.uk

Housed in Victorian splendour, as well as modern, state-of-the-art galleries, the V&A is the world's leading museum of art and design, with its collection spanning 5,000 years of furniture, glass, textiles, fashion, ceramics and jewellery.

The Victoria and Albert Museum (V&A) contains one of the world's broadest collections of art and design, with exhibits ranging from early Christian devotional objects to cutting-edge furniture. Originally founded in 1852 to inspire design students as the Museum of Manufactures, it was renamed by Queen Victoria in 1899 in memory of Prince Albert. The museum has undergone extensive renovation since the early 2000s, including the opening in 2017 of a new quarter on Exhibition Road, encompassing the Sackler Courtyard and the underground Sainsbury Gallery, and an expanded Photography Centre in 2018.

↑ The grand Cromwell Road entrance to the V&A

← The welcoming neon information desk at the museum

GALLERY GUIDE

The V&A has six levels. Level 1 houses the China, Japan and South Asia galleries, the Fashion gallery and the Cast Courts. The British galleries are on Levels 2 and 4. Level 3 contains the 20th-century galleries and silver, ironwork, paintings and photography. The glass display is on Level 4. The Ceramics galleries and Furniture are on Level 6. The fantastic European galleries from AD 300 to 1815 are on Level 1.

↑ The reading room of the National Art Library in the V&A

Did You Know?

The V&A was the first museum to have its own restaurant. The original refreshment rooms are still in use today.

↑ Large-scale works that were once part of buildings, in the Medieval & Renaissance Galleries

EXPERIENCE MORE

6 🏃 Ⓜ 🖥 🛍

Houses of Parliament

📍D4 🏠SW1 🚇Westminster 🚉Victoria 🚢Westminster Pier 🕐For details of tours and to buy tickets, check website 🔒Recesses: mid-Feb, Easter, Whitsun, summer (late Jul-early Sep), conference season (mid-Sep-mid-Oct), mid-Nov, Christmas 🌐parliament.uk/visit

There has been a Palace of Westminster here since the 11th century, though only Westminster Hall and the Jewel Tower survive from that time. The present Gothic-Revival-style structure was designed by architect Sir Charles Barry after the old palace was destroyed by fire in 1834.

Since the 16th century, the site has been the seat of the two Houses of Parliament, called the Commons and the Lords. The Commons is made up of elected Members of Parliament (MPs) of different political parties; the party – or coalition of parties – with the most MPs forms the Government, and its leader becomes Prime Minister. The Government formulates legislation which must be agreed to in both Houses before it becomes law. The Lords comprises appointed life peers, but also hereditary peers and Church of England bishops.

Take a tour of the palace to discover its grand interior and fascinating history, including the Gunpowder Plot of 1605, when Guy Fawkes attempted to blow up the king and Houses of Parliament.

↑ The Houses of Parliament, designed by Sir Charles Barry

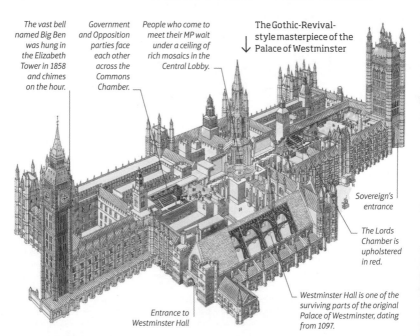

The vast bell named Big Ben was hung in the Elizabeth Tower in 1858 and chimes on the hour.

Government and Opposition parties face each other across the Commons Chamber.

People who come to meet their MP wait under a ceiling of rich mosaics in the Central Lobby.

The Gothic-Revival-style masterpiece of the ↓ Palace of Westminster

Sovereign's entrance

The Lords Chamber is upholstered in red.

Westminster Hall is one of the surviving parts of the original Palace of Westminster, dating from 1097.

Entrance to Westminster Hall

❼
Downing Street

📍 C3 🏠 SW1 🚇 Westminster
🔒 To the public

No 10 Downing Street has been the official residence of the British Prime Minister since 1732. It contains the Cabinet Room, in which government policy is decided, the impressive State Dining Room and a private apartment.

Next door, No 11 is the residence of the Chancellor of the Exchequer, who is in charge of the nation's financial affairs. Members of the public cannot visit Downing Street without authorized access.

❽
The Mall

📍 C3 🏠 SW1 🚇 Charing Cross, Green Park

This broad triumphal approach to Buckingham Palace was created by Aston Webb when he redesigned the front of the palace in 1911. It follows the course of a path at the edge of St James's Park, which was laid out in the reign of Charles II and became the city's most fashionable promenade.

The Mall is used for royal processions and the finish line of the London Marathon. Flagpoles down both sides fly the national flags of foreign heads of state during official visits. The Mall is closed to traffic on Sundays.

❾ 🍸 🍴 🖥 🏛
Tate Britain

📍 C4 🏠 Millbank SW1
🚇 Pimlico 🚆 Victoria, Vauxhall ⛴ Millbank Pier
🕐 10am–6pm daily (to 9:30pm first Fri of month, except Jan) 🔒 24–26 Dec
🌐 tate.org.uk

Founded in 1897, Tate Britain houses the nation's largest collection of British art,

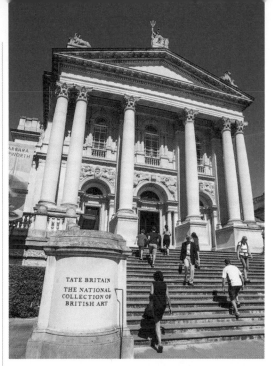

↑ The stately façade of Tate Britain, home of British art

spanning the 16th to the 21st centuries. The museum is named after the sugar merchant Henry Tate, whose private collection formed the basis of the museum.

Displays change frequently but highlights include John Constable's *Flatford Mill* (1816–17), John Everett Millais' *Ophelia* (1851–2) and Francis Bacon's *Three Studies for Figures at the Base of a Crucifixion* (c 1944)

The seven-room Clore Gallery contains the Turner Bequest, some 300 moody oil paintings, 300 sketchbooks and about 20,000 watercolours and drawings that were left to the nation by the great Romantic landscape painter J M W Turner.

TURNER PRIZE

Every other year, Tate Britain exhibits the shortlisted works for the prestigious and often controversial Turner Prize, which was established in 1984. Representing all visual arts, four contemporary artists are short-listed annually on the basis of their work during the preceding year, before a panel of judges picks the winner. Among the most sensational of the boundary-testing winners have been Damien Hirst's *Mother and Child, Divide*d (1995) and the ceramics of Grayson Perry *(right)* in 2003.

10 Royal Academy of Arts

📍C3 🏠Burlington House, Piccadilly W1 🚇Piccadilly Circus, Green Park 🕐10am-6pm daily (to 10pm Fri) 🚫24-26 Dec 🌐royalacademy.org.uk

Founded in 1768 to train artists and to promote and exhibit works of art, the Royal Academy (RA) is one of Britain's oldest art institutions. It's perhaps best known for its annual Summer Exhibition, between June and August, which comprises a mix of around 1,200 new works by established and unknown painters, sculptors, photographers and architects.

The collection is displayed across two palatial Italianate buildings – Burlington House and Burlington Gardens. The two are linked by a bridge, built to mark the RA's 250th anniversary in 2018. At the same time, new galleries, including the Vaults and the Collection Gallery, were built, allowing more space to display highlights from the exceptional permanent collection, which includes works by Michelangelo and Constable, as well as by contemporary artists.

Did You Know?

The Royal Academy was Britain's first independent fine arts school.

11 Leicester Square

📍C3 🏠WC2 🚇Leicester Sq, Piccadilly Circus

Named after the Earl of Leicester, who built a grand house here in 1635, this square was first laid out in the 1670s and soon became a fashionable place to live. In the 18th century residents included scientist Sir Isaac Newton, the painter Joshua Reynolds and the surgeon John Hunter.

The first music halls sprung up here in Victorian times and today it forms the heart of London's West End entertainment district. The Empire and Odeon cinemas are both used to screen major film premieres. Visit the TKTS booth, located in the square, for cut-price theatre tickets.

12 Trafalgar Square

📍C3 🏠WC2 🚇Charing Cross

London's main venue for rallies and outdoor public meetings was conceived by John Nash and was mostly constructed during the 1830s. The 52-m (169-ft) column in the centre of the square commemorates Admiral Lord Nelson, Britain's most famous sea lord, who died at the Battle of Trafalgar in 1805. It dates from 1842; 14 stonemasons held a dinner on its flat top before the statue of Nelson was finally installed. The north side of the square is taken up by the National Gallery, with Canada House on the west side and South Africa House on the east. Three plinths support statues of the

Looking across Trafalgar Square to St Martin-in-the-Fields ↓

great and the good; funds ran out before the fourth plinth, on the northwest corner, could be filled. It now hosts one of London's most idiosyncratic art displays, as artworks are commissioned specially for it, and change every year or two.

↑ Window-shopping and snacking in the Apple Market, Covent Garden

13 Ⓜ Ⓨ Ⓓ Ⓗ

National Gallery

📍 C3 🏠 Trafalgar Sq WC2 Ⓔ Charing Cross, Leicester Sq, Piccadilly Circus 🚉 Charing Cross 🕐 10am–6pm daily (to 9pm Fri) 🚫 1 Jan, 24–26 Dec Ⓦ nationalgallery.org.uk

London's leading art museum, the National Gallery has a collection of over 2,300 paintings. It was established in 1824, after Parliament agreed to purchase 38 major paintings, including works by Raphael and Rubens, at the instigation of art patron Sir George Beaumont. These became the core of a national collection of European art that spans late-medieval times to the 20th century.

Erected in the heart of the West End in order to be accessible to all, the imposing Greek-Revival-style main gallery building was designed by William Wilkins and opened in 1838. To its left lies the Sainsbury Wing, financed by the grocery family and completed in 1991. It houses the Early Renaissance (1200–1500) collection.

Works by artists such as Botticelli, Da Vinci, Monet and Goya are all on display in the National Gallery, and highlights include Jan van Eyck's *The Arnolfini Portrait* (1434), Diego Velázquez's *Rokeby Venus* (1647) and Vincent van Gogh's *Sunflowers* (1888). In 2014, the gallery purchased its first non-European work, *Men of the Docks* (1912), by American artist George Bellows.

Next door is the **National Portrait Gallery**, which holds over 215,000 portraits, spanning six centuries. In 2020, the gallery closed its doors for a major refurbishment; it is scheduled to re-open in 2023. During the closure, artworks from the collection will be displayed in the National Gallery, as well as at various locations across the UK.

National Portrait Gallery

Ⓨ Ⓔ Ⓓ 🏠 2 St Martin's Pl WC2 🚫 For refurbishment until 2023 Ⓦ npg.org.uk

---

SHOP

Fortnum & Mason

The finest foods in beautifully designed packaging are the hallmarks of Fortnum & Mason. Established in 1707, this is one of the city's most renowned and extravagant stores.

📍 C3 🏠 181 Piccadilly W1 Ⓦ fortnumand mason.com

---

14 Ⓨ Ⓓ Ⓗ

Covent Garden Piazza and Central Market

📍 D3 🏠 Covent Garden WC2 Ⓔ Covent Garden, Leicester Sq 🚉 Charing Cross Ⓦ coventgarden.london

One of London's most distinct and animated squares, Covent Garden comprises a bustling piazza filled with street performers and a market alive with shops, cafés and the occasional opera singer. The tradition of street entertainers in the piazza has endured since at least the 17th century.

The 17th-century architect Inigo Jones planned for the Covent Garden Piazza to be an elegant residential square, modelled on the piazza in the Tuscan town of Livorno, but the Victorian buildings on and around the square are now almost entirely commercial.

The central, covered Apple Market, designed in 1833 for fruit and vegetable whole-salers, today houses an array of stalls and small shops selling designer clothes, books, arts and crafts, decorative items and antiques.

↑ The London Eye observation wheel, on the River Thames

Charles Dickens Museum

⊛ ⊜ ⓖ ◨ 48 Doughty St WC1 ⊜ Chancery Lane, Russell Sq ◷ 10am–5pm Tue–Sun (last adm: 4pm; Dec: also Mon); check website for monthly late opening ◷ 1 Jan, 25 & 26 Dec, and occasionally for events ⓦ dickensmuseum.com

16 ⊛ ◨ ⓰
London Eye

◙ D3 ◨ Jubilee Gardens SE1 ⊜ Waterloo, Westminster ◷ From 10am daily; closing times vary, check website for details ⊜ Waterloo ⊜ London Eye Pier ◷ Two weeks in Jan for maintenance ⓦ londoneye.com

The London Eye is a 135-m (443-ft) observation wheel that was installed on the South Bank to mark the millennium; it immediately became one of the city's most recognizable landmarks, notable not only for its size, but also for its circularity amid the block-shaped buildings flanking it.

Its enclosed passenger capsules offer a 30-minute ride as the wheel makes a full turn, with breathtaking views over London and for up to 40 km (25 miles) around. Towering over one of the world's most familiar riverscapes, it has understandably captured the hearts of Londoners and visitors, and is one of the city's most popular attractions.

Trips on the wheel are on the hour and every half-hour.

17 ⊛ ◨ ⓨ ⓰
Tate Modern

◙ E3 ◨ Bankside SE1 ⊜ Blackfriars, Southwark ⊜ Blackfriars ◷ 10am–6pm Sun–Thu, 10am–10pm Fri & Sat ◷ 24–26 Dec ⓦ tate. org.uk/modern

Looming over the southern bank of the Thames, Tate Modern occupies the converted

---

15
Bloomsbury

◙ C2 ⊜ Russell Sq, Tottenham Court Rd

A traditional centre of the book trade, Bloomsbury is home to numerous writers and artists. This historic area is dominated by the British Museum *(p62)* and the University of London, and characterized by fine Georgian squares. These include leafy Russell Square, where the famed poet T S Eliot (1888–1965) worked for publisher Faber & Faber for 40 years; peaceful Queen Square, which contains a statue of Queen Charlotte, wife of George III; and Bloomsbury Square, laid out in 1661. A plaque here commemorates members of the Bloomsbury Group. Several members of the group, including prominent figures such as novelists

Virginia Woolf and E M Forster, lived in houses around Gordon Square. Charles Dickens lived at 48 Doughty Street during a brief but critical stage in his career; it was here that he completed *The Pickwick Papers* and where he wrote such classics as *Oliver Twist* and *Nicholas Nickleby*.

His former home is now the **Charles Dickens Museum**, which has a number of rooms laid out as they were in Dickens' time; other rooms display a varied collection of articles associated with him. The museum houses over 100,000 items in total – from manuscripts, paintings and personal items, to pieces of furniture from Dickens' other homes, and first editions of many of his best-known works. The museum also puts on special exhibitions and events, and runs a monthly "Housemaid's Tour".

⬙ GREAT VIEW
Top of the Tower

On Level 10 of the Tate Modern (the top floor of the fantastic Blavatnik Building extension), the 360-degree viewing terrace gives epic views of London. You can enjoy more of the same, taking in St Paul's Cathedral, the rest of the City and beyond, from the restaurant on Level 9.

Bankside power station, a dynamic space for one of the world's premier collections of modern and contemporary art. Opened to coincide with the new millennium, this Goliath of a gallery boasts a collection of over 70,000 works of modern art, featuring paintings and sculptures by some of the most significant artists of the 20th and 21st centuries, including Pablo Picasso and Francis Bacon.

The gallery's west entrance leads into the huge central Turbine Hall, which houses a newly commissioned installation every year. The galleries for the permanent collection and special exhibitions begin on level 2 and continue to level 4, with a bridge leading across the Turbine Hall into the Switch House. This striking ten-storey building opened in 2016 and displays work from 1960 to the present, with the basement space, formerly occupied by the power station's oil tanks, used for live art, film and video.

The displays in the permanent galleries are organized by different themes such as "Artist and Society" and "Materials and Objects". Some of the best works that have been on display at the Tate Modern include Picasso's *Weeping Woman* (1937), Henri Matisse's

→

Enjoying the sun outside the Queen Elizabeth Hall at the Southbank Centre

paper cut-out *The Snail* (1953) and Louise Bourgeois' giant spider sculpture *Maman* (1999).

(18) (🚫) (🍴) (💻) (🏛)
Southbank Centre

📍 D3 🏠 Belvedere Rd, South Bank SE1 🚇 Waterloo, Embankment 🚉 Waterloo, Waterloo East, Charing Cross 🚢 Festival Pier, London Eye Pier 🌐 southbankcentre.co.uk

With an art gallery and three world-class auditoriums for music, dance and other events lined up along the river, the Southbank Centre is one of London's pre-eminent cultural and performance venues.

London's high-profile and much-respected arts centre takes centre stage among the other great institutions on the South Bank: the National Theatre and the British Film Institute. The Southbank Centre itself comprises four main venues: the Royal Festival Hall, the Hayward Gallery, the Queen Elizabeth Hall and the Purcell Room. The centre is always buzzing, with bars and restaurants slotted into and between the terraces, platforms, walkways and rooftops of this concrete complex.

Performances focus on classical music, but there is also opera, folk, world music and all kinds of leftfield genres, plus comedy and dance. Regular festivals include the London Jazz Festival, Women of the World (WOW) Festival, the London Literature Festival and Meltdown.

DRINK

Queen Elizabeth Hall Roof Garden
There are great views of the River Thames from the lawn of this rooftop bar.

📍 D3 🏠 Southbank Centre ⏰ Apr-Oct 🌐 southbankcentre.co.uk

BFI Riverfront
A buzzing balcony bar facing the river under the curve of Waterloo Bridge. There are DJ sets on Saturdays.

📍 D3 🏠 BFI Southbank ⏰ Wed-Sat 🌐 benugo.com

↑ The imposing Tower of London, the setting for key historical events

19

The Shard

📍 E3 🚪 London Bridge St SE1 🚇 London Bridge 🕐 The View from the Shard: 10am–10pm daily (last adm: 9pm; sometimes closes earlier for events) 🌐 the viewfromtheshard.com

Designed by Italian architect Renzo Piano, the Shard is one of the tallest buildings in Western Europe. At 310 m (1,016 ft) high, this unique building dominates the skyline, its appearance changing with the weather due to the crystalline façade that reflects the sky. Its 95 floors are home to offices, apartments, the five-star Shangri-La hotel, half a dozen bars and restaurants, and Britain's highest observation gallery, The View from the Shard, which allows visitors 360-degree panoramas of up to 64 km (40 miles).

20

Shakespeare's Globe

📍 E3 🚪 21 New Globe Walk SE1 🚇 Blackfriars, London Bridge, Mansion House 🕐 Tours every 30 mins 9:30am–12:30pm; book online 🗓 24 & 25 Dec 🌐 shakespearesglobe.com

Opened in 1997, this striking circular building is a reproduction of an Elizabethan theatre, close to the site of the original

↑ The simple yet striking exterior of Shakespeare's Globe

Globe where many of William Shakespeare's plays were first performed. It was built using handmade bricks and oak laths, fastened with wooden pegs, and has the first thatched roof allowed in London since the Great Fire of 1666. Open to the elements (the seating area is covered), it operates only in the summer. Beneath the theatre, an exhibition covers many aspects of the Bard's work.

21

Tower of London

📍 F3 🚪 Tower Hill EC3 🚇 Tower Hill, Tower Gateway DLR 🚆 Fenchurch Street 🕐 9am–5:30pm Tue–Sat; 10am–5:30pm Sun & Mon (Nov–Feb: to 4:30pm) 🗓 1 Jan, 24–26 Dec 🌐 hrp.org.uk

Soon after William the Conqueror became king in

1066, he built a fortification here to guard the entrance to London from attack via the Thames Estuary. In 1097 the White Tower was completed in sturdy stone; other fine buildings, including Henry VIII's Medieval Palace, have been added over the centuries. The Tower has served as a royal residence, armoury, treasury and, most famously, as a prison. Prisoners escorted there entered from the river through "Traitor's Gate". Some were tortured, before meeting violent deaths on nearby Tower Hill. Among those who died here were Edward IV's young sons, the "Princes in the Tower", and two of Henry VIII's wives, Anne Boleyn and Catherine Howard.

The Tower has been an attraction since the reign of Charles II (1660–85), when both the Crown Jewels and the Line of Kings collection of armour were first shown to the public. Other exhibits include a display on the Peasants' Revolt of 1381, the only time the Tower's walls were breached.

The most celebrated residents are the ravens; legend has it that the kingdom will fall if they desert the Tower.

22 ⚽ Ⓜ

Tower Bridge

⑨ F3 **📍 SE1** **🚇 Tower Hill** **🕐 9:30am–5:30pm daily** **📅 24–26 Dec** **🌐 tower bridge.org.uk**

This striking piece of Victorian engineering, designed by Sir Horace Jones, was completed in 1894 and soon became a symbol of London. Its two Gothic towers contain the mechanism for raising the roadway to permit large ships to pass through, or for special occasions. The bridge is 60 m (200 ft) wide and 40 m (135 ft)

high when raised. The towers are made of a steel framework clad in stone, linked by two high-level walkways.

The bridge houses the Tower Bridge Exhibition, with interactive displays bringing its history to life. There are fine river views from the walkways, including through the glass floor, as well as a magnificent Victorian steam engine room, which powered the lifting machinery until 1976, when the system was electrified.

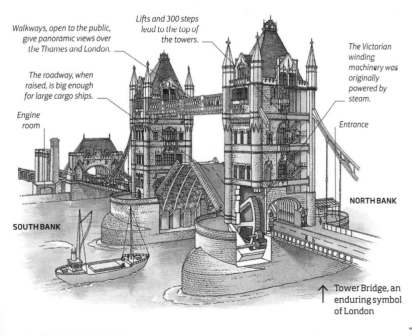

Walkways, open to the public, give panoramic views over the Thames and London.

Lifts and 300 steps lead to the top of the towers.

The roadway, when raised, is big enough for large cargo ships.

Engine room

The Victorian winding machinery was originally powered by steam.

Entrance

SOUTH BANK

NORTH BANK

↑ Tower Bridge, an enduring symbol of London

←

The huge skeleton of a blue whale in the Natural History Museum

24 Science Museum

📍A4 🚪Exhibition Rd SW7
🚇South Kensington
🕐10am-6pm daily (last adm: 5:15pm) 🌐science museum.org.uk

Centuries of continuing scientific and technological development lie at the heart of the Science Museum's massive collections. The hardware displayed is magnificent: from steam engines to aeroengines; spacecraft to the very first mechanical computers. Equally important is the social context of science – what discoveries and inventions mean for day-to-day life – and the process of discovery itself.

23 Natural History Museum

📍A4 🚪Cromwell Rd SW7
🚇South Kensington
🕐10am-5:50pm daily (to 10pm last Fri of month) 🌐nhm.ac.uk

The richly sculpted stonework of the cathedral-like Natural History Museum (NHM) conceals an iron and steel frame, a revolutionary construction technique when the museum opened in 1881. The imaginative displays tackle fundamental issues such as the planet's ecology and evolution, the origin of species and the development of human beings – all explained through the latest technology, interactive techniques and traditional displays.

The central Hintze Hall showcases the museum's collections and explores humanity's relationship with the planet. It is dominated by the huge suspended skeleton of a blue whale.

The museum is divided into four sections: the Blue Zone, Green Zone, Red Zone and Orange Zone. In the Blue Zone, the Ecology exhibition explores the complex web of the natural world through a replica of a moonlit rainforest buzzing with the sounds of insects. One of the most popular exhibits is the Dinosaur Gallery, which includes animatronic models of dinosaurs. The Vault, in the Green Zone, holds a dazzling collection of gems, crystals, metals and meteorites from around the world. The Darwin Centre is the largest curved structure in Europe. The eight-storey-high cocoon houses a vast collection of insects and plants.

TOP 5 UNMISSABLE EXHIBITS IN THE NHM

Triceratops Skull
The gigantic skull of a plant-eating three-horned dinosaur.

Latrobe Gold Nugget
A rare crystallized gold nugget from Australia weighing 717 g (25 oz).

Butterflies
A tropical butterfly house (open Mar-Sep).

Archaeopteryx
This valuable fossil of a feathered dinosaur provided the link between birds and dinosaurs.

Earthquake Simulator
Experience the effects of an earthquake in this simulation.

The museum is spread over five floors and includes the high-tech Wellcome Wing at its western end. The basement features excellent hands-on galleries for children, including The Garden. The Energy Hall dominates the ground floor and is dedicated to steam power, with the still-operational Harle Syke Mill Engine of 1903. Here too are Exploring Space and Making the Modern World, a highlight of which is the display of the scarred Apollo 10 spacecraft, which carried three astronauts to the moon and back in May 1969.

In Challenge of Materials, on the first floor, our expectations of materials are confounded by exhibits such as a bridge made of glass and a steel wedding dress, while the renovated Medicine galleries chart some of the most extraordinary achievements in the world of medicine over the last 400 years. The Flight gallery, on the third floor, is packed with early flight contraptions, fighter planes, aeroplanes and the Launchpad.

The Wellcome Wing offers four floors of interactive technology, including "Who Am I?" (first floor), a fascinating exhibition exploring the science of you. With an IMAX 3D Cinema and the SimEx simulator ride, it is a breathtaking addition to the museum.

Royal Albert Hall

A3 **Kensington Gore SW7** **South Kensington** **For performances & tours daily; box office: 9am-9pm daily** **royalalberthall.com**

The vast oval hall named after Queen Victoria's beloved consort, Prince Albert, was opened in 1871 and has mainly functioned as a concert venue, but it has also hosted a wide variety of other events over the years, including comedy shows and sporting contests. Today, it is probably most famous for the summer "Proms".

A short walk to the north of the Albert Hall, in Kensington Gardens, is the grandiose **Albert Memorial**. Designed by leading Victorian architect George Gilbert Scott and completed in 1876, it is made up of a vast decorative Gothic canopy within which sits a gilded statue of Prince Albert sculpted by John Foley.

Eight large allegorical sculptures stand at the corner of the memorial and at the base of the steps leading up to it: four representing industry; the other four the Empire.

Albert Memorial
South Carriage Dr, Kensington Gardens W2
6am-dusk daily
royalparks.org.uk

←

The Prince Consort statue in front of the Royal Albert Hall

A SHORT WALK
COVENT GARDEN

Distance 1.5 km (1 mile) **Time** 25 minutes
Nearest Tube Leicester Square

Although no longer alive with the calls of fruit and vegetable market traders going about their business, visitors, residents and street entertainers throng Covent Garden Piazza, much as they would have done centuries ago. Pause to people-watch as you stroll through this buzzing area, popping into vibrant boutiques and historic pubs along the way.

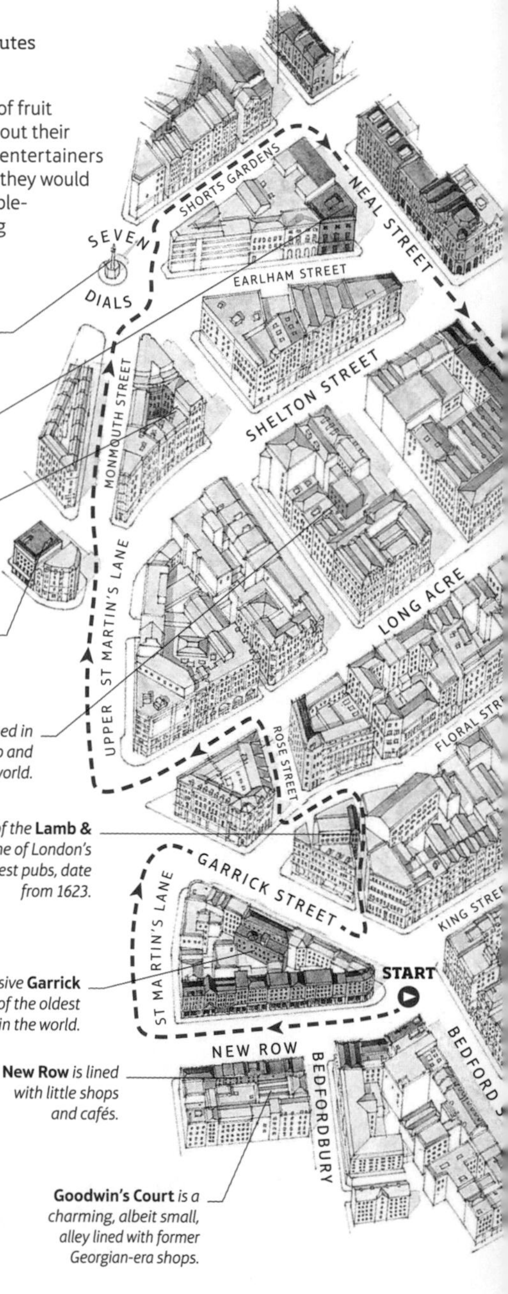

*Bright and colourful **Neal Street** and **Neal's Yard** are home to lots of charming shops and cafés.*

*A replica of a 17th-century monument marks the junction at **Seven Dials**.*

*The airy **Thomas Neal's Centre** houses designer shops and the Donmar Warehouse Theatre.*

***Ching Court** is a Post-Modernist courtyard by architect Terry Farrell.*

***St Martin's Theatre** is home to the world's longest-running play: The Mousetrap.*

***Stanfords**, established in 1852, is the largest map and guide retailer in the world.*

*Parts of the **Lamb & Flag**, one of London's oldest pubs, date from 1623.*

*The exclusive **Garrick Club** is one of the oldest in the world.*

***New Row** is lined with little shops and cafés.*

***Goodwin's Court** is a charming, albeit small, alley lined with former Georgian-era shops.*

SEVEN DIALS

SHORTS GARDENS

NEAL STREET

EARLHAM STREET

SHELTON STREET

MONMOUTH STREET

LONG ACRE

FLORAL STREET

ST MARTIN'S LANE

UPPER ST MARTIN'S LANE

ROSE STREET

GARRICK STREET

KING STREET

ST MARTIN'S LANE

NEW ROW

BEDFORDBURY

BEDFORD ST

START

Did You Know?

Eliza Doolittle, of George Bernard Shaw's *Pygmalion* (1913), was a flower seller in Covent Garden.

Locator Map
For more detail see p56

↑ Plants in a wooden market
barrow in Covent Garden

*Covent Garden
station*

Many of the world's greatest
classical singers and dancers
have appeared on the **Royal
Opera House**'s stage.

Bow Street Police Station *housed
London's first police force, the Bow
Street Runners, in the 18th century. It
is being converted into a hotel.*

*A theatre has stood on the site of
the* **Theatre Royal Drury Lane** *since
1663, making it London's oldest theatre.
It is owned by composer Andrew Lloyd
Webber and stages popular musicals.*

8 Russell Street, *now
a French bakery, is
where Dr Johnson first
met his biographer,
James Boswell.*

*The history of the city's
public transport system
is brought to life in
the intriguing* **London
Transport Museum**.

*Performers of all kinds – jugglers, clowns,
acrobats and musicians – entertain
the crowds in* **Covent Garden Piazza** *and
under cover in the Central Market (p73).*

Jubilee Market *sells
clothes and bric-a-brac.*

Despite appearances, **St Paul's
Church** *faces away from the
piazza. Its grand portico serves
as a stage for a colourful cast
of street performers.*

Rules restaurant *is
frequented by the
rich and famous for its
typically English food.*

FINISH

0 metres 100
0 yards 100

N ↑

A SHORT WALK
WHITEHALL AND WESTMINSTER

Distance 1.5 km (1 mile) **Time** 30 minutes
Nearest Tube St James's Park

London has comparatively little monumental architecture, but a stroll through the historic seat of both the Government and the Established Church uncovers broad, stately avenues designed to overawe with pomp. On weekdays the streets are crowded with members of the civil service, while at weekends they teem mainly with tourists visiting some of London's most famous sights.

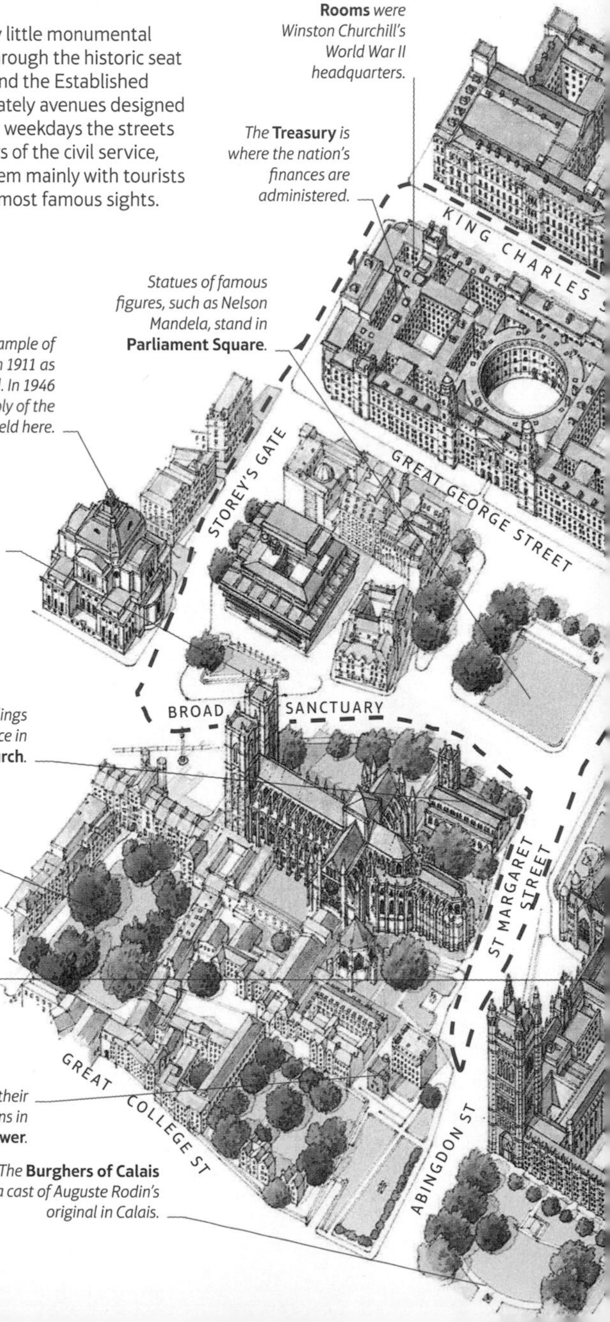

The meticulously preserved **War Rooms** were Winston Churchill's World War II headquarters.

The **Treasury** is where the nation's finances are administered.

Statues of famous figures, such as Nelson Mandela, stand in **Parliament Square**.

Central Hall is a florid example of the Beaux Arts style, built in 1911 as a Methodist meeting hall. In 1946 the first General Assembly of the United Nations was held here.

Westminster Abbey is London's most important church (p60).

Society weddings often take place in **St Margaret's Church**.

Westminster School was founded in Dean's Yard in 1540.

Richard I's statue, by Carlo Marochetti (1860), depicts the 12th-century Coeur de Lion (Lionheart).

Kings once stored their most valuable possessions in the **Jewel Tower**.

The **Burghers of Calais** is a cast of Auguste Rodin's original in Calais.

KING CHARLES S

STOREY'S GATE

GREAT GEORGE STREET

BROAD SANCTUARY

ST MARGARET STREET

GREAT COLLEGE ST

ABINGDON ST

FINISH

British prime ministers have lived on **Downing Street** since 1732 (p71).

A mounted guard is ceremonially changed at **Horse Guards Parade** every day.

Dover House, a stately mansion dating from 1787, now houses the Scotland Office.

Inigo Jones designed the elegant **Banqueting House**, which has a Rubens ceiling, in 1622.

DOWNING ST

WHITEHALL

LONDON

Whitehall and Westminster

Locator Map
For more detail see p56

Depicting wartime uniforms, the **Monument to the Women of World War II** was unveiled by the Queen in 2005.

Edwin Lutyens' **Cenotaph** dates from 1920.

RICHMOND TERRACE

The Commons Chamber might relocate to **Richmond House** in the mid-2020s while the Palace of Westminster undergoes renovation work.

PARLIAMENT STREET

VICTORIA EMBANKMENT

Westminster Pier is a starting point for riverboat excursions.

Portcullis House provides offices for Members of Parliament.

Boudicca, the British queen who resisted the Romans, was portrayed by Thomas Thornycroft in the 1850s.

BRIDGE STREET

START

Westminster station

The **Houses of Parliament** and **Big Ben** were designed by Charles Barry in 1834, when the Palace of Westminster burned down (p70).

0 metres   100
0 yards   100

N

→ The Burghers of Calais statue, by the Houses of Parliament

KENT AND SUSSEX

England's southeast corner has been an arrival point for newcomers throughout history, including Iron Age Celts, Romans, Saxons, Christian missionaries and countless other visitors from Europe and even further afield.

The Romans arrived in Kent in the 1st century AD and built towns and villas between the coast and their new city of Londinium. In the 6th century, St Augustine came to Kent to convert the Anglo-Saxons to Christianity and make Canterbury the centre of the English Church, as it remains today.

As London consolidated its status as the focus and capital of the country, the counties between the city and the coast became favoured places for the monarchs and the nobility to show their wealth and prestige, and a number of lavish mansions arose. Kent also came to be known as the "Garden of England" due to the fertility of its fruit farms and the beauty of its spectacular gardens.

Around the coast, ports such as Dover, Hastings and Rye – which is now 3 km (2 miles) from the sea – grew rich in the Middle Ages on Continental trade. More recently, this shoreline became one of the first centres of the seaside holiday, with long shingle beaches and a range of resorts. These include Margate – affectionately dubbed Shoreditch-on-Sea following a recent influx of London creatives swapping city life for sea air – and Brighton, the cosmopolitan, free-spirited jewel of the south coast.

KENT AND SUSSEX

Must Sees
1. Canterbury
2. Brighton

Experience More
3. Margate
4. Leeds Castle
5. Rochester
6. Whitstable
7. Dover
8. Royal Tunbridge Wells
9. Sissinghurst
10. Knole
11. Ightham Mote
12. Chartwell
13. Hever Castle
14. Romney Marsh
15. Rye
16. Bodiam Castle
17. Winchelsea
18. Hastings
19. Eastbourne
20. Lewes
21. Charleston
22. Arundel Castle
23. Steyning
24. Petworth House
25. Chichester

LONDON
p54

HAMPSHIRE AND WILTSHIRE
p108

0 kilometres   20
0 miles   20

N

❶

CANTERBURY

⚑F1 **⌂Kent** **🚃🚌** **ℹThe Beaney, 18 High St; www.canterbury.co.uk**

The beautiful city of Canterbury has been a major Christian pilgrimage site for the last 900 years, since the building of its glorious cathedral in 1070 and the martyrdom of Thomas Becket a century later.

Canterbury's position on the London to Dover route meant it was an important Roman town even before the arrival of St Augustine in 597 to convert the Anglo-Saxons to Christianity. The town soon became the centre of the Christian Church in England.

The first Norman archbishop, Lanfranc, ordered a new **cathedral** to be built on the ruins of the Anglo-Saxon cathedral in 1070. It was enlarged and rebuilt many times and as a result embraces examples of all styles of medieval architecture. The most poignant moment in its history came in 1170 when Thomas Becket was murdered here. Four years after his death a fire devastated the cathedral and the Trinity Chapel was built to house Becket's remains. The shrine quickly became an important religious site. The Trinity Chapel also holds the world-renowned Miracle Windows. Dating from the early 13th century, these stunning glass panels depict pilgrims in various guises travelling to Canterbury.

For a glimpse into the city's ancient past, visit the **Canterbury Roman Museum**, which harbours the remains of a Roman townhouse complex, as well as some beautiful mosaics. Beyond here lie the ancient city walls, which include the Westgate Towers, England's oldest surviving medieval gateway, which stands on the bank of the Great Stour river.

A wonderful way to see the city is from the river in a punt. Glide under bridges, alongside historic buildings and through a medieval tunnel on a guided tour. Punts depart from Westgate Bridge and Water Lane.

Canterbury Cathedral

♿🅿🕐 ⌂11 The Precincts, Canterbury 🕐9am–5:30pm Mon–Sat (to 5pm winter), 12:30–4pm Sun 🌐canterbury-cathedral.org

Canterbury Roman Museum

♿ ⌂Longmarket, Butchery Lane 🕐10am–5pm daily 🌐canterburymuseums.co.uk

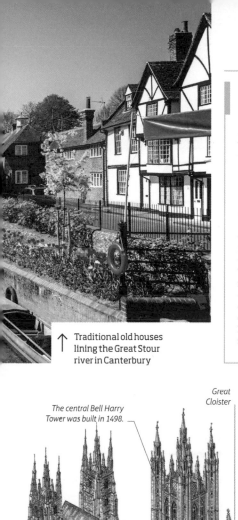

↑ Traditional old houses lining the Great Stour river in Canterbury

GEOFFREY CHAUCER

Considered to be the first great English poet, Geoffrey Chaucer (c 1345–1400) wrote what is thought by many to be one of the greatest and most entertaining works of early English literature, the *Canterbury Tales* – a rumbustious account of a group of pilgrims travelling from London to Becket's shrine in 1387. The pilgrims represent a cross-section of 14th-century English society.

Illustration showing ↓ some of the highlights of Canterbury Cathedral

The central Bell Harry Tower was built in 1498.

Great Cloister

The quire (choir), completed in 1184, is one of the longest in England.

The site of the tomb of St Thomas Becket is marked by a lighted candle.

The tomb of Edward III's son, who died in 1376.

Trinity Chapel

The circular Corona Chapel

The South West Porch (1426)

The nave is 60 m (197 ft) in length.

The medieval southwest transept window

The Great South Window (1958)

St Augustine's Chair

2

BRIGHTON

🅐 D2 🚉 East Sussex 🚆 Brighton 🚌 Pool Valley
ℹ️ Brighton Centre, King's Rd; www.visitbrighton.com

London's nearest south-coast resort, Brighton has always attracted a sophisticated crowd. The spirit of the Prince Regent lives on, not only in his splendid Pavilion, but in the city's buzzing nightlife, independent shops, thriving LGBT+ scene and progressive politics.

① 🍴 🖥️

Brighton Palace Pier

🅐 Madeira Drive
🌐 brightonpier.co.uk

Opened in 1899, the large Brighton Palace Pier (also known simply as Brighton Pier) retains a Victorian ambience while catering for modern visitors with game arcades, bars, fish and chip restaurants and funfair rides, such as a roller-coaster, dodgems and carousels.

②

West Pier

🌐 westpier.co.uk

A distinctive landmark west of Brighton Pier, the now-derelict West Pier was built in 1866 and had a popular concert hall in its heyday. Its popularity declined from the 1950s and it eventually closed in 1975.

③ 🚲 🖥️ 🛍️

Brighton Museum & Art Gallery

🅐 Royal Pavilion Gardens
🕙 10am–5pm Tue–Sun
🌐 brightonmuseums.org.uk

This lovely museum and art gallery, part of the Royal Pavilion Estate, has wonderfully varied exhibits ranging from art and design, fine art and fashion to natural sciences and archaeology, all enhanced by state-of-the-art interactive displays.

→
Displays in the Brighton Museum & Art Gallery

↑ Brighton's Victorian pleasure pier, also known as the Palace Pier

④ 🚃

Volk's Electric Railway

🅰 Aquarium Station to Black Rock Station 🕐 Spring and summer 🆆 volkselectric railway.co.uk

Opened in 1883, Volk's is the world's oldest operating public electric railway. It provides a fun ride along the Brighton seafront from the pier to the marina in season, taking about 12 minutes, and can carry up to 80 passengers.

The son of a German clockmaker, Magnus Volk, who designed the railway, was an inventor and pioneering electrical engineer born in Brighton in 1851.

Did You Know?

Brighton's West Pier is one of just two Grade I listed piers in Britain.

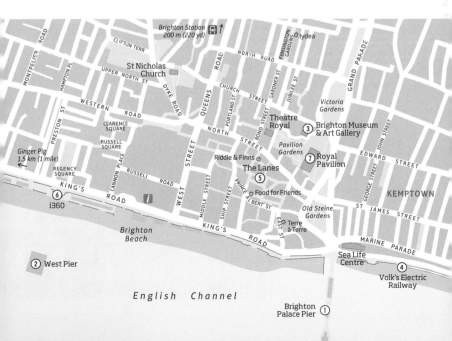

EAT

Food for Friends
Knockout vegetarian and vegan delights in a light-filled interior.

📍17-18 Prince Albert St
🌐 foodforfriends.com

£££

Ginger Pig
A traditional but classy pub just off the seafront offering delicious British food sourced from local suppliers.

📍3 Hove St, Hove
🌐 thegingerpigpub.com

£££

Terre à Terre
An acclaimed restaurant in the Lanes serving world-inspired vegetarian dishes.

📍71 East St 🕒Mon Oct-Feb 🌐terreaterre.co.uk

£££

Iydea
This award-winning vegetarian café serves delicious, freshly prepared dishes.

📍17 Kensington Gardens 🕒From 5:30pm
🌐iydea.co.uk

£££

Riddle & Finns
The flagship of this champagne-and-oyster bar chain in the Lanes serves superb fresh seafood and fish in a casual setting.

📍12B Meeting House Lane 🌐riddleand finns.co.uk

£££

⑤ 🛍️ 🍴 ☕

The Lanes
The original streets of the fishing village of Brighthelstone, this is the oldest part of Brighton. The maze of narrow alleys, completed around the middle of the 18th century, is full of independent shops and boutiques and forms the city's most popular shopping district. It is packed with all sorts of shops, from antiques stores and jewellers to gift shops and clothes boutiques. Head north of the Lanes for North Laine, another lively shopping district full of independent shops lining wider thoroughfares.

⑥ 🎢 🍴

i360

📍Lower King's Rd
🕒10am-7:30pm daily (to 9:30pm Fri & Sat)
🌐britishairwaysi360.com

This breathtaking "vertical cable car" is a sleek glass pod that rises 137 m (450 ft) up a

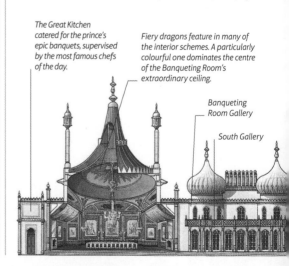

The Great Kitchen catered for the prince's epic banquets, supervised by the most famous chefs of the day.

Fiery dragons feature in many of the interior schemes. A particularly colourful one dominates the centre of the Banqueting Room's extraordinary ceiling.

Banqueting Room Gallery

South Gallery

LGBT+ BRIGHTON

Brighton has the most renowned LGBT+ scene in England and, outside of London, the liveliest and most vibrant. Today's thriving LGBT+ community is thought to make up as much as 15 per cent of the city's population. The epicentre is the seafront Kemptown district, also known as Camp Town, and the annual Pride Festival, held in the first week of August, is among the biggest in Europe, attracting superstar music acts to the main venue at Preston Park.

↑ Colourful bunting adorning the Lanes shopping area

giant silver needle to provide superb 360-degree vistas. At the foot of the needle is a fine beachside restaurant. Inside the pod is the "Skybar", open at night for a unique view of the stars over the sea.

> **As sea bathing became increasingly popular in the 18th century, Brighton became England's most fashionable seaside resort.**

Royal Pavilion

⊙ Old Steine, Brighton
⊙ Apr–Sep: 9:30am–5:45pm daily; Oct–Mar: 10am–5:15pm daily (last adm: 45 mins before closing)
⊙ 25 & 26 Dec ⊙ brighton museums.org.uk

The Prince of Wales's opulent seaside retreat, designed to echo the palaces of Mughal India, epitomizes the extravagant pleasures of Brighton in its 19th-century heyday and its quirky charm today. As sea bathing became increasingly popular in the 18th century, Brighton became England's most fashionable seaside resort. Its gaiety soon appealed to the rakish Prince of Wales, who became George IV in 1820. When, in 1785, at the age of 23, he secretly

married Mrs Fitzherbert, a 29-year-old Catholic widow, it was here that they conducted their liaison. He acquired a former farmhouse near the shore and in 1815, once he had become Regent – just one small step to the throne – he employed Henry Holland and later John Nash to transform it into a lavish Oriental palace.

Completed in 1823, the exterior of this seaside retreat has remained largely unaltered. Queen Victoria sold the Pavilion to the town of Brighton in 1850. The delightful Regency Pavilion Gardens have been restored following Nash's original 1820s plans.

The splendid Royal Pavilion, constructed ↓ with Bath stone, with an exuberant interior

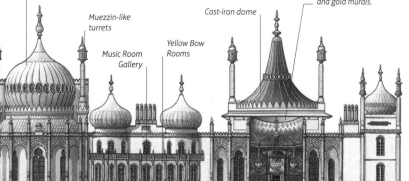

The central dome is an imposing onion dome decorated with delicate tracery. Nash drew heavily from Islamic buildings such as the Taj Mahal, but called this design his "Hindu style".

A 70-piece orchestra played for the prince's guests in the exquisitely decorated Music Room, with crimson and gold murals.

Muezzin-like turrets

Cast-iron dome

Music Room Gallery

Yellow Bow Rooms

EXPERIENCE MORE

③ Margate

⚑G1 ⬤Kent 🚆🚌 🛈The Droit House, Stone Pier; www.visitthanet.co.uk

A classic seaside resort, with fine sand beaches, Margate is a draw not only for its amusement park, Dreamland, but also for the **Turner Contemporary** art gallery. This spectacular modern building celebrates the town's connections with J M W Turner and hosts eclectic exhibitions.

Just south is a 19th-century estate, **Quex Park**. The adjoining **Powell-Cotton Museum** has a fine collection of predominantly African art and artifacts, as well as wildlife dioramas.

To the west is a Saxon church, built within the remains of the bleak Roman coastal fort of Reculver. Access to Reculver is any time during daylight hours.

Turner Contemporary

☺🏠 ⬤Rendezvous
🕐10am–6pm Tue–Sun
🌐turnercontemporary.org

Quex Park & Powell-Cotton Museum

⬡☺🏠 ⬤Birchington
🕐10am–5pm Tue–Sun
(Museum: closed for reno-vation) 🌐quexpark.co.uk

④ Leeds Castle

⚑F1 ⬤Maidstone, Kent
🚉Bearsted, then bus
🕐10am–6pm daily
(Oct–Mar: to 5pm)
🗓1st Sat & Sun in Nov
🌐leeds-castle.com

Surrounded by a lake that reflects the warm buff stone of its crenellated turrets, Leeds is among the most beautiful castles in England. Celebrating its 900th anniversary in 2019, it has been continuously inhabited and its present appearance is the result of centuries of rebuilding and extensions, most recently in the 1930s.

Leeds has many royal connections, going back to 1278, when it was given to Edward I by a courtier seeking favour. Henry VIII loved the castle and visited it often to escape the plague in London. It contains a life-sized bust of Henry VII from the late 16th century. Leeds passed out of royal ownership when Edward VI gave it to Sir Anthony St Leger in 1552, as a reward for helping to pacify the Irish.

↓ The striking architecture of the Turner Contemporary art gallery in Margate

CHARLES DICKENS

The greatest novelist of the Victorian era, Charles Dickens (1812–70) was born in Portsmouth, but moved to Chatham aged five. He set many of his stories in the Rochester area. Although he later moved to London, Dickens kept up his Kent connections and spent his last years at Gad's Hill, near Rochester. The town honours him with an annual Dickens festival each June.

⑤ Rochester

⚑E1 ⬤Kent 🚆🚌 🛈95 High St; www.visitmedway.org

Clustered at the mouth of the River Medway are the towns of Rochester and Chatham, both rich in naval history.

England's tallest Norman keep is at **Rochester Castle**, worth climbing for views over the Medway. The town's medieval history is still visible, with the original city walls on view in the High Street, along with wall paintings in the cathedral, built in 1088.

In Chatham, the **Historic Dockyard** is now a museum of shipbuilding and the Age of Sail. **Fort Amherst** nearby was built in 1756 to protect the dockyard from attack, and has 1,800 m (5,906 ft) of tunnels that were hewn by Napoleonic prisoners of war.

↑ Sea view from the top of the iconic white cliffs of Dover

Rochester Castle

⊛ 🏛 ♿ 🅿 Castle Hill
📞 01634 335882
🕐 10am–4pm daily (Apr–Sep: to 6pm; last adm: 45 mins before closing)

Historic Dockyard

⊛ 🍴 🏛 ♿ 🅿 Dock Rd, Chatham 🕐 Apr–Oct: 10am–5pm daily (Feb & Mar: to 4pm)
🌐 thedockyard.co.uk

Fort Amherst

⊛ 🏛 ♿ 🅿 Dock Rd, Chatham 🕐 8am–4pm Mon–Fri; 9am–3pm Sat
🌐 fortamherst.com

7

Dover

🅰 G2 🅰 Kent 🚉🚌🚢
ℹ Dover Museum, Market Sq; www.whitecliffs country.org.uk

Its proximity to the European mainland makes Dover the leading port for cross-Channel travel. Its famous white cliffs are an iconic British landmark.

Due to its strategic position and large natural harbour, Dover has played a key role in the nation's defences. Built on the site of a Saxon fort, **Dover Castle** helped defend the town from 1198, when Henry II first built the keep, right up to World War II, when it was used as the command post for the Dunkirk evacuation.

Some 3 km (2 miles) inland, one of the most significant sites in England's early history is the ruin of **Richborough Roman Fort**. Now a grassy site, this was where, in AD 43, Claudius's Roman invaders made their first landing.

Dover Castle

⊛ 🍴 🏛 🅿 ♿ 🅰 Castle Hill
🕐 Times vary, see website
🌐 english-heritage.org.uk

Richborough Roman Fort

⊛ 🏛 ♿ 🅰 Richborough
🕐 Apr–Sep: 10am–6pm daily; Oct: 10am–5pm Wed–Sun; Nov–Mar: 10am–4pm Sat & Sun 🌐 english-heritage.org.uk

---

6

Whitstable

🅰 F1 🅰 Kent 🚉🚌

Celebrated for its oysters since Roman times, Whitstable is the prettiest of the old fishing towns on the North Kent coast, with brightly painted buildings, atmospheric alleyways, a busy little harbour and a long shingle beach lined with colourful huts. Plenty of lively restaurants specialize in delicious local seafood. The bustling Whitstable Oyster Festival takes place each July, a tradition dating from Norman times. There are also many unique art and craft shops. On the beach, the walk westwards is especially lovely.

EAT

Whitstable Oyster Company
Kentish oysters headline the menu at this seafood specialist.

🅰 F1 🅰 Horsebridge, Whitstable
🌐 whitstableoyster company.com

£££

Hantverk & Found
An unconventional seafood café-restaurant with a daily changing, locally sourced menu.

🅰 G1 🅰 16–18 King St, Margate
🕐 Mon–Wed & Sun pm
🌐 hantverk-found.co.uk

£££

The Allotment
Unpretentious yet stylish, this restaurant serves local meat dishes and afternoon teas.

🅰 G2 🅰 9 High St, Dover
🕐 Sun & Mon
🌐 theallotment restaurant.com

£££

←

Alfresco eating at the elegant Pantiles, Royal Tunbridge Wells

(p41), who had grown up at Knole, and her husband, the diplomat and author Harold Nicholson (1886–1968), who acquired the 16th-century castle in the 1930s.

Working as an "artist-gardener", Sackville-West spurned traditional ideas of formal garden design and instead created different garden "rooms" around the old house, each with plants chosen by colour, texture and season to match a particular theme, most spectacularly in the celebrated White Garden.

Inside the house, the library is full of items collected by Vita and Harold, while the Elizabethan Tower offers a lovely overview of the gardens.

DRINK

The Mount Edgcumbe

Sup local ales and craft beers in a number of intimate spaces, including a sandstone cave, at this pub with a terrace overlooking the expansive Tunbridge Wells Common.

Ⓐ E2 **Ⓐ The Common, Royal Tunbridge Wells** **ⓦ themount edgcumbe.com**

The Duke of York

At the heart of the Pantiles, this 18th-century pub with a wooden ceiling offers a cosy spot for a pint in the winter and outside tables in the summer.

Ⓐ E2 **Ⓐ 17 The Pantiles, Royal Tunbridge Wells** **ⓦ dukeofyork tunbridgewells.co.uk**

The Bucks Head

A classic English country pub near Knole with oak beams, a log fire and panelling.

Ⓐ E2 **Ⓐ Park Lane, Godden Green, near Knole** **ⓦ bucks headsevenoaks.co.uk**

❽
Royal Tunbridge Wells

Ⓐ E2 **Ⓐ Kent** **🚌🚆**
ⓘ The Corn Exchange, The Pantiles; www.visit tunbridgewells.com

Helped by royal patronage, this town became a popular spa after mineral springs were discovered in 1606. The Pantiles – the colonnaded and paved promenade – was laid out in the 1700s.

Nearby manor house **Penshurst Place**, built in the 1340s, has an 18-m- (60-ft-) high Great Hall.

Penshurst Place

 **Ⓐ Tonbridge, Kent** **Ⓒ Apr-Oct: daily (House & Toy Museum: 11:30am-3:30pm; Gardens: 10am-5pm)** **ⓦ penshurstplace.com**

---

❾
Sissinghurst

Ⓐ E2 **Ⓐ Cranbrook, Kent** **Ⓑ Staplehurst, then taxi** **Ⓒ Mar-Oct: 11am-5:30pm daily** **ⓦ nationaltrust.org.uk**

The most famous of Kent's many gardens was begun by writer Vita Sackville-West

→

The moat around Hever Castle, where Anne Boleyn lived as a young woman

❿ Ⓐ Ⓜ Ⓐ Ⓐ NT
Knole

Ⓐ E1 **Ⓐ Sevenoaks, Kent** **Ⓑ Sevenoaks, then taxi** **Ⓒ Mar-Oct: 11am-5pm Tue-Sun; Park: dawn-dusk daily** **ⓦ national trust.org.uk**

This huge Tudor mansion was built in the late 15th century and was seized by Henry VIII from the Archbishop of Canterbury at the Dissolution. In 1566 Queen Elizabeth I gave it to her cousin Thomas Sackville. His descendants

have lived here ever since, including the writer Vita Sackville-West. The house is well known for its 17th-century furniture, such as the elaborate bed made for James II.

The 405-ha (1,000-acre) park has deer and lovely walks.

11

Ightham Mote

🅰 **E1** 🏠 **Ivy Hatch, Sevenoaks, Kent** 🚈 **Hildenborough, then taxi** 🕐 **House: Mar–Oct: 11am–5pm daily, Dec: 11am–3pm daily; Gardens: 10am–5pm daily (Nov & Dec to 4pm)** 🌐 **nationaltrust.org.uk**

A little-known gem, nestled in a lush green valley, Ightham (pronounced "item") is the most complete medieval manor house in England, with parts dating back to the 1320s. This stone-and-timber building has over 70 rooms and a grand courtyard (complete with a Grade I listed 19th-century dog kennel). Rooms are decorated in a range of styles from across the centuries, including a 15th-century chapel with an ornate 16th-century painted oak ceiling and a drawing room with hand-painted 18th-century Chinese wallpaper. The house is surrounded by a placid moat, crossed by three bridges, and is set in manicured gardens.

For 300 years, the manor was home to the Selby family, who were involved in the Gunpowder Plot to blow up Parliament in 1605. It is said that the ghost of Dorothy Selby, who accidentally gave away the plotters, still lives in Ightham's tower.

12

Chartwell

🅰 **E1** 🏠 **Mapleton Rd, Westerham, Kent** 🚈 **Edenbridge** 🕐 **Times vary, check website** 🌐 **nationaltrust.org.uk**

This grand Victorian house was the home of one of Britain's most famous politicians, Sir Winston Churchill, from the 1920s until his death in 1965. Before he became Prime Minister in 1940, he expended a lot of his energy on improving Chartwell and created a magnificent garden. Look out for the famous wall that he built himself when he took up bricklaying as a hobby. His greatest pleasure, though, was painting, and his specially built studio is lined with his landscapes and portraits.

After Winston died, Lady Churchill left the house almost immediately, and the main

rooms are still preserved almost exactly as the couple left them, with books, family photos, cigar stubs, letters, memorabilia and gifts from various world figures, giving a rich flavour of Sir Winston's varied life and personality.

---

13 ✏️ 🎨 🍴 🖥️ 🏛️

Hever Castle

🅰 **E2** 🏠 **Edenbridge, Kent** 🚈 **Edenbridge** 🕐 **Mid-Feb–Mar & Nov: 10:30am–4:30pm daily; Apr–Oct: 10:30am–6pm daily** 🌐 **hevercastle.co.uk**

This small, moated castle, the oldest parts of which date back to 1270, was the 16th-century home of Anne Boleyn, the doomed second wife of Henry VIII, executed for adultery. She lived here as a young woman, and the king often visited her while staying at Leeds Castle. Today, visitors can still see her bedroom and other apartments.

In 1903, Hever was bought by William Waldorf Astor, who began a restoration programme, building a Neo-Tudor village alongside it for guests and servants.

Don't miss the lovely gardens, which are filled with beautiful sculptures, hidden grottoes and imaginative topiary.

14

Romney Marsh

🅰 F2 🅰 Kent 🅰 Ashford
🚃 Ashford, Hythe
ℹ️ Dymchurch Rd, New
Romney; www.kent
wildlifetrust.org.uk

Once upon a time, Romney Marsh and its neighbour Walland Marsh were entirely covered by sea at high tide. The Romans drained the Romney section, and Walland Marsh was reclaimed during the Middle Ages. Together they formed a large area of fertile land, particularly suitable for the Romney Marsh sheep, bred for the quality of their wool.

Fourteen medieval churches are scattered over the marsh. Dungeness, a desolate spot at the southeastern tip of the area, is dominated by a lighthouse and a nuclear power station. It is also the southern terminus of the Romney, Hythe & Dymchurch Light Railway. This takes passengers 23 km (14 miles) up the coast to Hythe on trains one third the conventional size. The full timetable is at www.rhdr.org.uk.

The Kent Wildlife Trust Visitor Centre explores the marsh's history and wildlife.

15

Rye

🅰 F2 🅰 East Sussex 🚃🚌
ℹ️ Town Hall, Market St;
www.visit1066country.
com/destinations/rye

In 1287, a huge storm diverted the River Rother so that it met the sea at Rye, and for more than 300 years thereafter, this charming fortified town was one of the main Channel ports. The brick-and-timber warehouses on Strand Quay survive from the prosperous days when Rye was a thriving port. In the 16th century the harbour began to silt up, and the town is now 3 km (2 miles) inland.

Cobbled Mermaid Street, lined with houses jutting out at unlikely angles, has hardly altered since the 14th century. On this street, the Mermaid Inn, rebuilt around 1420, is Rye's largest medieval edifice. On nearby West Street, Lamb House was the residence of Henry James from 1897 to 1914. Built in 1722, this fine Georgian house is now a writer's museum. Ypres Tower on Pump Street, built under Henry II in 1250 as a defence against the French, contains a museum with exhibits of medieval artifacts.

About 6 km (4 miles) southeast of Rye, Camber Sands is a popular beach for swimming and kite- and windsurfing. West of the beach, near Brede Lock, are the ruins of Camber Castle, one of the coastal forts built by Henry VIII.

↑ Novices' chamber, part of the Battle Abbey ruins on the site of the Battle of Hastings

Bodiam Castle

🅰E2 🅝Nr Robertsbridge, East Sussex 🚉Robertsbridge then taxi 🕙10am-5pm daily (Nov-Feb: to 4pm) 🆆nationaltrust.org.uk

Surrounded by a wide moat, this late 14th-century castle, with its wooden portcullis and spiral staircases, is one of the most romantic in England.

Previously believed to have been built as a defence against French invasion, it is now thought to have been intended as a home for a Sussex knight. During the Civil War in 1642–51 (*p49*), Parliamentary soldiers removed the roof to restrict the castle's use as a base for Charles I's troops. It has been uninhabited since. With the exception of the roof, it was restored in 1919 by Lord Curzon, who gave it to the nation.

To the east is **Great Dixter**, a 15th-century manor house restored by Sir Edwin Lutyens in 1910. The late Christopher Lloyd created a magnificent garden with a blend of terraces and borders, and a great nursery, too.

←

Charming half-timbered houses lining cobbled Mermaid Street, Rye

Great Dixter

🅝Northiam, Rye 🕙Apr-Oct: 11am-5pm Tue-Sun & public hols 🆆greatdixter.co.uk

---

⓱
Winchelsea

🅰F2 🅝East Sussex 🚉🚌 🅸www.winchelsea.com

Just 3 km (2 miles) south of Rye is the small town of Winchelsea. At the behest of Edward I, it was moved to its present position on higher ground in 1288, after most of the Old Town on lower land to the southeast was submerged by the same storm that diverted the River Rother in 1287. Winchelsea is probably Britain's first coherently planned medieval town. Although not all of it was built as originally planned, its rectangular grid survives today, as does the Church of St Thomas Becket (begun c 1300) at its centre. The church has several well-preserved, superbly carved medieval tombs in the chantry. The three windows (1928–33) in the Lady Chapel were designed by Douglas Strachan as a memorial to those who died in World War I.

The beach below the town is one of the finest on the southeast coast.

⓲
Hastings

🅰F2 🅝East Sussex 🚉🚌 🅸Muriel Matters House, Breeds Place; www.visit 1066country.com/ destinations/hastings

This seaside town was one of the first Cinque Ports (a confederation of five port towns founded for military and trade purposes) and is still a thriving port. In the 19th century, the area to the west of the Old Town was built up as a seaside resort, which left the narrow, characterful streets of the old fishermen's quarter intact.

Some 11 km (7 miles) from Hastings is the small town of Battle, whose central square is dominated by the gatehouse of **Battle Abbey**. William the Conqueror built this on the site of his great victory, reputedly placing the high altar where Harold fell, but the abbey was destroyed in the Dissolution. Visitors can take an evocative walk around the actual battlefield.

Battle Abbey

🅝High St, Battle 🕙Apr-Oct: 10am-6pm daily; Nov-Mar: 10am-4pm Sat & Sun 🆆english-heritage.org.uk

---

BATTLE OF HASTINGS

In 1066, William the Conqueror's army from Normandy, France, landed on the south coast of England, aiming to take Winchester and London. Hearing that King Harold and his army were camped just inland from Hastings, William confronted them. He won the battle after Harold was mortally wounded by an arrow to the eye. Audio guides, along with displays and a film at the visitor's centre, bring the battle to life.

⑲ Eastbourne

Ⓐ E2 Ⓐ East Sussex 🚃🚌
ⓘ Welcome Building, Compton St; www.visit eastbourne.com

With its pier and beachside promenade, Eastbourne is a classic Victorian seaside resort. It is also the starting point of the South Downs Way (p106), and an excellent base for touring the South Downs. The path begins at Beachy Head, the 163-m (536-ft) chalk cliff just on the outskirts of the town. From here it is a bracing walk to Birling Gap, with views to the Seven Sisters. To the west of Eastbourne is the 280-ha (690-acre) **Seven Sisters Country Park**.

Just north is the village of Alfriston, with an ancient market cross and a 15th-century inn, The Star. Nearby is the 14th-century **Clergy House**, which became the first National Trust property in 1896.

Bexhill-on-Sea, 19 km (12 miles) east of Alfriston, features the 1935 Art Deco **De La Warr Pavilion**, which hosts art exhibitions and has a café with fabulous views.

Seven Sisters Country Park

🛈🚻 Ⓐ Exceat, Seaford
🕒 Apr–Sep: 10:30am–4:30pm daily; Mar & Nov: 11am–4pm Sat & Sun; Oct: 11am–4pm daily 🖳 sevensisters.org.uk

Clergy House

🛈🚻Ⓝⓣ Ⓐ Alfriston
🕒 Mar–Oct: 10:30am–5pm Sat–Wed (Jul & Aug: also Fri)
🖳 nationaltrust.org.uk

De La Warr Pavilion

🛈🚻🚻 Ⓐ Marina, Bexhill-on-Sea 🕒 10am–6pm daily
🖳 dlwp.com

⑳ Lewes

Ⓐ E2 Ⓐ East Sussex 🚃
ⓘ 187 High St; www.visit lewes.co.uk

The ancient town of Lewes was a strategic site for the Saxons because of its high vantage point. William the Conqueror built a wooden castle here in 1067. In 1264 Lewes was the site of a critical battle in which Simon de Montfort and his barons defeated Henry III, enabling

🔍 HIDDEN GEM
Farleys House

Tucked in the country-side 16 km (10 miles) east of Lewes is the former home of photographer Lee Miller and Surrealist artist Roland Penrose, where they lived for 35 years from 1949. It displays their works and those by their friends, who included Picasso and Man Ray (www. farleyshouse.co.uk).

them to establish the first English Parliament, though this victory was shortlived.

The Tudor **Anne of Cleves House** is a museum of local history, although Anne of Cleves, Henry VIII's fourth wife, never actually lived here.

On Guy Fawkes Night on 5 November lighted tar barrels are rolled to the river and effigies, including of notable figures of the year, are burned. This commemorates the town's 17 Protestant martyrs burned at the stake by Mary I.

Nearby are the 16th-century **Glynde Place**, a fine courtyard house, and **Glyndebourne**, a private opera house which hosts the famous annual festival from May to August.

Anne of Cleves House

⊗⊜⊕ 🅰52 Southover High St 🕐Times vary, check website 🅦sussexpast.co.uk

Glynde Place

⊗⊗⊜⊕ 🅰Lewes 🕐May-Jun: 2–5pm Wed, Thu & Sun 🅦glynde.co.uk

Glyndebourne

⊗⊗⊜⊕ 🅰Lewes 🅦glyndebourne.com

㉑ ⊗⊗⊜⊕

Charleston

🅰E2 🅰Firle, East Sussex 🅡Lewes, then taxi 🕐Mar-Oct: 11:30am–5pm Wed-Sat, noon–5pm Sun 🅦charleston.org.uk

An artistic time capsule, this pretty, secluded farmhouse is

inseparable from the circle of avant-garde artists, designers and writers known as the Bloomsbury Group – after the area of London in which they first met in the early 1900s (p74). Members included novelist Virginia Woolf, her husband Leonard, writers Lytton Strachey and E M Forster, and economist J M Keynes. In 1916, Virginia Woolf's sister Vanessa Bell and her lover Duncan Grant, both artists, moved to this Sussex farmhouse, and it soon became the group's favourite country retreat.

Over the years, Bell and Grant, with help from their family and friends, decorated the house with post-Impressionist-style paintings, textiles and ceramics. The house soon amassed an art collection that includes works by Picasso, Derain and Renoir, among others. The grounds also feature a distinctive walled garden created by Bell and Grant.

The house and garden have been carefully preserved and restored as they were when Bell and Grant left, and host varied events, including an arts festival every year in May.

EAT

Limetree Kitchen

The eclectic menu at this Lewes eatery features Asian flavours. There's a stripped-back, shabby-chic interior and a simple terrace.

🅰E2 🅰14 Station St, Lewes 🕐Sun pm, Mon & Tue 🅦limetree kitchen.co.uk

ⓔ⒠⒠

Tiger Inn

This country pub, near Eastbourne, has a log fire for cold days and outdoor tables in the summer. The menu offers hearty dishes, such as ploughman's lunch and bangers and mash.

🅰E2 🅰East Dean, Eastbourne 🅦beachyhead.org.uk

ⓔ⒠⒠

↑ Walking along the beach by the huge Seven Sisters chalk cliffs near Eastbourne

22 🛡️ 🖥️ 🍴 🛍️

Arundel Castle

📍D2 🏠Arundel, West Sussex 🚉Arundel 🕐Apr-Oct: 10am-5pm Tue-Sun & public hols (Aug: daily; last adm: 4pm) 🌐arundelcastle.org

Dominating the small riverside town, this vast hilltop castle was originally built for the Norman earl Roger de Montgomery in 1067. In the 16th century its owners, the Fitzalans, merged by marriage with the Howards, the country's senior Roman Catholic family. With this wedding, the castle became the seat of the Duke of Norfolk, whose descendants still live here today.

The Howards played a major role in the English Civil War and the castle was rebuilt after the original was virtually destroyed by Parliamentarians in 1643. The building was remodelled once more in Gothic Revival style in the 19th century.

Today, visitors can explore the castle's beautiful gardens and interior, which houses fine furniture as well as portraits by the likes of Van Dyck, Gainsborough and Reynolds.

23

Steyning

📍D2 🏠West Sussex 🚌 ℹ️9 Causeway, Horsham; visitsteyning.co.uk

This charming little town below the South Downs is full of well-preserved timber-framed houses dating from the Tudor era and earlier. In Saxon times, Steyning was an important port on the River Adur, and a splendid 12th-century church is evidence of its medieval prosperity. The town's fortunes changed in the 14th century, when the river silted up, but it later became an important coaching stop.

Just to the southeast of the centre of Steyning in Bramber, once a separate village, are the gaunt ruins of a Norman motte-and-bailey defensive fort, Bramber Castle. Also here is **St Mary's House**, a timber-framed manor built around 1470, with fine panelled rooms and beautiful gardens with topiary figures.

St Mary's House

🏛️ 🖥️ 🏠Bramber 🕐May-Sep: 2-6pm Thu, Sun & public hols (also Wed in Aug) 🌐stmarysbramber.co.uk

24 🛡️ 🍴 🖥️ 🛍️ NT

Petworth House

📍D2 🏠Petworth, West Sussex 🚉Pulborough, then taxi 🕐House: 11am-5pm daily (Nov-Feb: 10:30am-4pm daily); Park: 8am-8pm daily (Nov-Feb: to 6pm) 🌐nationaltrust.org.uk

This late 17th-century house was immortalized in a series of famous views by the painter J M W Turner, who was often welcomed as a guest by his friend and

The stately Arundel Castle, home of the Dukes of Norfolk ↓

patron, the third Earl of Egremont (1751–1837). Some of his best paintings are on display here and are part of Petworth's outstanding art collection, which also includes works by Titian, Van Dyck and Gainsborough. Also well represented is ancient Roman and Greek sculpture, notably the 4th-century BC *Leconfield Aphrodite*, widely thought to be by Praxiteles.

The Carved Room is decorated with intricately carved wood panels of birds, flowers and musical instruments, by Grinling Gibbons (1648–1721).

The large deer park includes some of the earliest work of "Capability" Brown.

↑ The interior of Chichester Cathedral, seen from the choir

25

Chichester

🅰 C2 🅰 West Sussex 🚉🚌
ℹ️ The Novium, Tower St; www.visitchichester.org

This well-preserved cathedral city, with a 16th-century market cross at its centre, is dominated by **Chichester Cathedral**, consecrated in 1108. The spire is said to be the only English cathedral spire visible from the sea. Also of interest is the cathedral's unique detached bell tower, dating from 1436.

There are two carved stone panels in the choir, dating from 1140. Modern works include paintings by Graham Sutherland (1903–80) and a stained-glass window by Marc Chagall (1887–1985).

Chichester was an important Roman settlement, and sections of its 3rd-century AD Roman city walls can still be seen. Just outside of Chichester is the refurbished **Fishbourne Roman Palace**, the largest

Roman villa in Britain. Discovered in the 1960s, it was built around AD 75, had over 100 rooms and featured advanced technology, such as underfloor heating and indoor plumbing for baths. It was destroyed by fire in 285. The north wing has some of the finest mosaics in Britain, including one of Cupid.

To the north is **Goodwood House**, built in the 18th century and home to the Duke of Richmond. Its magnificent art collection features a number of works by Canaletto (1697–1768) and Stubbs (1724–1806). Goodwood is also well known for its sporting events, with a motor-racing circuit that hosts the Festival of Speed in June and July, and a horse-racing track that is the venue for the annual Glorious Goodwood festival in late July.

Bosham is a sleepy village set on Chichester Harbour. Its Saxon Holy Trinity Church is thought to have been used by King Canute and appears in the Bayeux Tapestry, as King Harold heard Mass here before sailing to Normandy.

> **ENGLISH WINE**
>
> There are more than 500 vineyards in Britain, most of them in the English southern counties of Kent and Sussex, where the drier, warmer climate provides better growing conditions. Sparkling varieties make up the bulk of production, such as Denbies (Surrey), Chapel Down (Kent) and Breaky Bottom (Sussex). Still whites are now appearing in increasing numbers, too.

Chichester Cathedral
♿😊🏛 🅰 West St
🕐 Times vary, check website; tours at 11am & 2:30pm Mon–Sat
🌐 chichestercathedral.org.uk

Fishbourne Roman Palace
♿😊🏛 🅰 Roman Way
🕐 Mar–Oct: 10am–5pm daily; Feb & Nov–Dec: 10am–4pm daily 🌐 sussexpast.co.uk

Goodwood House
♿😊🍴😊🏛 🅰 Goodwood
🕐 Mar–Oct: 1–4:30pm Mon & Sun; Aug: 1–4:30pm Sun–Thu
🅰 For special events; check website 🌐 goodwood.com

Bosham is a sleepy village set on Chichester Harbour. Its Saxon Holy Trinity Church is thought to have been used by King Canute and appears in the Bayeux Tapestry.

A DRIVING TOUR
ASHDOWN FOREST

Length 18 km (11 miles) **Stopping-off points** Pubs serve food in each village. The Gallipot Inn in Upper Hartfield and the Hatch Inn in Coleman's Hatch are recommended.

Once a hunting reserve, Ashdown Forest is a broad expanse of wild, ancient heathland, intermixed with dense woods and hilltop clumps of tall pines. The forest is associated with A A Milne (1882–1956), who lived in Hartfield during the 1920s while he wrote his *Winnie the Pooh* stories. With his young son – the model for Christopher Robin – he explored the woods, and many of "the enchanted places" featured in the stories can be found here. Discover these for yourself on a drive around the forest.

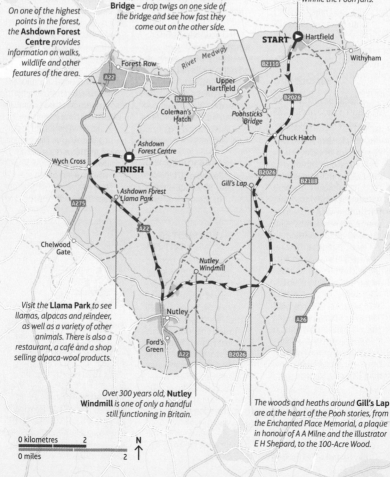

Hartfield is home to the Pooh Corner shop and tearoom, a must-visit for Winnie the Pooh fans.

*Play Poohsticks on **Poohsticks Bridge** – drop twigs on one side of the bridge and see how fast they come out on the other side.*

*On one of the highest points in the forest, the **Ashdown Forest Centre** provides information on walks, wildlife and other features of the area.*

*Visit the **Llama Park** to see llamas, alpacas and reindeer, as well as a variety of other animals. There is also a restaurant, a café and a shop selling alpaca-wool products.*

*Over 300 years old, **Nutley Windmill** is one of only a handful still functioning in Britain.*

*The woods and heaths around **Gill's Lap** are at the heart of the Pooh stories, from the Enchanted Place Memorial, a plaque in honour of A A Milne and the illustrator E H Shepard, to the 100-Acre Wood.*

0 kilometres 2
0 miles 2

N

↑ Ducks and geese wandering
under stunning autumn foliage
in Ashdown Forest

A LONG WALK
SOUTH DOWNS WAY

Distance 160 km (100 miles) **Walking time** 8-9 days **Terrain** The path leads mostly along farm tracks. Except for some steep slopes, walking conditions are reasonably easy.

The South Downs is a range of steep chalk ridges extending across Sussex into Hampshire. The South Downs Way runs along the tops of the downs for 160 km (100 miles) from Eastbourne to Winchester, providing views over the Weald countryside to the north, and southwards down to the sea. There are lovely walks around beauty spots along the path. Iron Age hillforts are also dotted across the downs, built to take advantage of the high ground.

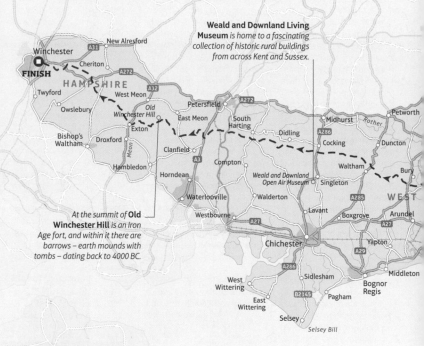

Weald and Downland Living Museum *is home to a fascinating collection of historic rural buildings from across Kent and Sussex.*

At the summit of **Old Winchester Hill** *is an Iron Age fort, and within it there are barrows – earth mounds with tombs – dating back to 4000 BC.*

← The traditional stone Elizabethan Parham House, built in 1557 below the South Downs

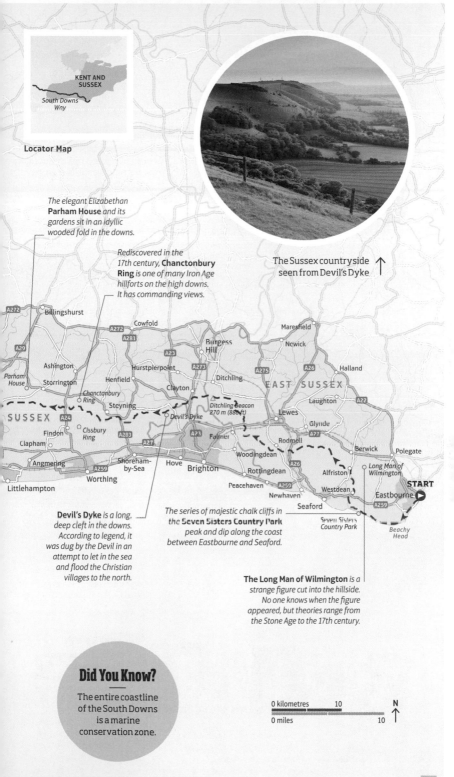

KENT AND SUSSEX

South Downs Way

The elegant Elizabethan **Parham House** and its gardens sit in an idyllic wooded fold in the downs.

Rediscovered in the 17th century, **Chanctonbury Ring** is one of many Iron Age hillforts on the high downs. It has commanding views.

The Sussex countryside seen from Devil's Dyke ↑

Billingshurst

Cowfold

Maresfield

Newick

Burgess Hill

Ditchling

EAST SUSSEX

Halland

Ashington

Hurstpierpoint

Parham House

Storrington

Henfield

Clayton

Ditchling Beacon 270 m (880 ft)

Laughton

Chanctonbury Ring

Steyning

Lewes

Glynde

SUSSEX

Devil's Dyke

Findon

Cissbury Ring

Falmer

Rodmell

Berwick

Polegate

Clapham

Woodingdean

Angmering

Shoreham-by-Sea

Hove

Brighton

Rottingdean

Alfriston

Long Man of Wilmington

START

Littlehampton

Worthing

Peacehaven

Newhaven

Westdean

Eastbourne

Devil's Dyke is a long, deep cleft in the downs. According to legend, it was dug by the Devil in an attempt to let in the sea and flood the Christian villages to the north.

The series of majestic chalk cliffs in the **Seven Sisters Country Park** peak and dip along the coast between Eastbourne and Seaford.

Seaford

Seven Sisters Country Park

Beachy Head

The Long Man of Wilmington is a strange figure cut into the hillside. No one knows when the figure appeared, but theories range from the Stone Age to the 17th century.

Did You Know?

The entire coastline of the South Downs is a marine conservation zone.

0 kilometres 10

0 miles 10

N ↑

HAMPSHIRE AND WILTSHIRE

Around 5,000 years ago, Wiltshire's Salisbury Plain was home to early settlers who created the mysterious stone circles of Stonehenge and Avebury. From Roman times onwards, the grasslands of the plain provided pasture for sheep, whose wool was exported across Europe, making towns such as Bradford-on-Avon and Devizes wealthy.

Saxon settlers arrived in the 4th century, and occupied the valleys around the plain. Winchester, on the River Itchen, became the capital of Saxon Wessex and the first capital of England. Subsequent kings also valued the area and, in 1079, William the Conqueror made a corner of Hampshire a royal hunting reserve forever known as the New Forest.

Later aristocrats built magnificent country mansions set in glorious parks and gardens, such as Beaulieu, Stourhead and Longleat. In the 18th century, these grand houses and Hampshire's quiet, leafy villages inspired the stories of one of the county's most famous residents, Jane Austen.

Much of the region's history is entangled with Britain's naval endeavours. With their natural harbours on the Solent – the stretch of sea between the coast and the Isle of Wight – Southampton and Portsmouth have played a central role in Britain's maritime history, from the earliest days of shipbuilding to today's era of recreational yachting.

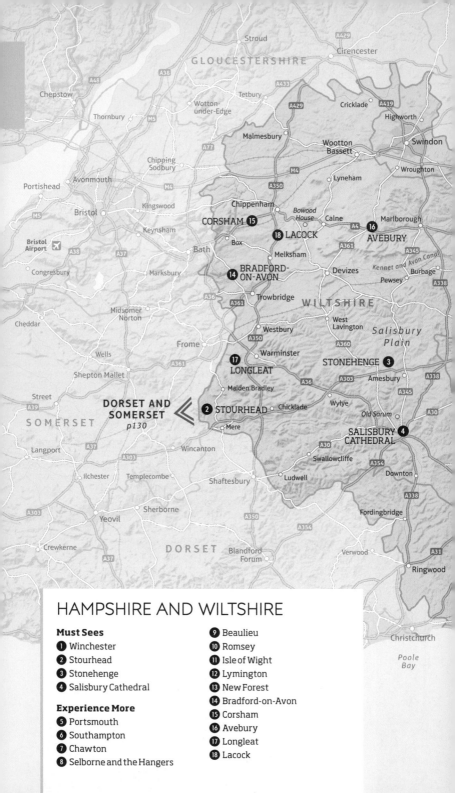

HAMPSHIRE AND WILTSHIRE

Must Sees

1. Winchester
2. Stourhead
3. Stonehenge
4. Salisbury Cathedral

Experience More

5. Portsmouth
6. Southampton
7. Chawton
8. Selborne and the Hangers
9. Beaulieu
10. Romsey
11. Isle of Wight
12. Lymington
13. New Forest
14. Bradford-on-Avon
15. Corsham
16. Avebury
17. Longleat
18. Lacock

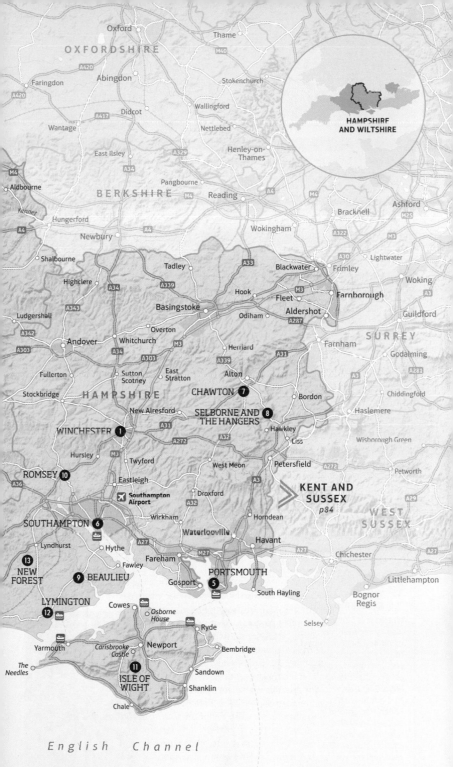

❶

WINCHESTER

🅰B2 🅿Hampshire 🚃🚌 ℹGuildhall, High St;
www.visitwinchester.co.uk

Capital of the ancient kingdom of Wessex, the city of
Winchester was also the headquarters of the Anglo-
Saxon kings until the Norman Conquest. Today, a
statue of King Alfred the Great (848–99) looks over
the main street and King Arthur's legendary Round
Table hangs in the Great Hall. Between these two
sites are cobbled streets and a magnificent cathedral.

💬 **INSIDER TIP**
**Take a
Guided Tour**

Winchester's long
history can feel over-
whelming. Fortunately,
the city's council runs
walking tours focusing
on topics, including
Royal Scandals,
Medieval Jewish
Winchester and Jane
Austen. They also have
tours for locals and
children *(www.visit
winchester.co.uk)*.

---

❶ 🖉 🛍

Westgate Museum

🅰High St 📞01962 869864
🕐Mid-Feb-Oct: Sat & Sun
(Jul-Sep daily)

Housed above one of the two
surviving 12th-century
gatehouses in the city wall,
this room (once a prison) has
walls covered in prisoners'
graffiti and a 16th-century
painted ceiling, moved here
from Winchester College,
England's oldest fee-paying,
or "public", school. There are
great views from the roof.

---

❷ 🖉 🛍

Great Hall and
Round Table

🅰Castle Ave 🕐11am-3pm
Fri-Wed 🌐hants.gov.uk/
greathall

The 13th-century Great Hall is
the only part of the former
Winchester Castle (founded
by William the Conqueror
in 1067) that was spared
destruction by Oliver Cromwell
in the 17th century and is
one of the finest surviving
medieval aisled halls in
England. On the wall is the
iconic Round Table, designed

← The historic city of Winchester on the edge of the South Downs

④ Winchester College

🏛 College St ⏰ For guided tours only 🌐 winchester college.org

Established by William Wykeham, Bishop of Winchester, in 1393, this distinguished private school offers daily guided tours of the beautiful Gothic chapel, the dining hall, cloisters and a 17th-century open classroom where exams still take place.

⑤ Hospital of St Cross

🏛 St Cross Rd ⏰ Apr-Oct: 9:30am-5pm Mon-Sat, 1-5pm Sun; Nov-Mar: 10:30am-3:30pm Mon-Sat 🌐 hospitalofstcross.co.uk

The Hospital of St Cross is an almshouse founded in the 12th century by Henry of Blois, a grandson of William the Conqueror, and is said to be the oldest charitable institution in England. A secular establishment, it is run by the 25 Brothers of St Cross, who are appointed by the Hospital Trust. In the Middle Ages it sheltered and provided food and drink for those in need. Today weary strangers may still claim the "Wayfarer's Dole" from the Brothers – a horn (cup) of ale and a crust of bread, given out since medieval times.

EAT

Wykeham Arms
Dating to 1755, when it was a coaching inn, this wonderful historic pub is full of bric-a-brac and serves a wide range of drinks to accompany a varied menu. Lord Nelson is said to have stayed here.

🏛 75 Kingsgate St 🌐 wykehamarms winchester.co.uk

£ £ £

in legend by King Arthur, who had it shaped so none of his knights could claim precedence. It was said to have been built by the wizard Merlin but was actually made in the 13th century.

③ Wolvesey Castle

🏛 College St ⏰ Apr-Oct: 10am-5pm daily; Nov-Mar: 10am-4pm Sat & Sun 🌐 english-heritage.org

Winchester has been an ecclesiastical centre for many centuries. Wolvesey Castle (built around 1110) was the home of the cathedral's bishops in the Middle Ages. The extensive ruins evoke the former grandeur of the castle. In 1554 Queen Mary and Prince Philip II of Spain celebrated their wedding with a banquet here.

← The Round Table in Winchester's Great Hall, steeped in history and myth

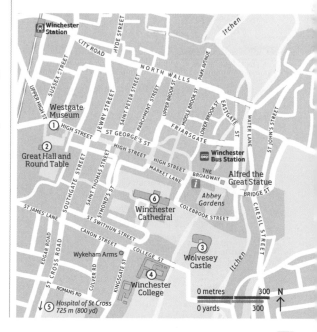

⑥ ◈ Ⓜ ▭ 🛍

WINCHESTER CATHEDRAL

🅰 The Close 🕒 9am–4:30pm Mon–Sat, 12:30–3pm Sun
🆆 winchester-cathedral.org.uk

This magnificent building is one of the largest Gothic cathedrals in Europe. The first church was built here in 648, but the present building was begun in 1079 and was originally a Benedictine monastery. Much of the Norman architecture remains, although some of the domestic buildings used by the monks, including the refectory and cloister, were destroyed during the Dissolution of the Monasteries.

Among the highlights of the cathedral are the exquisitely beautiful 12th-century illuminated Winchester Bible, intricately carved medieval choir stalls and wall paintings. The cathedral is also the resting place of Saxon royalty, bishops and the writer Jane Austen, who died in Winchester in 1817 and is buried near the entrance in the north aisle of the nave. Informative guided tours of the crypt and the cathedral are included in the admission price. For an additional fee, the tower tour takes you up onto the nave roof, from where there are superb views across Winchester.

WILLIAM WALKER

The water table is very near the surface here, so when, in the early 20th century, the cathedral's east end was in dire need of work to underpin its foundations, it had to be done underwater. From 1906 to 1911, William Walker, a deep-sea diver, worked 6 hours a day laying sacks of cement beneath the unsteady walls until the building was safe.

Jane Austen's grave

Main entrance

The 12th-century black Tournai marble font

The perpendicular nave is the highlight of the building.

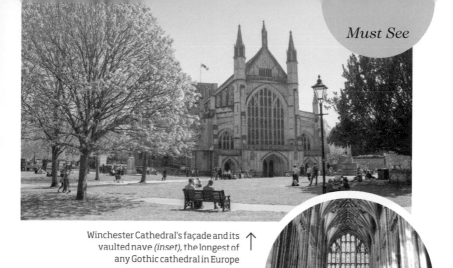

Winchester Cathedral's façade and its vaulted nave *(inset)*, the longest of any Gothic cathedral in Europe

The magnificent choirstalls (c 1308) are England's oldest.

The Lady Chapel was rebuilt by Elizabeth of York (c 1500) after her son was baptized here.

Author Izaac Walton (1593–1683) is depicted in the 1914 stained-glass Anglers' Window.

← The cathedral, sitting amid green space and historic buildings

The library has over 4,000 books, including the 12th-century Winchester Bible.

Prior's Hall

The Close still retains some lovely timber-framed buildings dating to the time when this was the Priory of St Swithun.

The Norman Chapterhouse ceased to be used in 1580. Only the Norman arches survive.

② ⊘ ⑯ ⑲ ⊡ ⑪ Ⓝ🇹

STOURHEAD

🅰G4 **⊕Stourton, Wiltshire** **🚉Gillingham (Dorset) then taxi**
🕘9am–6pm daily (winter: to 5pm) **🖳nationaltrust.org.uk**

Located at the source of the River Stour, Stourhead is a large estate with stunning landscape gardens and a Palladian villa set among ancient woods and farmland.

Among the finest examples of 18th-century landscape gardening in Britain, the garden was begun in the 1740s by Henry Hoare (1705–85), who inherited the estate and transformed it into a breathtaking work of art. He created the lake as the centrepiece of the garden, surrounding it with rare trees and plants, and Neo-Classical Italianate temples, mystical grottoes, ornate follies and bridges. The Palladian-style house, built by Colen Campbell (1676–1729), dates from 1724.

Did You Know?

C Hoare & Co, founded in 1672 by Richard Hoare, is the oldest privately owned bank in the UK.

The Grotto is an artificial cave with a pool and a life-size statue of the guardian of the River Stour, sculpted by John Cheere in 1748.

Modelled on the Pantheon in Rome, this elegant temple was designed by architect Henry Flitcroft. It was built as a visual centrepoint for the garden.

Gothic Cottage (1806)

Iron Bridge

A walk of 3 km (2 miles) around the lake provides artistically contrived vistas.

Stourhead's famous lake was created by damming the River Stour in the 1750s. The path around it evokes the journeys of Aeneas in Virgil's Aeneid.

Inspired by Italian originals and dedicated to the sun god Apollo, this circular temple was also created by architect Henry Flitcroft.

Turf Bridge

📷 **PICTURE PERFECT**
Floral Photos

Stourhead is beautiful all year round, but in spring, the rhododendrons, and in autumn, the vibrant colours of the trees, make for exceptional photos. The view from the Temple of Apollo is particularly attractive.

Fragrant rhododendrons bloom in the spring, and azaleas explode into colour later in the summer. There are also many fine cypresses, Japanese pines and other exotic trees.

The Temple of Flora (1744) is dedicated to the Roman goddess of flowers.

The parish church of St Peter contains monuments to the Hoare family. The medieval Bristol Cross, nearby, was brought from Bristol in 1765.

Stourhead estate, with its picturesque lake and sweeping gardens ↑

←

The expansive land-scaped gardens, with Iron Bridge and the Pantheon in view

→

The Regency library at Stourhead, with a lunette window by Francis Eginton

Reconstructed after a fire in 1902, Stourhead House contains fine Chippendale furniture. The art collection reflects Henry Hoare's Classical tastes and includes The Choice of Hercules *(1637) by Nicolas Poussin.*

Pelargonium House contains a collection of over 100 species of the pelargonium plant and its cultivars.

The reception has a helpful visitor information centre.

Stourton village was incorporated into Hoare's overall design.

STONEHENGE

🅰A2 🏠Off A303, Wiltshire 🕐Apr, May & Sep–mid-Oct: 9:30am–7pm; Jun–Aug: 9am–8pm; mid-Oct–Mar: 9:30am–5pm (Stone Circle Experience visit available outside these hours); book ahead 🌐english-heritage.org.uk

Built in several stages from about 3000 BC, Stonehenge is Europe's most famous prehistoric monument, a masterpiece of Neolithic engineering and building. No trip to the south of England is complete without visiting the vast, awe-inspiring stone circle.

We can only guess at the rituals that took place at Stonehenge, but the alignment of the stones leaves little doubt that the circle is connected with the sun and the passing of the seasons, and that its builders possessed an understanding of both arithmetic and astronomy. Despite popular belief, the circle was not built by the Druids, an Iron Age priestly cult in Britain from around 250 BC – Stonehenge was abandoned more than 1,000 years before this time. Its monumental scale is all the more impressive given that the only tools available were made of stone, wood and bone. Its builders must have been able to command immense resources and vast numbers of people to transport and erect the stones.

Ringing the horizon around Stonehenge are scores of pre-historic circular barrows, or burial mounds, where members of the ruling class were honoured with burial close to the temple site. Ceremonial bronze weapons and other finds excavated around Stonehenge and other local prehistoric sites can be seen in the visitor centre at Stonehenge and Salisbury Museum.

> **The alignment of the stones leaves little doubt that the circle is connected with the sun and the passing of the seasons.**

WILTSHIRE'S OTHER PREHISTORIC SITES

The open countryside of the Salisbury Plain made this area a major centre of prehistoric settlement, and today it is covered in many ancient remains.

Built out of chalk blocks around 2750 BC, Silbury Hill is Europe's largest prehistoric earthwork, but its purpose remains a mystery. Nearby, West Kennet Long Barrow is the biggest chambered tomb in England. Built as a huge communal burial site around 3250 BC, it was in use for several centuries.

Old Sarum, a 400 BC Iron Age hillfort, is located just north of Salisbury. The Romans, Normans and Saxons all left their mark here. Visitors can walk along the Iron Age ramparts, which give great views, and see the remains of the 11th-century castle and cathedral.

The Heel Stone casts a long shadow straight to the heart of the circle on Midsummer's Day.

The Slaughter Stone, named by 17th-century historians who believed Stonehenge to be a place of human sacrifice, is one of a pair marking the entrance to the interior.

The Bluestone Circle was built around 2500 BC out of some 80 slabs quarried in the Preseli Hills in south Wales.

Horseshoe of Bluestones

The Avenue forms a ceremonial approach to the site.

The Sarsen Circle was erected around 2500 BC and is capped by lintel stones held in place by mortise and tenon joints.

Horseshoe of Sarsen Trilothons

The Outer Bank, dug around 3000 BC, is the oldest known phase of Stonehenge.

↑ Illustration of Stonehenge showing what it probably looked like about 4,000 years ago

💬 **INSIDER TIP**
A Close Encounter

Visitors can get up close to the stone circle itself on a Stone Circle Experience session; these last one hour and take place outside normal opening hours. Tickets must be booked in advance.

↑ The mysterious Stonehenge circle of standing stones

④ 〰 ⓜ 🍴 🛍

SALISBURY CATHEDRAL

🅰B2 🏠The Close, Salisbury 🚉 🕐9am–5pm Mon–Sat, noon–4pm Sun 🌐salisburycathedral.org.uk

An outstanding example of Early English Gothic architecture, Salisbury Cathedral was built in the 13th century over the short space of 38 years. Its landmark spire – the tallest surviving in England – was an inspired afterthought added in 1280–1310.

The cathedral was built between 1220 and 1258 from locally sourced Purbeck marble and Chilmark stone. The Gothic design is typified by tall, sharply pointed lancet windows. Highlights include the West Front façade, decorated by rows of symbolic figures and saints in niches, and the soaring octagonal spire, which was an astounding accomplishment for its medieval builders. The Chapter House, meanwhile, contains the best preserved of only four surviving original Magna Cartas issued in 1215; this landmark document laid the foundations for an independent legal system and granted certain rights.

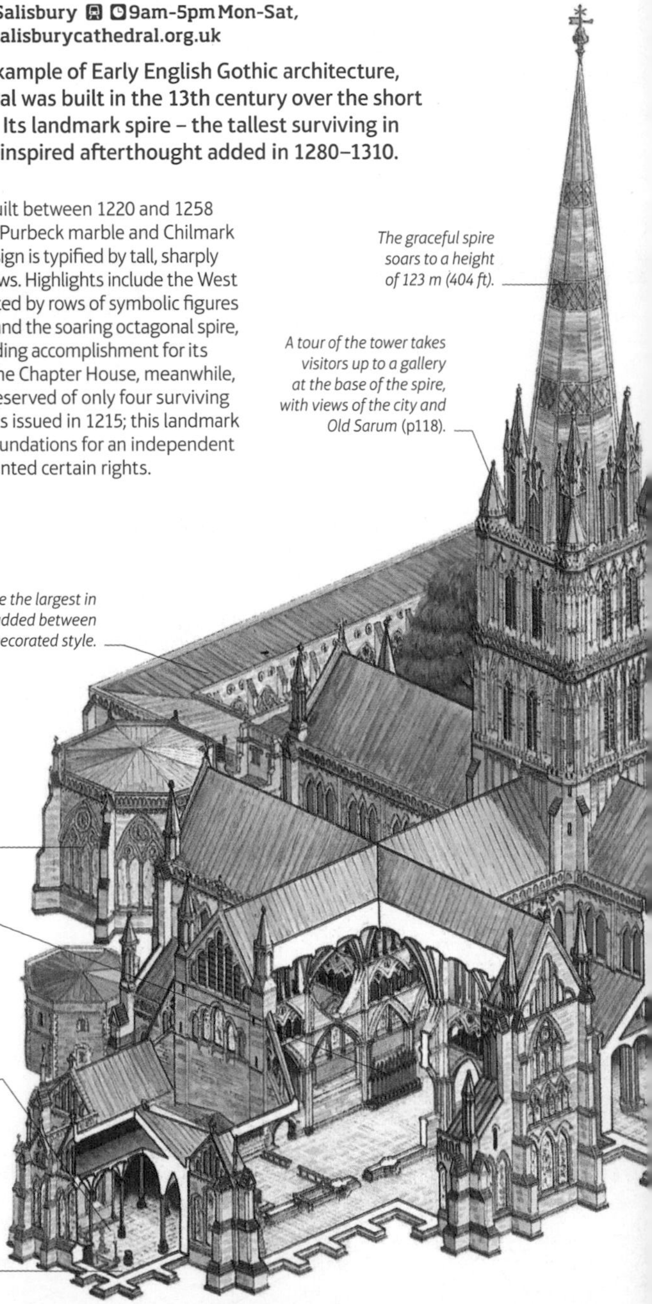

The graceful spire soars to a height of 123 m (404 ft).

A tour of the tower takes visitors up to a gallery at the base of the spire, with views of the city and Old Sarum (p118).

The Cloisters are the largest in England. They were added between 1263 and 1284 in the Decorated style.

The Chapter House has an original of the Magna Carta. Its walls have stone friezes showing scenes from the Old Testament.

Choirstalls

The Trinity Chapel contains the tomb of St Osmund, who was bishop of Old Sarum from 1078 to 1099.

Bishop Audley's Chantry, a magnificent 16th-century monument, is one of several chapels around the altar.

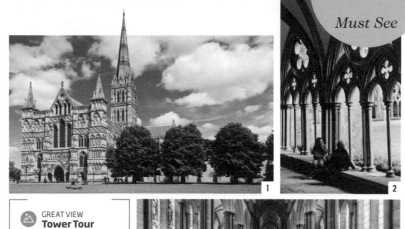

GREAT VIEW
Tower Tour

Take a 100-minute tour of the tower and climb 332 steps to the base of the spire, where there are panoramic views of the city and the surrounding countryside. Advance booking online is recommended.

Numerous stained-glass windows depict stories from the Bible.

The clock, dating from 1386, is believed to be the oldest working mechanical clock in the world.

The nave is divided into ten bays by columns of polished Purbeck marble.

North transept

↑ Salisbury Cathedral, with its elegant Gothic architecture and spire

① The West Front façade is decorated with elaborate statues and columns.

② The expansive Cloister Garden is a peaceful place for visitors to relax.

③ Designed by William Pye, the font was added in 2008. Its water reflects the cathedral's elegant ceiling.

WHAT ELSE TO SEE IN SALISBURY

Founded in 1220, Salisbury is full of historic sights. Its medieval centre is home to the 13th-century Church of St Thomas, with its carved timber roof, and the striking Poultry Cross, built in the 14th century as a covered poultry market. There's also the Salisbury and South Wiltshire Museum, housed in the medieval King's House, which displays archaeological finds from Old Sarum, Stonehenge (p118) and other prehistoric sights.

EXPERIENCE MORE

5

Portsmouth

🏛C2 🅰Hampshire
🏠🚌🚆 *i* The Hard
Interchange; www.
visitportsmouth.co.uk

A vital port for centuries, this vibrant city has a fascinating naval history. **Portsmouth Historic Dockyard** is the hub of the city's main sights. Among these is the hull of the *Mary Rose*, the greatest of Henry VIII's warships, which capsized on its maiden voyage in 1545. Recovered from the seabed in 1982, it is exhibited in the **Mary Rose Museum**, along with many of the 19,000 16th-century objects that have been raised from the wreck.

Nearby is the Dockyard's most famous exhibit, HMS *Victory*, the English flagship on which Admiral Nelson was killed at Trafalgar. Here, visitors get a vivid idea of life at sea in the early 19th century. Compare this ship with the nearby mid-19th-century HMS *Warrior*, one of the first armour-plated warships. Portsmouth's other major military memorial is **The D-Day Story**, which tells the story of the 1944 Allied landing in Normandy.

Less-warlike attractions include the **Charles Dickens Birthplace Museum**, the modest house where the famous Victorian novelist was born in 1812, and the striking **Spinnaker Tower**, which rises 170 m (558 ft) above Portsmouth; the views from the top are magnificent.

Portsmouth Historic Dockyard

♿🛈🚻🍴🛍 🅰Victory Gate, HM Naval Base ⏰10am–5:30pm daily (Nov–Mar: to 5pm) 🌐historicdockyard.co.uk

Mary Rose Museum

♿🛈🚻🍴🛍 🅰Portsmouth Historic Dockyard ⏰10am–5:30pm daily (Nov–Mar: to 5pm) 🌐maryrose.org

The D-Day Story

♿🚻🛍 🅰Clarence Esplanade ⏰10am–5:30pm daily (Oct–Mar: to 5pm) 🌐theddaystory.com

Charles Dickens Birthplace Museum

♿🛍 🅰393 Old Commercial Rd ⏰Apr–Sep & 7 Feb

27,831

dives were made to the *Mary Rose* during the ship's excavation.

(Dickens' birthday): 10am–5:30pm Fri–Sun 🌐charlesdickensbirthplace.co.uk

Spinnaker Tower

♿🚻🛍 🅰Gunwharf Quays ⏰10am–5:30pm daily 🌐spinnakertower.co.uk

6

Southampton

🏛B2 🅰Hampshire
✈🚢🏠🚌🚆 *i* www.
visitsouthampton.co.uk

This city has been a flourishing port since the early Middle Ages. Its city walls, extended by King Edward III in the 14th century, show its importance as a

←
HMS *Victory*, one of the highlights of Portsmouth Historic Dockyard

medieval royal harbour. Southampton – like its neighbour, Portsmouth – was one of the ports where the *Mayflower* called before it sailed to America with the Pilgrim Fathers in 1620. In the 19th century, it became Britain's foremost departure point for transatlantic liners – the *Titanic* left from here on its maiden and ultimately tragic voyage in 1912.

A well-marked walk runs around the remains of the city walls, which include the Bargate, the most elaborate surviving medieval gatehouse in England. It still has its 13th-century drum towers and is decorated with beautifully intricate 17th-century armorial carvings.

Southampton's maritime past is showcased in the **SeaCity Museum**, with absorbing interactive displays on the city's role as "gateway to the world", including special exhibits on ocean liners and the *Titanic*, with a large-scale model of the ship.

SeaCity Museum
⊛⊜🏛 🅰 Havelock Rd
🕐 10am–5pm daily
🅦 seacitymuseum.co.uk

Chawton

🅰 C2 🅰 Hampshire 🅰 Alton, then bus or taxi 🚌 🛈 The Library, The Square, Petersfield; www.visit-hampshire.co.uk

This tranquil village, with its woods, ponds and old cottages, is the site of **Jane Austen's House**, where the author lived with her mother and sister for the last eight years of her life. Chawton is where she wrote all her major novels, including *Sense and Sensibility* and *Pride and Prejudice*. Now a museum, the house displays Austen's letters and furniture.

Just outside the village is **Chawton House**, a 1580s manor house that once

↑ The home of 18th-century naturalist Gilbert White, in the pretty village of Selborne

belonged to Austen's brother Edward, who added a pretty walled rose garden. The house is now a centre for the study of women's writing between 1600 and 1830.

Jane Austen's House
⊛⊜🏛 🅰 Chawton Village Green 🕐 Feb–May & Sep–Dec: 10:30am–4:30pm daily; Jun–Aug: 10am–5pm daily 🕐 Jan
🅦 janeaustens.house

Chawton House
⊛⊜🏛 🅰 Chawton 🕐 House: Feb–Dec 11am–4:30pm daily; Library: by appt all year 🕐 Jan
🅦 chawtonhouse.org

Selborne and the Hangers

🅰 C2 🅰 Hampshire 🅰 Alton, then bus or taxi 🚌 🛈 The Library, The Square, Petersfield; www.visit-hampshire.co.uk

Eastern Hampshire has a unique landscape made up of a series of precipitous ridges, called Hangers because they

are so steep that trees and bushes seem to hang from them rather than stand on top.

On one of the highest Hangers is the village of Selborne, where naturalist Gilbert White was parish priest for over 40 years and wrote his 1789 *Natural History of Selborne*. An idyllic Georgian rectory, **Gilbert White's House** was later owned by the family of Captain Lawrence Oates, who died on the 1912 Scott Expedition to Antarctica, and the museum also has exhibits on Oates' polar exploration and family. Away from the museum, there's a zigzag path, laid out by Gilbert White, which descends the Hanger.

The Hangers are great for walking, with superb views. A circular path snakes around Hawkley, one of the prettiest villages, and the 33-km (21-mile) Hangers Way runs all the way from Alton to Petersfield.

Gilbert White's House
⊛⊜🏛 🅰 The Wakes 🕐 Jan–Mar, Nov & Dec: 10:30am–4:30pm Tue–Sun; Apr–Jun & Oct: 10:30am–5pm Tue–Sun; Jul–Sep: 10:30am–5pm daily
🅦 gilbertwhiteshouse.org.uk

←

Visitors admiring a vintage car at Beaulieu, home to the National Motor Museum

Buckler's Hard

ⓘⓘⓘ 🅰Beaulieu ⏰10am-4:30pm daily (Apr-Sep: to 5pm) 🅦bucklershard.co.uk

---

⑩

Romsey

🅰B2 🅰Hampshire 🅱🅱
ℹ13 Church St; www.visitromsey.org

This charming market town is perhaps best known for being home to **Broadlands**, seat of the Mountbattens, the family of the Duke of Edinburgh. Queen Elizabeth II and Prince Philip even honeymooned in this elegant Palladian mansion in 1947, as did Prince Charles and Princess Diana in 1981.

The town itself grew up around **Romsey Abbey**, built around 1130 on the remains of an older Saxon church. Nearby, **King John's House** is one of the oldest surviving houses in England, complete with graffiti left by medieval knights in 1306.

About 8 km (5 miles) north of Romsey, **Mottisfont Abbey** is a historic house with sections that date from the 13th to the 18th century. Inside is a permanent art collection with works by Degas and Rex Whistler.

Broadlands

ⓘⓘⓘⓘⓘ 🅰Broadlands Park ⏰Times vary, check website 🅦broadlands estates.co.uk

Romsey Abbey

ⓘⓘ 🅰Church Lane ⏰7:30am-6pm Mon-Sat, 9am-6pm Sun 🅦romsey abbey.org.uk

King John's House

ⓘⓘⓘ 🅰Church St ⏰10am-4pm Mon-Sat 🅦kingjohnshouse.org.uk

EAT

Boathouse

A beautiful spot on the Isle of Wight to enjoy freshly caught fish, lobster and crab.

🅰C3 🅰Steephill Cove, Ventnor, Isle of Wight ⏰Wed & Oct-Apr 🅦steephill-cove.co.uk

££££

The Elderflower

Imaginative seasonal dishes as well as crowd-pleasers like fish and chips are offered at this New Forest eatery.

🅰B2 🅰4-5 Quay St, Lymington ⏰Sun pm, Mon & Tue 🅦elderflower restaurant.co.uk

££££

The Terrace

Local game and seafood are on this Beaulieu restaurant's menu, along with produce from the kitchen garden.

🅰B2 🅰The Montagu Arms, Beaulieu ⏰Mon & Tue 🅦montagu armshotel.co.uk

££££

---

⑨ 🅰🅰🅰

Beaulieu

🅰B2 🅰Hampshire 🅰Brockenhurst, then taxi 🅱 ⏰10am-5pm daily (May-Sep: to 6pm) 🅦beaulieu.co.uk

Home to the Montagu family since 1538, the Beaulieu estate is not called "beautiful place" without reason. The estate centres on Palace House, once the gatehouse of Beaulieu Abbey (founded in 1204 by King John for Cistercian monks). The vast estate can be toured by monorail and sights include an *Alice in Wonderland*-themed topiary garden, an exhibit on monastic life and the National Motor Museum. Established by the current Lord Montagu's father in 1952, it is home to one of the world's finest collections of vintage cars. A single ticket is valid for all the attractions.

A beautiful walk south along the river takes you to **Buckler's Hard**, a well-preserved village built by Lord Montagu in the 18th century. It was once a centre for shipbuilding, using timber from the New Forest to construct hulls for Royal Navy vessels, and employed 4,000 men at its peak. It fell into decline when steel began to be used. Today, a maritime museum hosts exhibitions on shipwright skills. Boat cruises are also available.

Mottisfont Abbey

⊘⊜🗑ℕ 🅰Near Romsey
🕐Times vary, check website
🌐nationaltrust.org.uk

⓫

Isle of Wight

🅰B-C3 🅰Hampshire
🚢From Lymington,
Southampton, Portsmouth
ℹSouth St, Newport; www.
visitisleofwight.co.uk

The diamond-shaped Isle of Wight prides itself on being slightly apart from the bustle of the mainland. For a small island, it has remarkably varied scenery and plenty of historical associations, particularly with sailing – Cowes is the birthplace of modern regattas.

> **COWES WEEK**
>
> Cowes Week is one of the largest regattas in the world. Every August, as many as 1,000 boats compete across dozens of racing classes, animating the waters of the Solent. The first race was held in 1826, when just seven yachts took part.

A visit to **Osborne House**, the favoured seaside retreat of Queen Victoria and Prince Albert, is worth the ferry ride from the mainland alone. Furnished much as they left it, the house provides a great insight into royal life. Don't miss the Swiss Cottage, built for the children to play in, and the bathing machine used by the queen to preserve her modesty while swimming.

Another attraction on the island is the 11th-century **Carisbrooke Castle**. The climb to the top of its keep offers spectacular views.

Osborne House

⊘🍽⊜🗑🅱ℍ 🅰East Cowes
🕐Times vary, check website
🌐english-heritage.org.uk

Carisbrooke Castle

⊘🅿⊜🗑🅱ℍ 🅰Newport
🕐Times vary, check website
🌐english-heritage.org.uk

⓬

Lymington

🅰B2 🅰Hampshire 🚃🚢
ℹthenewforest.co.uk

With a Georgian high street, cobbled lanes, restaurants and a busy Saturday market,

Lymington has plenty of charm. Its location on the Solent facing the Isle of Wight makes it a popular sailing harbour, and there are three marinas. Near the harbour is the **Sea Water Baths**, an open-air seawater swimming pool built in 1833.

Sea Water Baths

⊘⊜ 🅰Bath Rd 🕐Apr-Jun: 2:30-6pm Mon-Fri, 10am-6pm Sat & Sun; Jul-Sep: 10am-6pm daily
🌐lymingtonseawater
baths.org.uk

⓭

New Forest

🅰B2 🅰Hampshire
🚃🚢Brockenhurst,
Lymington ℹHigh St,
Lyndhurst; www.thenew
forest.co.uk

Despite its name, this vast expanse of heath and woodland is one of the few primeval oak woods in England. It was a popular hunting ground of Norman kings.

Walk, cycle or drive *(p128)* through this national park for a chance to see New Forest ponies, unique to the area, and over 1,500 fallow deer.

↑ A grey pony and her foal on the expansive heathland of the New Forest

14 Bradford-on-Avon

🗺 G3 🚩 Wiltshire 🚉
ℹ 50 St Margaret St; www.
bradfordonavon.co.uk

This lovely Cotswold-stone town is full of houses built by wealthy merchants in the 17th and 18th centuries. One fine Georgian example is Abbey House, on Church Street. Further along, St Laurence Church is a remarkably complete Saxon building founded in the 8th century. Converted to a school and cottage in the 1100s, it was rediscovered in the 19th century when a vicar recognized the characteristic cross-shaped roof.

At one end of the medieval Town Bridge is a small stone cell, built as a chapel in the 13th century but later used as a lockup for vagrants. A short walk away is the spectacular 14th-century **Tithe Barn** (used for storing rents and tithes).

Tithe Barn

🏛 🚩 Pound Lane
🕐 10:30am–4pm daily
🌐 english-heritage.org.uk

---

15 Corsham

🗺 G3 🚩 Wiltshire
🚉 Chippenham, then taxi ℹ 31 High St; www.
corsham.gov.uk

The streets of Corsham are lined with stately Georgian

> **INSIDER TIP**
> **Wadworth Brewery Tour**
>
> In Devizes, southeast of Corsham, Wadworth Brewery (www.wadworth.co.uk) runs tours that illustrate the company's history and brewing techniques. Tastings are included.

↑ A summer's day at a riverside pub near the Town Bridge in Bradford-on-Avon

houses in Cotswold stone. St Bartholomew's Church has an elegant spire and the carved alabaster tomb (1960) of Lady Methuen, whose family founded Methuen publishers. The family acquired **Corsham Court** in 1745, with its collection of Flemish, Italian and English paintings.

Corsham Court

💠 🚩 Off A4 🕐 Mid-Mar–Sep: 2–5:30pm Tue–Thu, Sat & Sun; Oct–mid-Mar: 2–4:30pm Sat & Sun 🚫 Dec 🌐 corsham-court.co.uk

---

16 🖥 🏛 🏛 🅴🅷 🅽🆃 Avebury

🗺 A1 🚩 Wiltshire
🚉 Swindon, then bus
🌐 nationaltrust.org.uk

Built around 2500 BC, the Avebury Stone Circles surround the village of Avebury and were probably once some form of religious centre. Although the stones used are smaller than those at Stonehenge, the outer circle itself is larger. In the 18th century, superstitious

villagers smashed many of the stones, believing the circles to have been a place of pagan sacrifice.

The original form of the circles is best appreciated by a visit to the **Alexander Keiller Museum** to the west of the site, which illustrates in detail the construction of the circles.

Another attraction of note in Avebury is St James's Church, which has a rare 15th-century choir screen.

Alexander Keiller Museum

💠 🍽 🖥 🏛 🅽🆃 🚩 Off High St
🕐 Times vary, check website
🌐 nationaltrust.org.uk

→ The imposing Gothic Revival architecture of Lacock Abbey

17 ⊘ ⊜ Ⓜ ⓦ ⓐ

Longleat

🅰G4 🄰Warminster,
Wiltshire 🄴Frome, then
taxi 🄾Times vary, check
website 🅆longleat.co.uk

The architectural historian
John Summerson coined the
term "prodigy house" to
describe the exuberance and
grandeur of Elizabethan
architecture that is so well
represented at Longleat. The
house was started in 1540,
when John Thynne bought
the ruins of a priory on the
site for £53. Over the centuries,
subsequent owners have
added their own touches, not
least the late 7th Marquess of
Bath, Alexander Thynn, who
was renowned for his erotic
murals. Less controversial are
the Breakfast Room and
Lower Dining Room (dating
from the 1870s), modelled on
the Venetian Doge's Palace.
Today, the Great Hall is the
only remaining room that
belongs to John Thynne's time.

Part of the estate,
landscaped by "Capability"
Brown, was turned into an
expansive safari park in
1966, where wolves,
rhinos and other
animals roam freely;
there are myriad other
attractions too, such as a
large hedge maze, a mini-
train and an adventure castle.

18

Lacock

🅰G3 🄰Wiltshire
🄴Chippenham, then taxi

The picturesque village of
Lacock has provided the
backdrop to many costume
dramas, including *Downton
Abbey*. The meandering River
Avon forms the boundary to
the north side of the churchyard, where humorous stone
figures look down from
St Cyriac Church. Inside the
15th-century church is the
splendid Renaissance-style
tomb of Sir William Sharington
(1495–1553). He acquired
Lacock Abbey after the
Dissolution, but it was a later
owner, John Ivory Talbot, who
had the building remodelled
in the Gothic Revival style.
The abbey is famous for the
window (in the south gallery)
from which his descendant
William Henry Fox Talbot, an
early pioneer of photography,
took his first
picture in 1835.
A 16th-century
barn has
been

converted to the **Fox Talbot
Museum**, which has displays
on his experiments.

Designed by Robert Adam
in 1769, **Bowood House**
includes the laboratory where
Joseph Priestley discovered
oxygen in 1774, and a fine
collection of sculpture,
costumes, jewellery and
paintings. Italianate gardens
surround the house, while the
lake-filled grounds, landscaped
by "Capability" Brown, contain
a Doric temple and grotto.

Lacock Abbey

⊘ ⊜ ⓐ Ⓜ 🄰Lacock
🄾11am–5pm daily (Nov–Feb:
11:30am–3pm Sat & Sun)
🅆nationaltrust.org.uk

Fox Talbot Museum

⊘ Ⓜ 🄰Lacock 🄾10:30am–
5:30pm daily (Nov–Feb:
11am–4pm) 🅆national
trust.org.uk

Bowood House

⊘ ⓦ ⊜ ⓐ 🄰Derry Hill, nr
Calne 🄾Apr–Oct: 11am–
6pm daily 🅆bowood.org

A DRIVING TOUR
NEW FOREST

Length 77 km (48 miles) **Stopping-off points** Each town has cafés and pubs serving food. In Fordingbridge, the George is located beside the River Avon.

The New Forest got its name when it was made a new royal hunting preserve by William the Conqueror a few years after he seized England in 1066. Now a national park, it retains some ancient laws – especially the right for local inhabitants to graze animals across the entire forest. These include the famous New Forest ponies, which roam freely through the villages. Look out for England's largest deer herds as you drive through the gorgeous mix of heath and woodland scenery.

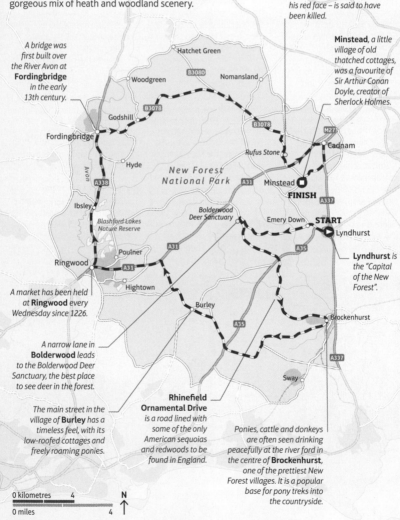

Rufus Stone marks the spot where cruel King William II – known as Rufus because of his red face – is said to have been killed.

Minstead, a little village of old thatched cottages, was a favourite of Sir Arthur Conan Doyle, creator of Sherlock Holmes.

*A bridge was first built over the River Avon at **Fordingbridge** in the early 13th century.*

Hatchet Green

Woodgreen
B3080
Nomansland

Godshill
B3078

Fordingbridge
B3078

Hyde

Rufus Stone
M27
Cadnam

New Forest
National Park
A31
Minstead
FINISH

Ibsley

Blashford Lakes
Nature Reserve

Bolderwood
Deer Sanctuary
Emery Down
START
Lyndhurst

Pouliner
A31

Ringwood
A31
Hightown

Burley
A35

Brockenhurst

Sway

A337

*A market has been held at **Ringwood** every Wednesday since 1226.*

Lyndhurst is the "Capital of the New Forest".

*A narrow lane in **Bolderwood** leads to the Bolderwood Deer Sanctuary, the best place to see deer in the forest.*

*The main street in the village of **Burley** has a timeless feel, with its low-roofed cottages and freely roaming ponies.*

Rhinefield Ornamental Drive is a road lined with some of the only American sequoias and redwoods to be found in England.

*Ponies, cattle and donkeys are often seen drinking peacefully at the river ford in the centre of **Brockenhurst**, one of the prettiest New Forest villages. It is a popular base for pony treks into the countryside.*

0 kilometres 4
0 miles 4

N

6,500
The number of animals that graze in the New Forest freely.

Gorgeous scenery and vibrant flowers at a common in the New Forest at sunrise ↑

DORSET AND SOMERSET

From fossilized dinosaurs to Georgian spas, this region has a long and diverse history. It was the Romans who first put the area on the map when they built England's first spa resort at Bath in the 1st century AD. Once the Romans left, the southwest of England became a stronghold of Celtic resistance, with the mythical King Arthur leading the fight against the Saxons in the early 6th century – legend suggests that he and his queen Guinevere were buried at Glastonbury Abbey.

The region's biggest city, Bristol became Britain's main transatlantic port after John Cabot, a Genoese navigator, set off from there to explore America in 1497 – the city's grand buildings are a testament to the wealth acquired from the subsequent slave trade. Nearby, Bath is also defined by grand architecture. In the 18th century, its spa waters came back into fashion with the Georgians, who built the stunning Palladian-style city seen today, while George III's regular visits to Weymouth kickstarted Dorset's reputation as one of the country's favourite seaside destinations.

Ancient fossils had always been collected along the rugged stretch of coast between Exmouth and Studland Bay, but it was in the 19th century, with the birth of paleontology and the work of Mary Anning, that this stretch of Dorset's shoreline became known as the Jurassic Coast.

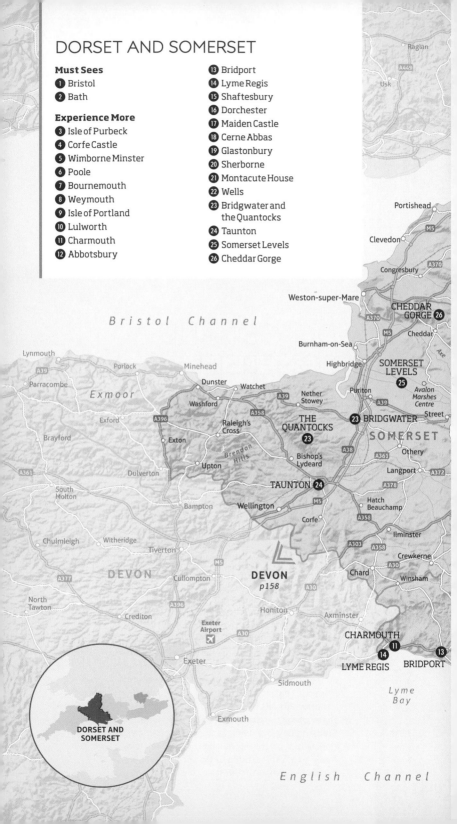

DORSET AND SOMERSET

Must Sees

1. Bristol
2. Bath

Experience More

3. Isle of Purbeck
4. Corfe Castle
5. Wimborne Minster
6. Poole
7. Bournemouth
8. Weymouth
9. Isle of Portland
10. Lulworth
11. Charmouth
12. Abbotsbury
13. Bridport
14. Lyme Regis
15. Shaftesbury
16. Dorchester
17. Maiden Castle
18. Cerne Abbas
19. Glastonbury
20. Sherborne
21. Montacute House
22. Wells
23. Bridgwater and the Quantocks
24. Taunton
25. Somerset Levels
26. Cheddar Gorge

EXPERIENCE Dorset and Somerset

① BRISTOL

F3 Bristol Bristol Temple Meads
The Galleries, Broadmead; www.visitbristol.co.uk

A major port at the mouth of the Avon, Bristol grew rich on the maritime trade of wine, tobacco and, in the 17th century, enslaved people. The oldest part of the city lies around Broad, King and Corn streets. In the lively dock area, bars, cafés and galleries line the waterside.

① Clifton Suspension Bridge

Leigh Woods; www.cliftonbridge.org.uk

The defining symbol of Bristol, the Clifton Suspension Bridge was designed by Isambard Kingdom Brunel, who won the commission at the age of 23. Completed in 1864, the bridge spans the dramatic Avon Gorge from Clifton to Leigh Woods. The brilliant visitor centre provides an interesting and entertaining background to its history. From Easter to October, there are excellent free tours of the bridge, starting from the toll booth at 3pm on Saturdays, Sundays and bank holidays.

② Brunel's SS Great Britain

Gas Ferry Rd 10am-6pm (Mar-Nov: to 4:30pm) daily ssgreatbritain.org

It was from Bristol that, in 1497, John Cabot sailed on his historic voyage to North America. In the 19th century, the city pioneered the era of the ocean-going steam liner with the construction of the SS *Great Britain*. Designed by Isambard Kingdom Brunel, this was the world's first large iron passenger ship. Launched in 1843, she travelled 32 times round the world before being abandoned in the Falkland Islands in 1886. The ship has been restored and contains an exhibition, Being Brunel.

③ St Mary Redcliffe

Redcliffe Way Daily stmaryredcliffe.co.uk

This magnificent 14th-century church was claimed by Queen Elizabeth I to be "the fairest in England". The church owes much to the generosity of William Canynge the Elder and Younger, both famous mayors of Bristol. Inscriptions on the tombs of merchants and sailors tell of lives devoted to trade. Look out for the maze roof boss in the north aisle. Regular musical events are held here.

BANKSY

As mysterious as he is prolific, Bristol-born Banksy is the world's best-known, yet secretive, graffiti artist. There are excellent tours taking in his works around the city (which include *Mild Mild West* and *Masked Gorilla*), together with other excellent street art. Alternatively, you can devise your own itinerary at *www.bristol-street-art.co.uk*.

↑ The Bristol skyline with the university buildings in the foreground

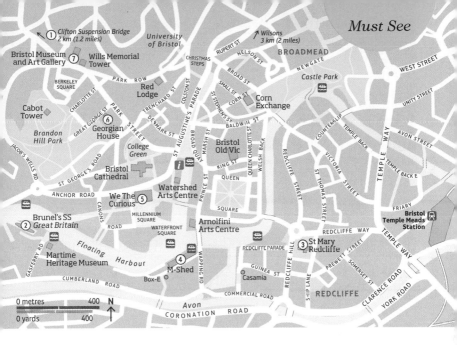

④ 🖥 🏛
M-Shed

🏛 Princes Wharf 🕒 10am–5pm Tue–Sun 🌐 bristol
museums.org.uk

The city's history is told in this museum in a 1950s harbourside transit shed, through film, photographs and objects. There are also several historic vessels moored in the Wharf.

⑤ ✍ 🖥 🏛
We The Curious

🏛 Anchor Rd 🕒 10am–5pm daily (to 6pm Sat & Sun) 🌐 wethecurious.org

On the harbourside, this exciting science centre has

several hundred interactive, hands-on exhibits to enable you to explore the inner workings of the world around you, and a 3-D planetarium with full surround-sound.

⑥
Georgian House

🏛 7 Great George St 🕒 Apr–Oct: 11am–4pm Sat–Tue 🌐 bristolmuseums.org.uk

Daily life in a wealthy 1790s Bristol merchant's house is reimagined here in rooms including the drawing room and the servants' area.

⑦ 🖥 🏛
Bristol Museum and Art Gallery

🏛 Queen's Rd 🕒 10am–5pm Tue–Sun 🌐 bristol museums.org.uk

The varied collections include Egyptology, fossils, Roman finds, Chinese glass and fine paintings. Bristol artists include Sir Thomas Lawrence, Francis Danby and Banksy.

Did You Know?

The world's first bungee jump took place from Clifton Suspension Bridge in 1979.

EAT

Box-E
Fantastic little outfit in an old shipping container with a small but ambitious menu.

🏛 Unit 10, 1 Cargo Wharf 🌐 boxebristol.com

€€€

Casamia
Spanish-run, Michelin-starred restaurant for a special occasion.

🏛 The General, Lower Guinea St 🌐 casa miarestaurant.co.uk

€€€

Wilsons
Food of great distinction, combined in exciting dishes.

🏛 24 Chandos Rd 🌐 wilsonsbristol.co.uk

€€€

↑ Bath Abbey, built, like much of the city, from the local warm-toned Bath stone

②

BATH

🅰 G3 🅰 Somerset 🚇 Bath Spa 🛈 Bridgwater House, 2 Terrace Walk; www.visitbath.co.uk

The beautiful and compact city of Bath is set among the rolling green hills of the Avon valley. Its lively, traffic-free heart is full of museums, cafés and enticing shops, while its characteristic honey-coloured Georgian houses form an elegant backdrop to city life.

① 🏛

Bath Abbey

🏛 Abbey Churchyard 🕐 Times vary, check website 🌐 bathabbey.org

This splendid abbey was supposedly designed by divine agency. According to legend, Bishop Oliver King dreamed of angels going up and down to heaven, which then inspired the ladders carved on the west front façade. The bishop began work in 1499, rebuilding a church that had been founded in the 8th century. Memorials cover the walls and the varied Georgian inscriptions make fascinating reading. The spacious interior is remarkable for the fan vaulting of the nave, an addition made by Sir George Gilbert Scott in 1874.

---

②

No. 1 Royal Crescent

🏛 Royal Crescent 🕐 10am-5pm daily 🚫 1 Jan, 25 & 26 Dec 🌐 no1royalcrescent. org.uk

Bath rose to prominence in the 18th century as one of England's most fashionable spa towns, and as a result the city now has some of the finest Georgian architecture in the country. Highlights are the Circus, a daring circular "square" of distinguished townhouses designed by John Wood the Elder (1704–54), and, above all, the magnificent Royal Crescent, created by his son, John Wood the Younger, in the 1770s.

No. 1 Royal Crescent is now a handsome museum that gives visitors a taste of what life was like for 18th-century aristocrats, such as the Duke of York, who stayed here. You can also see the servants' quarters, the spit powered by a dog made to run in a wheel, and Georgian mousetraps.

JANE AUSTEN

The one name most synonymous with Bath is Jane Austen, whose six years here informed some of her greatest novels, notably *Persuasion*. Devotees will certainly want to pay a visit to the Jane Austen Centre on 40 Gay Street, whose exhibits include the only known waxwork of the author. A plaque outside the door at No. 4 Sydney Place marks her first dwelling in Bath.

> According to legend, Bishop Oliver King dreamed of angels going up and down to heaven, which inspired the ladders carved on the Abbey's west front façade.

③ 🛹 🖥 🛍
Holburne Museum

📍 Great Pulteney St
🕐 10am-5pm daily (from 11am Sun & public hols)
🚫 1 Jan, 24-26 Dec
🌐 holburne.org

This historic building is named after William Holburne of Menstrie (1793–1874), whose collections form the nucleus of the display of fine and decorative arts, including superb silver and porcelain. Paintings by Gainsborough and Stubbs are on show.

④ 🛹 🖥 🛍
Assembly Rooms and Fashion Museum

📍 Bennett St 🕐 10:30am-5pm daily 🚫 25 & 26 Dec
🌐 fashionmuseum.co.uk

The Assembly Rooms were built in 1769 as a meeting place for the elite and as a backdrop for glittering balls. Jane Austen's *Northanger Abbey* (1818) describes the gossip and flirtation that went on here. In the basement is a collection of costumes from the 1500s to the present day.

EAT

Menu Gordon Jones

Seven-course tasting menus are cooked with imagination and flair; fantastic organic wines.

📍 2 Wells Way 🌐 menugordonjones.co.uk

£££

Noya's Kitchen

Homely but high-class Vietnamese; exquisite morsels form the five-course set menu.

📍 7 St James's Parade
🌐 noyaskitchen.co.uk

£££

Sotto Sotto

Consummate Italian restaurant located in an atmospheric brick-vaulted cellar.

📍 10 North Parade
🌐 sottosotto.co.uk

£££

↑ The Holburne Museum, a tranquil delight housing a splendid collection of fine and decorative arts

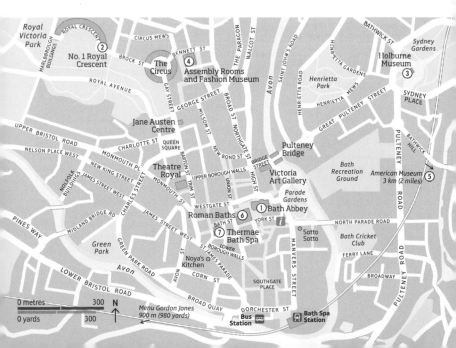

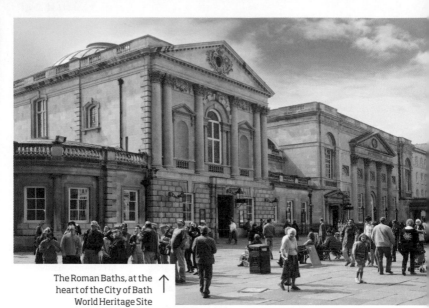

The Roman Baths, at the heart of the City of Bath World Heritage Site ↑

⑤ 〽️ 🖥️ 🏛️

American Museum

🏠 Claverton Manor, Claverton Down ⏰ Mid-Mar-Oct: 10am-5pm Tue-Sun 🌐 american museum.org

Founded in 1961, this was the first American museum to be established in Britain. The rooms in the 1820 manor house are decorated in many styles, from the rudimentary dwellings of the first settlers to the opulent style of 19th-century homes. The museum has special sections on Shaker furniture, quilts and American Indian art, and a replica of George Washington's Mount Vernon garden of 1785.

⑥ 〽️ 🖥️ 🏛️

Roman Baths

🏠 Entrance in Abbey Churchyard ⏰ Daily; times vary, check website 🚫 25 & 26 Dec 🌐 romanbaths.co.uk

According to legend, Bath owes its origins to the Celtic king Bladud, who discovered the curative properties of its natural hot springs in 860 BC. In the 1st century AD, the Romans built baths around the spring, as well as a temple dedicated to the goddess Sulis Minerva, who combined the attributes of the Celtic water goddess Sulis and the Roman goddess Minerva. The

← Impressive folk art on display at the American Museum

HIDDEN GEM
🔍 Victoria Art Gallery

Often overlooked, the Victoria Art Gallery on Bridge Street contains more than 1,500 decorative arts objects, sculptures and glassware. It is particularly strong on paintings by British artists from the 17th century to the present day (www.victoriagal.org).

medieval monks of Bath Abbey also exploited the spring's properties, but it was when Queen Anne visited in 1702–3 that Bath reached its zenith as a fashionable watering place. Beau Nash, Bath's Master of Ceremonies, commissioned the building of the adjoining Grand Pump Room, where Bath's high society gathered to meet and "take the waters". Gradually the whole complex was rebuilt in noble Neo-Classical style to echo the baths' Roman origins.

The Great Bath, at the heart of the Roman complex, was

only rediscovered in the 1870s. Leading off this magnificent pool were various bathing chambers which became increasingly sophisticated; extensive excavations have revealed the remarkable skill of Roman engineering. Artifacts from the digs and fragments of the original structure are displayed on the lower levels. The Pump Room remains an elegant tearoom.

⑦ 🛷 🖵 🛍

Thermae Bath Spa

🏛 Hot Bath St ⏰ 10am–9pm daily (last adm: 7pm); not open to under-16s ⌚ 1 Jan, 25 & 26 Dec 🌐 thermaebath spa.com

While bathing is not allowed in the Roman Baths, the opening of the Thermae Bath Spa in 2006 once again made Bath a popular day-spa destination. There are three pools fed by natural thermal waters: the New Royal Bath has two baths, including an open-air rooftop pool with superb views over the city; across the road, the oval Cross Bath is a more intimate open-air bath, ideal for shorter sessions. Also on offer are spa treatments and massages.

↑ A rooftop dip at Thermae Bath Spa overlooking the city

The dome (1897) is based on St Stephen Walbrook church in London.

↓ The Great Bath of Roman times in its present form

Around the edges of the bath are the bases of piers that once supported a barrel-vaulted roof.

The sacred spring was a focal point for worship in the Roman period.

The water flows from the spring into the corner of the bath at a constant temperature of 46° C (115° F).

Steps, column bases and paving stones around the edge of the bath date from Roman times.

A late 19th-century terrace bears statues of famous Romans such as Julius Caesar.

A SHORT WALK
BATH

Distance 1.5 km (1 mile) **Time** 15 minutes
Nearest bus station Dorchester St

Bath owes its magnificent Georgian townscape to the bubbling pool of water at the heart of the Roman Baths. The Romans transformed Bath into England's first spa resort and it regained fame as a spa town in the 18th century. At this time, the two John Woods (Elder and Younger), both architects, designed the city's Palladian-style buildings. Many houses bear plaques recording the numerous famous people who have resided here.

No. 1 Royal Crescent

Assembly Rooms and Fashion Museum

START

ROYAL CRESCENT

BROCK STREET

BENNETT STREET

THE CIRCUS

GAY STREET

GEORGE

No. 17 The Circus *is where the 18th-century painter Thomas Gainsborough lived.*

The Circus *is a daring departure from the typical Georgian square, by John Wood the Elder (1705–54).*

A permanent exhibition of film, costumes and books tells the story of the author's time in Bath at the **Jane Austen Centre**.

QUEEN

SQUARE

BARTON STREET

BEAUFORD SQUARE

Theatre Royal (1805)

←
The elegant façade of the Theatre Royal, a fine example of Georgian architecture

↑ The historic, shop-lined Pulteney Bridge spanning the River Avon in Bath's centre

The **Museum of Bath at Work** celebrates 2,000 years of Bath's working heritage.

Milsom Street and New Bond Street contain some of Britain's most elegant shops.

Built in the 1st century AD, the **Roman Baths** complex is one of Britain's greatest memorials to the Roman era.

0 metres 100
0 yards 100

N ↑

The charming **Pulteney Bridge** (1769–74), designed by Robert Adam, is lined with shops and links the city centre with the magnificent Great Pulteney Street.

FINISH

The splendid **Bath Abbey** stands at the heart of the old city in the Abbey Churchyard, a paved courtyard enlivened by buskers. Its unique façade features stone angels climbing Jacob's Ladder to heaven.

Courting couples came to the pretty riverside **Parade Gardens** for secret liaisons in the 18th century.

The tearooms in the **Pump Rooms** once formed the social hub of the 18th-century spa community.

Sally Lunn's House (1482) is one of Bath's oldest houses.

LANSDOWN ROAD
PARAGON
STREET
BROAD STREET
WALCOT STREET
MILSOM STREET
NEW BOND STREET
UPPER BOROUGH WALLS
UNION STREET
HIGH STREET
GRAND PARADE
ORANGE GROVE
PIERREPOINT STREET
CHEAP STREET
WESTGATE STREET
YORK STREET

EXPERIENCE MORE

3

Isle of Purbeck

🅐A3 🄾Dorset 🚊Wareham 🚌Shell Bay, Studland 🛈Shore Rd, Swanage; **www.swanage.gov.uk**

The Isle of Purbeck, which is in fact a peninsula, is the source of the grey shelly limestone, known as Purbeck marble, from which Corfe Castle and the nearby houses were built. The geology changes to the southwest at Kimmeridge, where the muddy shale is rich in fossils and oil reserves.

The Isle, a World Heritage Site, is fringed with unspoiled beaches like Studland Bay, with a nature reserve rich in birdlife. To best experience the Purbeck, walk along the South West Coast Path, taking in Lulworth (p145) along the way.

The main resort in the area is Swanage, the port where Purbeck stone was transported by ship to London. Unwanted masonry from demolished buildings was shipped back, and this is how Swanage got its ornate Town Hall façade.

4

Corfe Castle

🅐A3 🄾Dorset 🚊Wareham then bus 🕑10am–6pm daily (Oct to 5pm; Nov–Feb: to 4pm) 🆆**nationaltrust.org.uk**

The ruins of the 11th-century Corfe Castle crown a rocky pinnacle above the village that shares its name. In 1635 the castle was purchased by Sir John Bankes, whose wife and her retainers held out here against Parliamentary troops in a six-week siege during the Civil War (p49). The castle was taken and later blown up.

5

Wimborne Minster

🅐A2 🄾Dorset 🚌 🛈29 High St; **www.wimborne.info**

The fine collegiate church of Wimborne Minster, founded in 705 by Cuthburga, sister of King Ina of Wessex, fell prey to Danish raiders in the 10th century. Today's grey church dates from the refounding by Edward the Confessor in 1043. Stonemasons made use of the local Purbeck marble, carving beasts, biblical scenes and a mass of zigzag decoration.

The revamped **Museum of East Dorset** recalls the history of the local communities in this area; there's also an enchanting hidden garden here.

Kingston Lacy is a sumptuous mansion designed for the Bankes family after the destruction of Corfe Castle.

Museum of East Dorset
🅐29 High St 🕑Times vary, check website 🆆**museumofeastdorset.co.uk**

Kingston Lacy
🅐On B3082 🕑Times vary, check website 🆆**nationaltrust.org.uk**

→
Dramatic landscape of vertiginous cliffs on the Isle of Purbeck

←
People enjoying a drink
in the sunshine at a pub
on the quay, Poole

The original nave, dating from around 1093, is an impressive example of Norman architecture, but the highlight is the intricate stone reredos, which features a Tree of Jesse, tracing the lineage of Christ.

Hengistbury Head is well worth climbing for grassland flowers and sea views, while Stanpit Marsh, to the west of Bournemouth, is an excellent spot for viewing wading birds.

Compton Acres

⊛ⓨⓜ 🅿 Canford Cliffs Rd
🕙 10am-6pm daily (Nov-Good Friday: to 4pm)
🆆 comptonacres.co.uk

Russell-Cotes Art Gallery and Museum

⊛ 🅿 Eastcliff 🕙 10am-5pm Tue-Sun 🆆 russell cotes.com

Poole

🅰 A3 🅾 Dorset 🚊🚌🚢
🛈 4 High St; www.poole tourism.com

Situated on one of the largest natural harbours in the world, Poole is an ancient, still-thriving seaport. The quay is lined with old warehouses, modern apartments and a marina. The **Poole Museum**, partly housed in 15th-century cellars alongside the quay, has four floors of galleries. Nearby Brownsea Island is given over to a woodland nature reserve with herons, egrets and red squirrels.

Poole Museum

⊜🖐 🅿 4 High St 🕙 10am-5pm daily (Nov-Mar: to 4pm)
🆆 poolemuseum.co.uk

Brownsea Island

⊛🖐⊜🖐 Ⓝⓣ 🕙 Mid-Mar-Oct: daily (boat trips leave every 30 mins) 🆆 national trust.org.uk

Bournemouth

🅰 A3 🅾 Dorset 🚊🚍🚢
🛈 Pier Approach; www. bournemouth.co.uk

Bournemouth has an almost unbroken sweep of sandy beach, extending from the mouth of Poole Harbour to Hengistbury Head. To the west there are clifftop parks and gardens, interrupted by wooded river ravines known as "chines". The varied and colourful garden of **Compton Acres** was conceived as a museum of garden styles.

The **Russell-Cotes Art Gallery and Museum**, housed in a late Victorian villa, has an extensive collection, with an array of fine Asian and Victorian artifacts.

East of Bournemouth, Christchurch Priory is 95 m (310 ft) in length – one of the longest churches in England.

Colourful fishing cottages lining the busy harbourfront in Weymouth ↑

8

Weymouth

🅐G5 🅐Dorset 🚉🚌🚢
🅦visit-dorset.com

Weymouth's popularity as a seaside resort began in 1789, when King George III (1738–1820) paid the first of many summer visits to its glorious sandy beach. His statue is a prominent feature on the seafront. Here, gracious Georgian terraces look across to the beautiful expanse of Weymouth Bay, which hosted the sailing events in the 2012 Olympic Games.

North of the beach, **SEA LIFE Weymouth** is a popular attraction, particularly among young families. The centre runs an excellent conservation programme protecting the likes of sharks, penguins, rays and sea turtles.

Beyond the lifting Town Bridge, the Old Town has a traditional coastal character, with its many fishing boats and old seamen's inns that line the waterfront.

A short walk from the Old Town leads to the Victorian **Nothe Fort**, where displays of World War II memorabilia recall the time when the town played host to over 500,000 troops in advance of the 1944 D-Day Landings. The fort also offers fine views from its ramparts and the adjacent Nothe Gardens.

SEA LIFE Weymouth
♿🔊🕐 🅐Lodmoor Country Park 🕐Mar-Oct: 10am-5pm daily; Nov-Feb: 10am-4pm 🅦visitsealife.com

Nothe Fort
♿🔊🕐 🅐Barack Rd 🕐Apr-Oct: 10:30am-4:30pm daily; Mar & Nov: 10:30am-4:30pm Sun 🅦nothefort.org.uk

9

Isle of Portland

🅐G5 🅐Dorset 🚌

A rocky lump protruding dramatically above the coast, the Isle of Portland has been described as the Gibraltar of England. Many of the world's

finest buildings, including St Paul's Cathedral (p66), have been constructed using the Portland stone that has been quarried in the area for centuries. There are great views from the top of the island, which is home to two forts. The brooding Verne Citadel still serves as a prison, but it is possible to visit the other, **Portland Castle**, built under Henry VIII to protect the harbour. At the southern tip of the island is Portland Bill, an attractive headland capped by the **Portland Bill Lighthouse**, built in 1906. The visitor centre has a superb display on the island's history as well as the lighthouse's; the views from the top of the lighthouse are spectacular.

Portland Castle
⊛ ⊜ ⊕ ⊕ 🄰 Liberty Rd
🕒 Apr–Sep: 10am–6pm daily; Oct: 10am–5pm daily
🌐 english-heritage.org.uk

Portland Bill Lighthouse
⊛ ⊛ 🄰 Portland Bill 🕒 May–Sep: 10am–5pm daily; Oct, Mar–Apr: 10am–5pm Tue–Sun; Nov–Feb: 10am–3pm Sat & Sun 🄲 24 & 25 Dec
🌐 trinityhouse.co.uk

⑩
Lulworth
🄰 G5 🄰 Dorset 🚌

Sheltered Lulworth Cove is one of the prettiest and most popular coastal spots in Dorset, an almost circular shingle bay fringed by tall cliffs. A collection of former fishermen's houses nestle at the top of the bay, which is now occupied by numerous restaurants, pubs and cafés offering some of the freshest and tastiest seafood and local produce in the area.

The **Lulworth Visitor Centre**, near the main car park, explains the unusual coastal geology of the area, including the famous Durdle Door, Dorset's iconic rock arch. The arch can be reached by road or via a scenic 30-minute walk along the coast path. The steps that descend down to the shingle beach are very steep, but the views are well worth the effort.

Lulworth Visitor Centre
🄰 🄰 Main Rd 🕒 Mar–Oct: 10am–5pm daily; Nov–Feb: 10am–4pm daily
🌐 lulworth.com

DRINK

The Ship Inn
Creaky floorboards, cosy corners and classic ales: this historic pub is everything you'd want from a port town inn. Once the exclusive domain of salty seadogs, now all are welcome, including dogs of the non-seafaring variety.

🄰 G5 🄰 Custom House Quay, Weymouth
🌐 shipweymouth.co.uk

The Boat Shed
As well as homemade cakes, scrumptious cream teas and exquisite coffee, this nautically themed café also offers breakfasts and light lunches served with a side of Lulworth Cove's sea air.

🄰 G5 🄰 West Lulworth
📞 01929 400810
🕒 9:30am–5pm daily

← Durdle Door near Lulworth, part of the Jurassic Coast World Heritage Site

↑ Pretty ammonite fossils, a common find on Charmouth Beach

Charmouth is famed for its landslips: its dramatic coastal cliffs frequently crumble and fall into the sea, revealing fossils by the bucket-load.

⑪
Charmouth

ⒶF5 **Ⓐ**Dorset

A handsome village set on a pretty hillside by the coast, Charmouth is famed for its landslips: its dramatic coastal cliffs frequently crumble and fall into the sea, revealing fossils by the bucket-load. In 2000, a fossilized Scelidosaurus was found here, the only known example of this herbivorous dinosaur, while hundreds of tiny fossils of ammonites and belemnites (an extinct, squid-like creature) lie loose on the beach. Organized fossil tours take place from the **Heritage Coast Centre** next to the main car park. If you prefer to hunt for fossils independently, the chances of a find tend to be at their highest during winter, when bad weather and high winds erode the cliff-face. The beach is also quieter at this time. Visitors can also walk along the coastal path to the top of the Golden Cap, the highest cliff on the south coast at 191 m (627 ft).

Heritage Coast Centre
Ⓧ **Ⓐ**Lower Sea Lane
Ⓒ Easter–Oct: 10:30am–4:30pm daily; Nov–Easter: 10:30am–4:30pm Fri–Mon
Ⓦ charmouth.org/chcc

⑫
Abbotsbury

ⒶF5 **Ⓐ**Dorset **ⓘ**West Yard Barn, West St; www.abbotsbury-tourism.co.uk

The name Abbotsbury recalls the town's 11th-century Benedictine abbey, of which little but the huge tithe barn, built around 1400, remains. Nobody knows when the **Swannery** here was founded, but the earliest records date to 1393. Mute swans come to nest here in June, attracted by the reed beds along the Fleet, a brackish lagoon protected from the sea by a high ridge of pebbles called Chesil Beach. This 29-km (18-mile) shingle beach's wild atmosphere is captured in Ian McEwan's novel *On Chesil Beach* (2007).

Nature lovers will adore the **Abbotsbury Subtropical Gardens**, home to a stunning array of exotic plants. Many of its resident species were newly categorized by botanists in South America and Asia when they were introduced to the gardens. The latest addition is the Wonderland Sculpture Trail, which features celebrated characters from Lewis Carroll's classic tale, *Alice in Wonderland*.

On a hilltop above the village is St Catherine's Chapel. Visitors can enjoy wonderful views of the abbey ruins from this popular spot.

Swannery
Ⓧ Ⓜ **Ⓐ**New Barn Rd
Ⓒ01305 871858 Ⓒ Mid-Mar–Oct: 10am–5pm daily

Abbotsbury Subtropical Gardens
Ⓧ Ⓔ Ⓜ **Ⓐ**Off B3157 Ⓒ Apr–Oct: 10am–5pm daily; Nov–Mar: 10am–4pm daily Ⓒ 19 Dec–1 Jan Ⓦ abbotsbury-tourism.co.uk/gardens

⑬
Bridport

ⒶF5 **Ⓐ**Dorset **ⓘ**Town Hall, Bucky Doo Sq, South St; www.visit-dorset.com

The market town of Bridport was famed for its rope-making until the late 1700s, and its unusually wide streets

↑ Red stag sculptures near the Oriental Bridge in Abbotsbury Subtropical Gardens

↑ Looking out to sea and over the Jurassic Coast from the Cobb at Lyme Regis

date from the time when rope was hung between houses to be twisted. Since then it has acquired something of a foodie reputation thanks to a plethora of fine restaurants and a twice-weekly market. The town was a major port until the river silted up, but visitors can still walk alongside the River Brit to the nearest coast, West Bay, a fishing village with a broad shingle beach and towering sandstone cliffs, which formed the iconic backdrop to the popular British TV series *Broadchurch* (2013).

Lyme Regis

🅰F5 🏠Dorset 🅸Church St; www.lymeregis.org

Stretching 153 km (95 miles) between East Devon and Dorset, the landscapes of the Jurassic Coast record 185 million years of the Earth's history. The area is one of Britain's premier fossil-hunting regions, with Lyme Regis as its capital. It was here that pioneer fossil collector Mary Anning and her brother Joseph unearthed a 9-m- (20-ft-) long fossilized Ichthyosaur in 1811. Mary Anning's home is now

the **Lyme Regis Museum**, which traces the history of the town, including its role in the Monmouth Rebellion in 1685.

Lyme Regis takes its name (Regis) from the Royal Charter given by Edward I in 1284, and was a fashionable sea-bathing spot for the gentry in the late 18th and early 19th centuries. Jane Austen set parts of her novel *Persuasion* here.

Today it is a mix of fishermen's cottages and Victorian and Georgian townhouses, though its most famous structure is the Cobb, a 13th-century breakwater curling round the harbour. Visitors can walk out to sea along its massive walls – though do be aware that waves often crash over the Cobb, particularly when the seas are high and choppy.

Southwest of Lyme Regis, the South West Coast Path runs through the Undercliff, a serene wooded nature reserve that has grown up on the loose earth and rubble of former landslips.

Lyme Regis Museum

🧭 🏠Bridge St 🕙Easter-Oct: 10am–5pm Mon–Sat, 11am–5pm Sun; Nov–Easter: 11am–4pm Wed–Sun & school hols 🚫25 & 26 Dec 🌐lyme regismuseum.co.uk

---

TOP 5 FOSSILS TO FIND

Ammonites
The shells of extinct squid-like creatures, ammonites are easy to find in Charmouth.

Belemnites
Another ancestor of the squid, belemnites had a straight body, of which the tail section is often found as a fossil.

Ichthyosaur Bones
The backbones of Ichthyosaurs are fairly common around Lyme Regis and Charmouth, though tricky to find.

Jurassic Sea Shells
There are lots of types of fossilized sea shells found along the Jurassic Coast, including ancient relatives of oysters, clams and scallops.

Plesiosaur Remains
Thought to be the reptile the Loch Ness Monster was based on, rare Plesiosaur teeth and bones have been found along this coast.

↑ The main hall of the Dorset County Museum and (inset) its striking exterior

15
Shaftesbury

🅰G4 🅰Dorset 🚌 *i*8 Bell St; www.shaftesbury tourism.co.uk

Set on a hilltop commanding far-reaching rural views, the attractive town of Shaftesbury dates from Anglo-Saxon times. King Alfred the Great founded Shaftesbury Abbey here in 880 as a Benedictine nunnery – the first religious centre to be built for women. It quickly became one of the wealthiest and most powerful abbeys in the south, but was later dissolved under Henry VIII in 1539, during the English Reformation. Much of the surrounding town fell into disrepair during the years that followed. Today, little remains of the fortifications, 12 churches and four market crosses that once made this a town of some importance, although the impressive

14th-century St Peter's Church is one survivor. The foundations of the abbey now form part of the **Abbey Museum and Garden**, which explores the abbey's fascinating history, including details of King Canute's death here in 1035. The king was believed to have been visiting the tomb of the Saxon king Edward the Martyr, who was buried in the abbey after his murder at Corfe Castle (p142) in 978.

Today, Shaftesbury's charming cobbled streets and pretty 18th-century cottages are often used as a setting in films to give an atmospheric flavour of English rural history. The town's most famous sight is the picturesque Gold Hill, an extremely steep cobbled lane, which is lined on one side by quaint thatched cottages and, on the other, by a wall of the demolished abbey.

Abbey Museum and Garden
🅰 Park Walk
🕙Easter–Oct: 10am–5pm daily 🌐shaftesburyabbey. org.uk

16
Dorchester

🅰G5 🅰Dorset 🚉🚌 *i*The Library, Charles St; www. visit-dorset.com

Many parts of Dorchester, the county town of Dorset, are still recognizable as the place Thomas Hardy described in his novel The Mayor of Casterbridge (1886). Hardy lived at **Max Gate**, where rooms are open to visitors, but the original manuscript of his famous novel and a re-creation of his study can be seen in the **Dorset County Museum** on the High Street. This impressive galleried Victorian building also houses fossils and exhibits on the nearby Jurassic Coast (p147), along with archaeological finds.

Nearby is the Old Crown Court, where the famous Tolpuddle Martyrs were sentenced to transportation for demanding a wage increase; later pardoned, they are credited with founding the Trade Union movement. Today, this building is the location of the immersive **Shire Hall Historic Courthouse Museum**, where you can explore the old cells and stand in the dock where Hardy was once a magistrate.

Dorchester is home to Britain's only example of a

Roman Town House. The remains of this wealthy family villa include a fine mosaic and a Roman heating system. There are also finds from Iron Age and Roman sites on the outskirts of the town.

Just off Weymouth Avenue is Maumbury Rings, a Neolithic henge that was adapted for use as a Roman amphitheatre. It was later used for bear-baiting and executions, but it now hosts firework displays and other events.

Brewery Square, a former brewery, has been developed into a fashionable cultural quarter, comprising a cinema, theatre, arts centre and several shops and restaurants clustered around a central square.

Max Gate
⊘ ⓝⓣ 🚻 Arlington Ave ⏰ Mid Mar-Oct: 11am-5pm daily; Nov-mid-Mar: 10am-4pm Thu-Sun 🌐 nationaltrust. org.uk

Dorset County Museum
⊘ 🚼 🚻 🅿 ⏰ High West St 🚫 Closed for renovation until late 2021 🌐 dorsetcounty museum.org

Shire Hall Historic Courthouse Museum
⊘ 🚼 ⏰ 58-60 High West St ⏰ 10am-4pm Mon-Sat 🌐 shirehalldorset.org

Roman Town House
🚻 Colliton Park 🚫 Closed for renovation

---

17 ⓔⓗ
Maiden Castle

🅰 G5 🚻 Dorset 🌐 english-heritage.org.uk

Just southwest of Dorchester, barely out of the town suburbs, is the massive Maiden Castle, parts of which date back to around 3000 BC. It is one of Europe's largest Iron Age hillforts and from around 450 BC several hundred members of the Durotriges tribe resided in the safety of the fort, in a town

situated on a flat plateau at the top of the hill. You can still see where the fort's concentric lines of earthen ramparts and ditches follow the contours of the hill. These were once fortified by a series of fences and staggered gates that would have made the hilltop nigh-on impregnable to invading forces – at least until AD 43, when the Romans defeated the tribe in a bloody battle. Despite their victory, the Romans decided to settle in nearby Dorchester, building a temple on the hilltop in the 4th century that was later abandoned; the foundations survive today on a grassy hillock. Visitors can walk up the slopes to the top of Maiden Castle, now grazed by placid sheep that have little idea of the history beneath their feet.

18
Cerne Abbas

🅰 G5 🚻 Dorset 📧

Charming Cerne Abbas grew up around a Benedictine abbey, which was built in 987

and visited by kings John and Henry III. Though little of the abbey can still be seen, the village exudes history, with a magnificent medieval tithe barn and ancient cottages. Visitors can also see St Augustine's Well, the spring where St Augustine allegedly offered local shepherds a choice of water or beer. When they chose water, the saint struck the ground with his staff, making a spring gush from the ground. Ironically, the fresh water that bubbles up here subsequently supported a brewing trade that was so successful that the village once had 15 pubs.

Today, however, the village's most famous attraction is the Cerne Abbas Giant, a huge chalk figure carved into the hillside nearby. Many believe this 55-m- (180-ft-) high carving, with its large appendage, to be a fertility figure representing either the Roman god Hercules or an Iron Age warrior. Others argue that he may be a much later caricature of Oliver Cromwell. The figure has now been fenced off to avoid erosion and is best seen from the well-signed viewpoint on the hillside opposite, or via the Giant's Walk, a marked 90-minute trail from the village.

↑ The Cerne Abbas Giant, a large chalk figure etched onto the landscape

Cottages lining the cobbled street of Gold Hill in Shaftesbury

⑲ Glastonbury

🗺 F4 **🏛 Somerset** **🚌**
ℹ 1 Magdalene St; www. glastonburytic.co.uk

Shrouded in Arthurian myth and rich in mystical association, the town of Glastonbury was once one of the most important destinations for pilgrims in England. Today, thousands flock here for the annual music festival and for the summer solstice on Midsummer's Day (21 June).

Over the years, history and legend have become intertwined. In around 700, the monks who set up **Glastonbury Abbey** found it profitable to encourage the association between Glastonbury and the mythical "Blessed Isle" known as Avalon – alleged to be the last resting place of King Arthur and the Holy Grail. The great abbey was left in ruins after the Dissolution. Despite this, some magnificent remains survive, including parts of the Norman abbey church and the unusual Abbot's Kitchen (with its octagonal roof). Growing in the grounds is a cutting from the Glastonbury thorn, which is believed to have miraculously grown from the staff of St Joseph of Arimathea.

↑ The 15th-century ceiling of Sherborne's magnificent Abbey Church

According to myth, he was sent around AD 60 to convert England to Christianity. The thorn flowers at Christmas as well as in May.

A short walk away is the fascinating **Somerset Rural Life Museum**, located in a Victorian farmhouse. It offers a wonderful insight into the county's heritage, with themes ranging from religion and folklore to food production, in particular dairy farming and cider-making.

Glastonbury Abbey

⊘⊘🕐 **🏛 Chilkwell St**
🕐 10am–5pm Wed–Sat
w swheritage.org.uk

GLASTONBURY FESTIVAL

In 1970, farmer Michael Eavis decided to host a music festival at Worthy Farm in Pilton, near Glastonbury. Little did he know that the event would grow into one of the world's largest contemporary music festivals. Today, Glastonbury is held in late June and pulls in over 130,000 attendees. Its main draw is the quality of its music: top acts have ranged from David Bowie and Bob Dylan to Oasis and Adele.

Somerset Rural Life Museum

⊘⊘ **🏛 Chilkwell St**
🕐 10am–5pm Wed–Sat
w swheritage.org.uk

⑳ Sherborne

🗺 G4 **🏛 Dorset** **🚆🚌**
ℹ 3 Tilton Court, Digby Rd; www.visit-dorset.com

Few towns in England can rival Sherborne for its wealth of beautiful and unspoiled medieval buildings. In 1550, Edward VI founded the Sherborne School, thereby saving the **Abbey Church** that might otherwise have been demolished in the Dissolution (p48). The church's most striking feature is the 15th-century fan-vaulted ceiling.

The imposing **Sherborne Castle**, built for Sir Walter Raleigh (1552–1618) in 1594, anticipates Jacobean architecture with its flamboyant style. Raleigh also lived in the 12th-century **Old Castle**, which now stands in ruins, demolished during the Civil War (p49).

Abbey Church

⊘⊘🕐 **🏛 Abbey Close**
🕐 Apr–Oct: 8am–6pm daily; Nov–Mar: 8am–4pm daily
w sherborneabbey.com

Sherborne Castle

⊕⊝🏠 🚗New Rd 🕐Easter-Oct: 11am-5pm Tue, Thu, Sat & Sun 🌐sherbornecastle.com

Old Castle

⊕🏠♿ 🚗Off A30 📞01935 812730 🕐Easter-Oct: daily

㉑ ⊕ 🖰 (NT)

Montacute House

🅰F4 🚗Montacute
🕐House: mid-Mar-Oct: 11am-4:30pm daily; Gardens: Apr-Oct: 11am-4:30pm daily; Nov-Feb: 11am-4pm Wed-Sun
🌐nationaltrust.org.uk

West of Sherborne stands the magnificent Elizabethan Montacute House, set in the picturesque village of the same name. The house was built in the late 16th century for the wealthy politician Sir Edward Phelips, and stayed in the same family until the early 20th century. It is noted for its Long Gallery, tapestries, and Tudor and Elizabethan portraits, which are loaned

from the National Portrait Gallery. The house is set in 120 ha (300 acres) of grounds with formal gardens.

㉒

Wells

🅰F4 🚗Somerset
🛈Town Hall, Market Place; www.wellssomerset.com

The charming city of Wells is home to two impressive historic sights: **Wells Cathedral** and **Bishop's Palace**. The stunning cathedral was begun in the late 1100s, and is famous for its elaborate West Front and the "scissor arches" installed in 1338 to support the tower. The palace – the residence of the Bishop of Bath and Wells – is a beautiful medieval building, complete with a moat, 13th-century chapel and expansive gardens, as well as the ruins of the still-impressive Great Hall. The clear sacred spring that bubbles up from the ground near the palace, known as St Andrew's Well, is what gave the city its name

Wells Cathedral

⊕⊗⊝🏠 🚗Cathedral Green 🕐7am-6pm daily (except for events)
🌐wellscathedral.org.uk

Bishop's Palace

⊕⊝ 🚗Bishop's Palace
🕐10am-6pm daily (Nov-Mar: to 4pm)
🌐bishopspalace.org.uk

The Chain Gate (1460)

A graceful flight of steps curves up to the octagonal Chapter House, which has delicate vaulting dating from 1306. The 32 ribs fanning from the central column create a palm-tree effect.

13th century ruins of the Great Hall

The Vicars' Close was built in the 14th century for the Vicars' Choir. It is one of the oldest complete streets in Europe.

The West Front features 300 fine medieval statues of kings, knights and saints – many of them life-size.

Cloisters

The tombs of past bishops circle the chancel. The marble tomb in the south aisle is that of Bishop Lord Arthur Hervey, Bishop of Bath and Wells from 1869 to 1894.

Path leading round the moat

Moat with swans, which are trained to ring a bell by the gatehouse when they want to be fed.

The Bishop's Palace (1230–40)

↑ Wells Cathedral, begun in the late 12th century

23 Bridgwater and the Quantocks

F4 **Somerset** **quantockhills.com**

Famed for its annual Guy Fawkes carnival (held 1st Sun in Nov), Bridgwater grew as a bustling port and market town on the River Parrett. Its 16th-century **Blake Museum** details the town's history and its role in the failed Monmouth Rebellion in 1685, when the Duke of Monmouth, James Scott, attempted to overthrow King James II.

Bridgwater is also a useful base from which to explore the nearby Quantock hills. Now designated an Area of Outstanding Natural Beauty, the hills and surrounding countryside are said to have inspired the poet Samuel Taylor Coleridge (1772–1834). The pretty cottage where he wrote some of his best-known works lies in the village of Nether Stowey, 13 km (8 miles) west of Bridgwater.

From here, a well-worn footpath known as the Coleridge Way runs west for 82 km (51 miles) through Exmoor National Park (p164) to the coastal town of Lynmouth.

Blake Museum

5 Blake St **Easter-Oct: 10am-4pm Tue-Sat** **bridgwatermuseum.org.uk**

Cheddar Gorge is a spectacular ravine cut through the Mendip plateau by fast-flowing streams during the interglacial phases of the last Ice Age.

24 Taunton

F4 **Somerset** **Market House, Fore St; www.visitsomerset.co.uk**

Pretty Taunton lies at the heart of a fertile region famous for its apples and cider, but it was the wool industry that financed the massive church of **St Mary Magdalene** (1488–1514).

Taunton's castle was the setting for the Bloody Assizes of 1685, when "Hanging" Judge Jeffreys dispensed retribution on the Duke of Monmouth and his followers for an uprising against King James II. The 12th-century building houses the **Museum of Somerset**, with a Roman mosaic from a villa at Low Ham, depicting the story of Dido and Aeneas.

St Mary Magdalene

Church Sq **9:30am-4pm Mon-Fri, 9:30am-2pm Sat** **stmarymagdalene taunton.org.uk**

Museum of Somerset

Taunton Castle **10am-5pm Tue-Sat** **museumof somerset.org.uk**

---

25 Somerset Levels

F4 **Somerset** **Glastonbury** **Glastonbury**

The extensive Somerset Levels consist of ancient peat moors and grassland interspersed with dramatic hillocks such as the Glastonbury Tor, which some say was the mythical Isle of Avalon in Arthurian legend, though it has several other enduring mythological and spiritual associations. Glastonbury Tor has been a sight of spiritual significance for centuries; archaeological excavations have revealed artifacts that prove human visitation dating as far back as the Iron Age and Roman eras. Visible for miles around, the Tor is crowned by St Michael's Tower, which is all that remains of a 14th-century monastic church. The building was largely destroyed during the Dissolution of the Monasteries in 1536.

Though split by the Polden Hills, the Levels are prone to flooding and have been drained since the Middle Ages. Today, the wetlands – many formed from abandoned peat workings – are a magnet for wildlife. The various nature reserves at the beautiful Avalon Marshes are home to kingfishers, bitterns and great white egrets, and in winter massive murmurations of starlings blacken the sky in mesmerizing patterns.

There are some excellent walks and cycle rides that depart from the central **Avalon Marshes Centre**.

Avalon Marshes Centre

Shapwick Rd, Westhay **10am-5pm daily** **avalonmarshes.org**

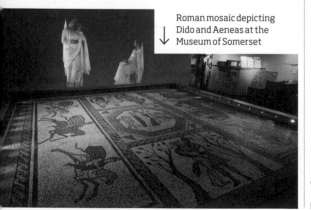

↓ Roman mosaic depicting Dido and Aeneas at the Museum of Somerset

26

Cheddar Gorge

A F4 **Q** The Cliffs, Cheddar, Somerset **S** From Weston-super-Mare **C** 10am–5pm daily **W** cheddargorge.co.uk

Described as a "deep frightful chasm" by novelist Daniel Defoe in 1724, Cheddar Gorge is a spectacular ravine cut through the Mendip plateau by fast-flowing streams during the interglacial phases of the last Ice Age. This narrow, winding limestone ravine rises almost vertically on either side to a height of 140 m (460 ft).

Of course, you don't have to pay to admire the gorge. The B3135 road winds its way around its 5-km (3-mile) base, making for a scenic drive, with numerous stopping points on the road. Other attractions have sprung up in the area, including escape rooms, climbing activities and the Museum of Prehistory, which displays "Cheddar Man", a 9,000-year-old skeleton.

Cheddar has given its name to a rich cheese that originates from the area, though now it is produced worldwide. The **Cheddar Gorge Cheese Company** is the only working Cheddar dairy in Cheddar. Visitors can see Cheddar being made, and taste and buy cheese in the store.

Cheddar Gorge Cheese Company

⊗ **Q** The Cliffs **C** 10am–4pm daily **W** cheddaronline.co.uk

---

GREAT VIEW
Clifftop Climb

Tackle the steep climb up Jacob's Ladder and Tower, which has some 274 steps, to reach the clifftop. From here, you'll be rewarded with stunning scenery over the gorge itself and the rolling Mendip Hills.

Hiking amid the majestic landscape of Cheddar Gorge, in the Mendip plateau ↑

A DRIVING TOUR
JURASSIC COAST

Length 146 km (91 miles) **Stopping-off points** Lulworth Cove Visitor Centre details the coastline's geology. Sample the seafood at The Hive Beach Café in Burton Bradstock.

The 153-km- (95-mile-) long Jurassic Coast is the only natural site in England with UNESCO World Heritage status. The area was given this accolade because of its extraordinary geology; incredibly rich in fossils, it reveals to scientists a landscape that has varied from swamp to arid desert over a period of 185 million years. Take a drive along Devon and Dorset's coast to discover the area's history and beauty.

*A favoured haunt of Jane Austen, **Charmouth** is great for fossil hunting, with new specimens exposed beneath one of Europe's largest coastal landslip areas.*

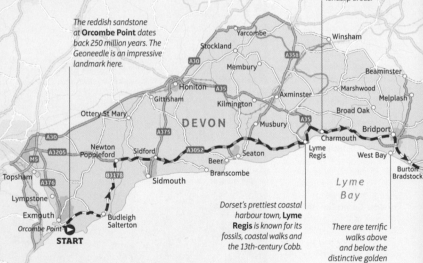

*The reddish sandstone at **Orcombe Point** dates back 250 million years. The Geoneedle is an impressive landmark here.*

*Dorset's prettiest coastal harbour town, **Lyme Regis** is known for its fossils, coastal walks and the 13th-century Cobb.*

*There are terrific walks above and below the distinctive golden cliffs of **West Bay**.*

START

← The striking Geoneedle obelisk at Orcombe Point

← Portland Bill Lighthouse, which was built in 1906, on the Isle of Portland

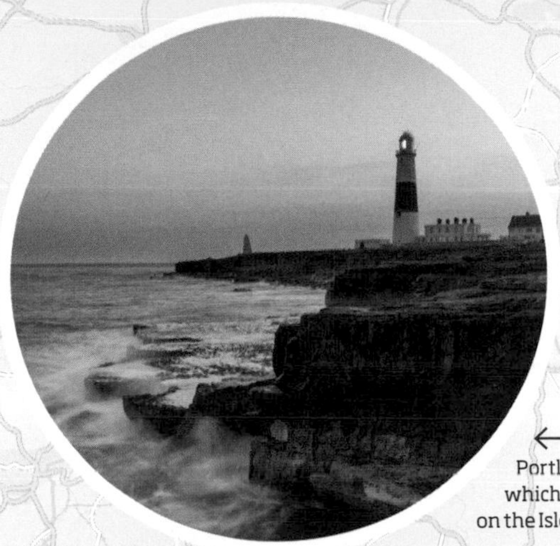

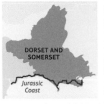

DORSET AND SOMERSET
Jurassic Coast

Locator Map

The former Iron Age hillfort on ***Wears Hill*** *provides superb views across the Fleet Lagoon.*

The sandy beach of ***Shell Bay*** *marks the end of the 1,014-km (630-mile) South West Coast Path.*

A short walk from the village of Studland, along the South West Coast Path, are the dramatic chalk stacks of ***Old Harry Rocks****.*

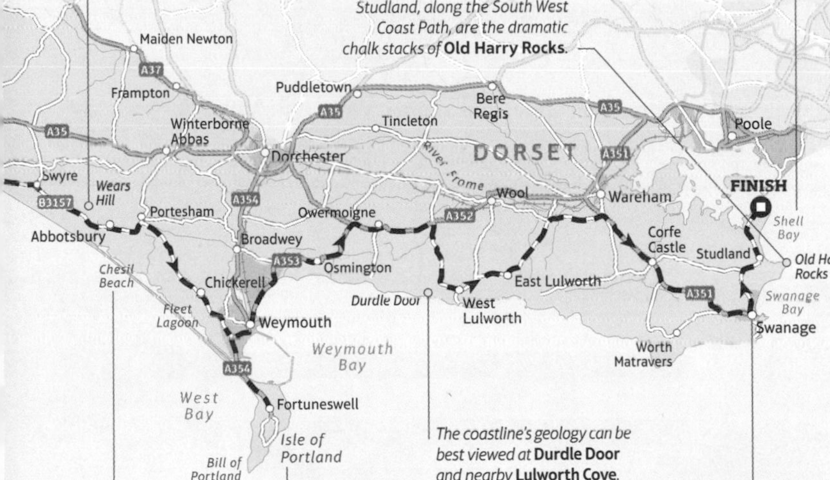

Maiden Newton
A37
Frampton
Puddletown
A35
Bere Regis
A35
Tincleton
Poole
A35
Winterborne Abbas
Dorchester
DORSET
A351
River Frome
Swyre
Wears Hill
B3157
Portesham
A354
Owermoigne
Wool
Wareham
FINISH
Shell Bay
Abbotsbury
Broadwey
A352
Corfe Castle
Studland
Old Harry Rocks
Chesil Beach
A353
Osmington
Chickerell
East Lulworth
Durdle Door
West Lulworth
A351
Swanage Bay
Fleet Lagoon
Weymouth
Swanage
Weymouth Bay
Worth Matravers
A354
West Bay
Fortuneswell
Isle of Portland
Bill of Portland
0 kilometres 10
0 miles 10
N

The coastline's geology can be best viewed at ***Durdle Door*** *and nearby* ***Lulworth Cove****.*

Connected to the mainland by a causeway, the ***Isle of Portland*** *is known for its sailing and diving.*

Visitors can enjoy fish and chips on the beach at the typical English seaside resort of ***Swanage****.*

With some 29 km (18 miles) of pebbles, ***Chesil Beach*** *provides a natural barrier between the sea and the Fleet Lagoon.*

DEVON

Renowned for its mild weather, Devon may have had a warmer climate than much of Britain in prehistoric times and it is the earliest known place in England to have been settled after the end of the last Ice Age. A jawbone discovered at Kents Cavern, near Torquay, is even thought to belong to the earliest modern human in northwest Europe. By 6000 BC, Dartmoor seems to have played a key role in Mesolithic and Neolithic culture – the bleak moorland holds the remains of the oldest surviving buildings in the country.

Only a few parts of Devon fell under Roman rule, and the county played a marginal role in British history until Tudor times, when the natural harbour at Plymouth was the point of departure for the navigators Sir Walter Raleigh and Sir Francis Drake.

Devon became an important destination during the Victorian era, as new train lines and a vogue for sea air and swimming saw the development of many seaside towns. Most famous were the resorts on the south coast – Torquay, Paignton and Brixham – which became known as the English Riviera for their relatively balmy climate, sub-tropical vegetation and palm-lined promenades. These towns continue to draw the crowds, and today tourism has overtaken agriculture as Devon's main source of income, though the two traditions still unite in the county's most famous delicacy – the Devonshire cream tea.

DEVON

Must Sees

1. Dartmoor National Park
2. Exmoor National Park
3. Exeter

Experience More

4. Beer
5. Torbay
6. Totnes
7. Dittisham
8. Buckfastleigh
9. Dartmouth
10. Salcombe and the South Hams
11. Burgh Island
12. Buckland Abbey
13. Plymouth
14. Morwellham Quay
15. Appledore
16. Barnstaple
17. Bideford
18. Clovelly
19. Lynton and Lynmouth
20. Ilfracombe
21. Broomhill Sculpture Gardens
22. Lundy Island

DORSET AND SOMERSET
p130

❶
DARTMOOR NATIONAL PARK

🅰D5 🏠Devon 🚊Exeter, Plymouth, Totnes then bus
ℹ️Tavistock Rd, Princetown; www.dartmoor.gov.uk

A mix of sheltered wooded valleys and barren moorland peppered with granite rock formations and Bronze Age remains, Dartmoor was one of the first areas in England to be designated a National Park, in 1951.

The dramatic landscape of central Dartmoor is one of contrasts, providing an impressive variety of striking vistas. The high, open moorland served as the eerie backdrop for the Sherlock Holmes tale *The Hound of the Baskervilles* (1902), while one of Britain's most famous prisons, Dartmoor Prison, is surrounded by weathered outcrops of stone

←

Haytor Rocks, one of the most remarkable of Dartmoor's many tors

TWO MOORS WAY

Walk across the splendid moorlands of Dartmoor and Exmoor along the Two Moors Way (also known as the Coast to Coast Path). Some 188 km (117 miles) in length, it starts at Wembury Bay in south Devon and finishes at Lynmouth on the North Devon coast, slicing through a small section of Somerset along the way. Suitable for both day and longer-distance walkers, the routes are explained on *www.twomoorsway.org*.

tors (rock formations) in Princetown village. Also dotting the landscape are scores of ancient remains of standing stones and mysterious hut circles that have survived thanks to the durability of granite. Creating pockets of tranquillity, streams tumble through wooded and boulder-strewn ravines forming waterfalls, and thatched cottages nestle in the sheltered valleys and villages around the margins of the moor. Dartmoor ponies, here for centuries, can be seen grazing on the moors.

↑ A walker looking out over the beautiful Dartmoor landscape at sunrise

St Michael de Rupe

▷ Legend has it that the Devil tried to prevent the construction of this church, perched atop Brent Tor, by moving the stones. Whatever the truth, there has been a church here since the 12th century. Reached by a footpath, there are stunning views over Dartmoor from here.

Postbridge

▽ In the centre of the moor and set on the River Dart, the village of Postbridge is a good starting point for walks on the moor. There is a medieval "clapper" bridge here, which was built to enable pack horses to carry mined tin across the river.

Lydford Gorge

There is a circular 5-km (3-mile) walk through this remote ravine.

Castle Drogo

This magnificent early 20th-century mock castle - said to be the last castle built in England - was designed by architect Edwin Lutyens for the grocery magnate Julius Drewe. From the house there are lovely walks through the gorge of the River Teign.

Hound Tor

▷ The remains of this village lie on the eastern edge of Dartmoor. The settlement consists of a cluster of 13th-century stone longhouses - in which the family lived at one end and the animals at the other - on land originally farmed in the Bronze Age.

Buckland-in-the-Moor

◁ One of the many pretty villages on the southeastern side of Dartmoor, Buckland-in-the-Moor has thatched stone cottages and a small granite church.

②

EXMOOR NATIONAL PARK

🅰E4 🏠Somerset/Devon 🚆Tiverton Parkway then bus 🛈National Park Centres: The Esplanade, Lynmouth; 7-9 Fore St, Dulverton; The Steep, Dunster; www.exmoor-nationalpark.gov.uk

For walkers, Exmoor offers 1,000 km (620 miles) of wonderful public paths and varied, dramatic scenery of moorland, river valleys and cliffs. The tamer perimeters of the national park offer less energetic attractions – everything from traditional seaside entertainments to picturesque villages and ancient churches.

The majestic cliffs plunging into the Bristol Channel along Exmoor's northern coast are interrupted by lush, wooded valleys carrying rivers from the high moorland down to sheltered fishing coves. Inland, wild rolling hills are grazed by sturdy Exmoor ponies, horned sheep and local wild red deer. Buzzards wheel over the bracken-clad terrain looking for prey.

←

A walker on Dunkery Beacon, Exmoor's highest point, at sunset

Exmoor ponies grazing on heather-covered moorland on Porlock Common, and *(inset)* Dunster Castle

SOUTH WEST COAST PATH

Running across the northern edge of Exmoor National Park is the wonderful South West Coast Path, which begins in Minehead in Somerset and then snakes its way around the coast of Cornwall to Poole in Dorset. Some 1,014 km (630 miles) in length, it is the longest national trail in England and passes through diverse, stunning scenery, taking in geology, wildlife and heritage along the way *(www.southwestcoast path.org.uk).*

Located in the heart of the national park is Exford. With its attractive village green, surrounded by shops, restaurants and hotels, it's a popular base for exploring Exmoor. The Exford circular walk is an easy route that offers quintessential Exmoor views of moorland covered in yellow gorse and purple heather. For a change of scene, try the Exe Valley Way, which connects Exford to the sea.

Lynmouth *(p180)* is an excellent starting point for coastal walks. There is a gorgeous 3-km (2-mile) trail that leads southeast to tranquil Watersmeet House, a former fishing lodge that is now a fabulous tearoom with a splendid garden. Set in a wooded valley, this is the spot where the East Lyn and Hoar Oak Water join together in a tumbling cascade.

East of here are charming Porlock village, with winding streets, thatched houses and a lovely old church, and Minehead, a major resort built around a pretty quay. Dunster is one of Exmoor's oldest villages, with an ancient castle, parts of which date to the 13th century, and an unusual octagonal Yarn Market (c 1609), where local cloth was once sold.

On the western edge of Exmoor, the village of Combe Martin lies in a sheltered valley. On the main street, lined with Victorian villas, is the 17th-century Pack o' Cards inn, built by a gambler to resemble a pack of cards, with 52 windows, one for each card in the pack.

> Inland, wild rolling hills are grazed by Exmoor ponies, horned sheep and local wild red deer. Buzzards wheel over the bracken-clad terrain looking for prey.

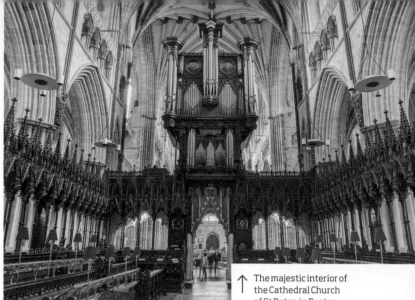

↑ The majestic interior of the Cathedral Church of St Peter, in Exeter

③

EXETER

Ⓐ E5 ✈ 🚉 🚌 ⓘ Dix's Field; www.visitexeter.com

Built high on a plateau above the River Exe, Exeter is encircled by substantial sections of Roman and medieval wall, and the street plan has not changed much since the Romans first laid out what is now the High Street. Cathedral Close has one of the country's finest Gothic churches, while atmospheric cobbled streets invite leisurely exploration.

①

Exeter Cathedral

Ⓐ 1 The Cloisters **⊙** 9am–5pm daily **ⓦ** exeter-cathedral.org.uk

Completed around 1400, the majestic Cathedral Church of St Peter is one of the most extravagantly ornamented cathedrals in Britain. Its West Front is intricately carved with tier upon tier of kings, angels, apostles and prophets – 66 in all, the largest single collection of medieval figure sculptures in England. Inside, breath-taking Gothic fan vaulting sweeps from one end of the church to the other, each join decorated with a unique gilded boss – the most famous depicts the assassination of Thomas Becket. The carved misericords, dating from 1220–30 and 1250–60, are the oldest complete set in England – the elephant is especially well known. A catflap in the door by the clock is a remnant from the days when the cathedral cat was paid a penny a week to catch mice.

Full of relaxed crowds listening to buskers perform on the green, the close that surrounds the cathedral contains a variety of architectural styles. One of the finest buildings here is Mol's Coffee House, built in 1596.

②

The Quay

Ⓐ Custom House: 46 The Quay **⊙** Apr–Oct: 10am–5pm daily; Nov–Mar: 11am–4pm Sat & Sun **ⓦ** exeter.gov.uk

Exeter's historic quay has been restored, with early 19th-century warehouses now home to a variety of unique and interesting shops and independent boutiques, selling everything from art and craft supplies to vintage clothes. Visitors will also find an eclectic mix of cafés, pubs and restaurants here. Boats and paddleboards can be hired from the quay for cruising down the canal, and there is also a climbing centre.

🔺 GREAT VIEW
The Riviera Line

Take the passenger train from Exeter St David's to Paignton for spectacular coastal views. The Riviera Line skirts the seafront, passing the seaside towns of Teignmouth, Dawlish and Torquay.

Located in the heart of the quayside is the opulent Custom House. Built in 1680, it now has a visitor centre with displays and presentations on Exeter's rich history.

③
The Guildhall

🏛 High St 🕐 Daily; times vary, call ahead 🌐 exeter. gov.uk

Among the many historic buildings that survived World War II is Exeter's magnificent Guildhall. Founded in 1330, it is claimed to be one of Britain's oldest civic buildings. It has functioned as a prison, a courthouse, a police station and a place for civic functions and celebrations.

④
St Nicholas Priory

🏛 Fore St 🕐 For restoration 🌐 exeter.gov.uk

Visitors can trace the fascinating history of this 12th-century Benedictine priory from its austere monastic beginnings to its post-Dissolution use as a residence for Protestant merchants. It is now decorated in the style of a typical Elizabethan town-house, with oak panelling and elaborate plasterwork ceilings.

⑤
Underground Passages

🏛 Paris St 🕐 Daily; times vary, call ahead 🌐 exeter. gov.uk

Under the city centre lie the remains of Exeter's medieval water-supply system. This mind-boggling system of underground passages was built in the 14th and 15th centuries on a slight gradient to bring in fresh water from springs outside the town. The tunnels were vaulted to allow access to the lead pipes so that they could be easily repaired if needed. Exeter is the only city in the UK to have developed such a system. An excellent interpretation centre and guided tours explain how the tunnels were built.

⑥
Royal Albert Memorial Museum and Art Gallery

🏛 Queen St 🕐 10am–5pm Tue–Sun 🌐 rammuseum. org.uk

This museum has a varied collection, including Roman remains, an Egyptian mummy and samurai armour.

↑ Pubs and restaurants at Exeter Quay on a fine summer day

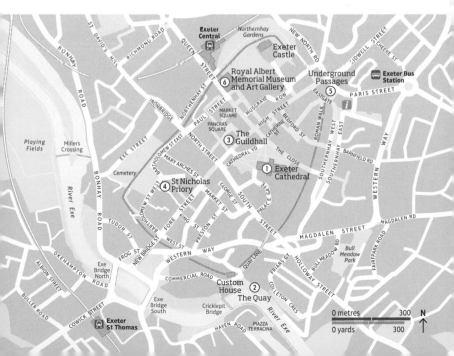

EXPERIENCE MORE

❹
Beer

🅰F5 🏛Devon 🚌Beer Cross
🛈The Underfleet, Seaton;
www.seatontourist
information.co.uk

Set on a fine shingle beach
backed by white limestone
cliffs, this fishing village derives
its name from the old Anglo-
Saxon word *bearu*, which
referred to the woodland that
once surrounded the settlement. It is one of the few
fishing villages without a
harbour; boats are winched
out of the sea over oiled logs
to ease their passage and
sit on the beach overnight.

Beer is famous for its local
stone, which has been used
in many cathedrals, including
St Paul's and Westminster
Abbey in London. The vast
underground complex of **Beer
Quarry Caves** was mined from
Roman times until the 1920s.
Today, you can take a guided
tour of the caves to discover
their diverse history, including
how they provided a place of
refuge for Catholics at times
of religious persecution and
served as an ideal hiding place
for smugglers.

Above ground, a key
attraction for children is
Pecorama, the home of the
iconic model railway manufac-
turers, Peco. The highlight
here is a ride on a miniature
steam train.

Further west along the
coast, the unspoiled seaside
town of Sidmouth lies in a
sheltered bay. It boasts an
eclectic array of architecture,
the earliest buildings dating
from the 1820s when
Sidmouth became a popular
summer resort. In the first
week of August the town
hosts Folk Week, a festival
of music and dance.

North of Sidmouth lies the
magnificent church at Ottery
St Mary. Built between 1338

and 1342, under the
supervision of Bishop
Grandisson, it is a scaled-
down version of Exeter
Cathedral (*p166*), which he
had helped build. Look out
for a memorial to the poet
Samuel Taylor Coleridge,
who was born in the town in
1772, in the churchyard wall.

Beer Quarry Caves
🚗Ⓓ👶🅿🍴 🏛Quarry Ln
Ⓒ Apr-Sep: 10am-4pm
daily: Oct: 10am-3pm daily
🌐beerquarrycaves.co.uk

Pecorama
🚗Ⓣ👶🅿🍴 🏛Underleys,
Seaton Ⓒ Apr-Oct: 10am-
5pm daily 🌐pecorama.co.uk

---

❺
Torbay

🅰E5 🏛Devon 🚊Paignton,
Torquay 🚌Dartmouth Rd,
Lymington Rd, Paignton
and Brixham Town Sq
🛈5 Vaughan Parade; www.
englishriviera.co.uk

The seaside towns of Torquay,
Paignton and Brixham form
an almost continuous resort
around the great sweep of

sandy beach and blue waters
of Torbay. Because of its mild
climate, semitropical gardens
and exuberant Victorian hotel
architecture, this popular
coastline has been dubbed
the English Riviera.

Torquay is perhaps the best
known town on the bay, with
a reputation dating back to
the 1840s, when the opening
of the railway first made the
town accessible. As a result,
droves of Victorians came
here to take to the waters.
The wealthiest built Italianate
villas, which can still be seen
today. Torquay's most famous

AGATHA CHRISTIE
(1890-1976)

One of the best-selling
authors of all time, Agatha
Christie spent much of her
childhood in Torquay.
Poirot, the detective in her
first novel, The *Mysterious
Affair at Styles* (1920),
was inspired by Belgian
refugees living in the town
during World War I. Several
attractions celebrate the
author, such as the Agatha
Christie Mile, which shows
her connections to Torquay,
and the Agatha Christie
Trail, which traces some of
the locations of her novels.

↑ Sunset falling on the marina at Torquay, one of the towns making up the Torbay area

resident was crime writer Agatha Christie, and the garden of **Torre Abbey** has a Potent Plants collection inspired by the poisons in her books. This mansion dates back to the 17th century and includes the remains of a monastery founded in 1196. Today, the abbey houses an art gallery and museum, but some rooms have been preserved as they were in the 1920s, when it was a private residence.

Nearby, the **Torquay Museum** also has a space dedicated to Christie, as well as natural history and archaeology exhibits, including finds from **Kents Cavern**, on the outskirts of the town. This is one of England's most important prehistoric sites, and the spectacular caves include displays on the people and animals who lived here 350,000 years ago. Stone Age living is now brought to life here with guided tours. The

Cavern also runs caving days for the more adventurous.

The charming miniature town of **Babbacombe Model Village** is 3 km (2 miles) north of Torquay, while 1.5 km (1 mile) inland is the lovely village of Cockington, where it is possible to visit the preserved Tudor manor house, church and thatched cottages and watch craftsmen at work.

Moving south along Torbay, Paignton is the quintessential seaside resort, complete with a funfair at the end of its pier and plenty of atmosphere. Further south still, Brixham is one of the busiest fishing ports in the country and, as a result, has a glut of good seafood restaurants.

Torre Abbey

⊛ ☺ 🏛 🏠 King's Dr, Torquay 🕐 Mar–May & Oct–Dec: 10am–5pm Wed–Sun; Jun–Sep: 10am–5pm daily 🚫 24–26 Dec & Jan–Feb 🌐 torre-abbey.org.uk

Torquay Museum

⊛ 🏛 🏠 529 Babbacombe Rd, Torquay 🕐 10am–4pm Mon–Sat (also Sun in summer) 🌐 torquaymuseum.org

Kents Cavern

⊛ ⊛ ☺ 🏛 🏠 91 Ilsham Rd, Torquay 🕐 10am–4pm daily

> **Paignton is the quintessential seaside resort, complete with a funfair at the end of its pier and plenty of atmosphere.**

🚫 25 Dec 🌐 kents-cavern. co.uk

Babbacombe Model Village

⊛ ⊛ ☺ 🏛 🏠 Hampton Ave, Torquay 🕐 Times vary, check website 🚫 25 & 26 Dec 🌐 model-village.co.uk

⑥
Totnes

🅰E5 🚉Devon 🚗🚌🚆
🌐englishriviera.co.uk

One of the most ecologically minded towns in the UK, vibrant Totnes is committed to sustainable food, energy and buildings. It is set at the highest navigable point on the River Dart, with the Norman **Totnes Castle** perched high on the hill above. Linking the two is the steep High Street, lined with bow-windowed Elizabethan houses and lots of independent shops and cafés. On Tuesdays in the summer, market stallholders dress in Elizabethan costume.

Bridging the street is the Eastgate, part of the medieval town wall. Life in the town's heyday is explored in the **Totnes Elizabethan Museum**, which also has a room devoted to the renowned mathematician Charles Babbage (1791–1871), who is regarded as the pioneer of modern computers. Nearby is the **Guildhall** and a church with a delicately carved and gilded rood screen.

A few miles north of Totnes, Dartington Hall has 10 ha (25 acres) of lovely gardens and hosts a music school every August, when concerts are held in the timbered 14th-century Great Hall.

Totnes Castle

♿ 🕐 🏠Castle St 🕐Apr-Oct: 10am-6pm daily; Nov-Mar: 10am-4pm Sat & Sun 🌐english-heritage.org.uk

Totnes Elizabethan Museum

🏠Fore St 🕐Apr-Sep: 10am-4pm Tue-Fri 🌐totnes museum.org

Guildhall

🏠Ramparts Walk 📞01803 862147 🕐Apr-Oct: 11am-3pm Mon-Fri 🚫Public hols

---

⑦
Dittisham

🅰E6 🚉Devon 🚆

Dittisham (pronounced "ditsum") is a pretty riverside village with pastel-painted cottages overlooking the quayside. Scattered around the village are cottages built by villagers who returned from the New Zealand gold rush in the 1860s.

A ferry shuttles across the river to **Greenway House**, a lovely cream stucco Georgian mansion which was bought by Agatha Christie in 1938. It now offers a programme of family-friendly activities, from croquet on the lawn to murder-mystery trails.

Greenway House

♿ 🚗 📷 NT 🏠Greenway Rd, Galmpton 🕐10:30am-5pm daily (Nov-Easter: 11am-4pm Sat & Sun) 🌐national trust.org.uk

Did You Know?

Totnes was the first UK town to introduce its own local currency.

8
Buckfastleigh

🅰E5 🏠Devon ℹ️80 Fore St, Buckfastleigh; 01364 644522

This market town, situated on the edge of Dartmoor (p162), is dominated by **Buckfast Abbey**. The original abbey, founded by King Canute in 1018, fell into ruin after the Dissolution of the Monasteries and it was not until 1882 that a group of French Benedictine monks set up a new abbey here. Work on the present building was carried out by the monks. The current abbey was completed in 1938 and has gardens, a restaurant and a shop selling tonic wine, honey and other products.

Nearby is the **Buckfast Butterfly Farm and Dartmoor Otter Sanctuary** and the **South Devon Steam Railway** terminus, where steam trains leave for Totnes.

Buckfast Abbey

🕙🏠 🏠Grange Rd 🕘9am–6pm Mon–Sat, noon–6pm Sun 🌐buckfasttourism.org.uk

Buckfast Butterfly Farm and Dartmoor Otter Sanctuary

🏠The Station 🕘Mar–Oct: 10am–5pm daily; Nov–Feb: 11am–3pm daily 🌐otters andbutterflies.co.uk

South Devon Steam Railway

🌐southdevonrailway.co.uk

9
Dartmouth

🅰E6 🏠Devon ℹ️Mayor's Ave; www.discover dartmouth.com

Dartmouth has long been a vital naval port. English fleets used to set sail from here to join the Second and Third Crusades. Sitting high on the hill above the River Dart is the Royal Naval College, where British naval officers have trained since 1905.

Several 18th-century houses adorn the cobbled quay of Bayards Cove, while carved-timber buildings line the 17th-century Butterwalk, home to the fascinating Dartmouth Museum. To the south of town is the imposing **Dartmouth Castle**, built in 1388.

Dartmouth Museum

🎟️🕙 🏠The Butterwalk, Duke St 🕘Apr–Oct: 10am–4pm daily; Nov–Mar: 1–4pm daily 🌐dartmouthmuseum. org

Dartmouth Castle

🎟️🕙🏠🅗 🏠Castle Rd 🕘10am–6pm daily (Nov–Easter: 10am–4pm Sat & Sun) 🌐english-heritage. org.uk

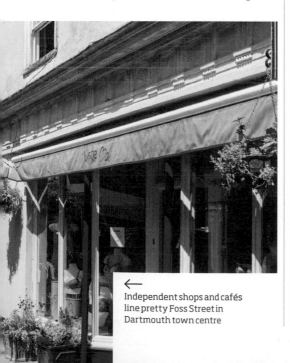

← Independent shops and cafés line pretty Foss Street in Dartmouth town centre

10

Salcombe and the South Hams

E6 **Devon** **Plymouth, Totnes** **From Plymouth and Totnes** **Timetable from the information centre and at Ferry Pier** **Market St; www.visit southdevon.co.uk**

Magnificently set on a steep hill at the mouth of the Kingsland Estuary, Salcombe is Devon's most exclusive resort, with the most expensive seaside real estate in the country. Once a humble port, where the main industries were sail-making and boat-building, it is now full of high-end boutiques, delis and restaurants, and is the birthplace of the yacht clothing chains Crew Clothing and Jack Wills.

For a taste of the Salcombe of old, head to the small, volunteer-run **Maritime Museum** below the tourist information centre, which beautifully evokes Salcombe's past with a collection of model boats, nautical paraphernalia, paintings, photographs and finds from the numerous ships wrecked on the coast nearby.

If you're looking to relax on the sand, there are two sheltered beaches just a short walk south of Salcombe. For fantastic coastal views, continue along the South West Coast Path to the rocky headland of Bolt Head. For those who do not want to walk, both beaches have car parks and there is a passenger

Low tide at the beach at Bigbury-on-Sea, looking towards Burgh Island ↑

ferry to South Sands. Beaches on the far side of the peninsula are also served by regular passenger ferries.

Salcombe is the perfect base for exploring the numerous villages, beaches and coves of the South Hams, an Area of Outstanding Natural Beauty. Highlights include the quaint fishing villages of Inner and Outer Hope, Burgh Island and Kingsbridge, a town at the head of the estuary that is famous for its quayside farmers' market (held on the first and third Saturday of each month). Another local foodie spot is the **South Devon Chilli Farm** at nearby Wigford Cross, which grows around 200 varieties of chilli.

Maritime Museum

The Old Council Hall, Market St Apr-Oct: 10:30am-12:30pm, 2:30-4:30pm daily salcombe museum.org.uk

South Devon Chilli Farm

Wigford Cross, Loddiswell, Kingsbridge 10am-4:30pm daily southdevonchillifarm.co.uk

INSIDER TIP
Sea Tractor

At low tide, Burgh Island is accessible on foot, but at other times, you must take the sea tractor. Built in 1969, it's the only one of its kind in the world and is the perfect way to reach the island's unique hotel in style.

DRINK

Pilchard Inn
Quench your thirst with a pint at this reputedly haunted 14th-century fisherman's inn on Burgh Island. Legend says that smugglers and wreckers also drank and slept here.

D6 **Burgh Island** **burghisland.com**

11

Burgh Island

D6 **Devon** **Plymouth, then bus to Bigbury-on-Sea** **The Quay, Kingsbridge; www.burghisland.com**

The short walk across the sands at low tide from Bigbury-on-Sea to Burgh Island takes visitors back to the era of the 1920s and 1930s. It was here that the millionaire Archibald Nettlefold built the luxury Burgh Island

hotel in 1929. Created in Art Deco style, with a natural rock sea-bathing pool, it was known as the "smartest hotel west of the Ritz" and, in its heyday, it was the exclusive retreat of figures such as the Duke of Windsor and English play-wright Sir Noël Peirce Coward. In later years, Churchill and Eisenhower met here prior to D-Day and the Beatles were among its guests. The island also served as the setting for two novels by Agatha Christie: *And Then There were None* and *Evil Under the Sun*. The hotel is the island's star attraction, and the restaurant is open to non-residents.

Other highlights include the Pilchard Inn and Huer's Hut. Until the early 19th century, a lookout was posted at this hut throughout the pilchard season, warning fishermen when a new shoal was spotted arriving.

Bigbury Beach, the golden sweep of sand leading to the island, offers safe swimming and rock pooling. Following the coast, Bantham Beach grants fabulous views of Burgh Island and is a great place to learn how to surf.

12 ⊘ Ⓜ Ⓝ

Buckland Abbey

Ⓐ D5 Ⓐ Yelverton Ⓒ Abbey: mid-Feb-Oct: 11am-5pm daily; Nov-Dec: for guided tours only; Garden: mid-Feb-Oct: 10am-5pm daily Ⓦ nationaltrust.org.uk

Founded by Cistercian monks in 1278, Buckland Abbey was converted into a house after the Dissolution and became the home of Sir Richard Grenville and his son Roger, who died on the *Mary Rose* (p122). The house's maritime connections continued when Sir Francis Drake purchased it in 1581 and his life, including his connections to slavery, is recalled through memorabilia in the house. The collection also includes *Self-portrait wearing a white feathered bonnet*, which was attributed to Rembrandt in 2014.

↑ Buckland Abbey, situated in a beautiful position in the Tavy Valley

⑬ Plymouth

🅐 D6 🏠 Plymouth 🚆🚌🚢
ℹ 3–5 The Barbican; www.
visitplymouth.co.uk

The tiny port from which Sir Francis Drake, Sir Walter Raleigh, James Cook and Charles Darwin all set sail on pioneering voyages around the world has since grown into a substantial maritime city.

It was, however, heavily bombed during World War II, and its fine Victorian centre was almost completely destroyed. Seen from a distance, it is the post-war redevelopments that now dominate Plymouth. The hills above the vast reach of its natural harbour, Plymouth Sound, are covered with triangular-roofed houses, a resonant testimony to the social optimism of the 1950s and 1960s. The city centre is also a fine example of 1960s architecture, with wide boulevards and imposing concrete blocks.

A more recent addition to the city centre is **The Box**. As its name suggests, this museum, gallery and archive is housed in a modern, cubic extension to an Edwardian building. Inside, the collection includes galleries dedicated to the history of Plymouth, the *Mayflower* and the mammoth.

What has survived of Old Plymouth clusters around the historic Barbican quarter and the Hoe, the famous patch of

↑ The coast seen from Mount Edgcumbe Park, Plymouth

turf on which Drake is said to have calmly finished his game of bowls as the Spanish Armada approached the port in 1588. Today, the Hoe is a pleasant park and parade ground surrounded by memorials to naval men, including Drake. On West Hoe Pier is a very different statue. Here, Anthony Gormley's *Look II*, a 3-m (12-ft) cast-iron sculpture of a human figure, looks out to sea. Just south is Tinside Lido, a lovely 1935 Art Deco swimming pool. Nearby is Charles II's

SIR FRANCIS DRAKE

Drake began his maritime career as a slave trader, leading multiple voyages to West Africa. He was the first Englishman to circumnavigate the globe, for which he was knighted by Elizabeth I, and his name was further immortalized after his Spanish Armada victory – it can now be spotted all over Plymouth.

Royal Citadel, built in 1660 to guard the harbour (visitors are advised to book in advance).

The fashionable Barbican waterfront (the western and northern sides of Sutton Harbour) is a hot spot for lively bars, restaurants and art shops. It is also home to the **National Marine Aquarium**, the largest public aquarium in the UK. Just west is the Mayflower Stone and Steps, the spot where the Pilgrim Fathers set sail for the New World in 1620. The fascinating **Mayflower Museum** explores the story of the *Mayflower* and the creation of the harbour; the museum features a large display model of the famous ship as well.

A short walk from the museum is the **Plymouth Gin Distillery**, which is housed in a former Dominican monastery and produces a popular local gin. Visitors can opt for a tour of the distillery which includes a complimentary gin and tonic. True aficionados should book in advance for the Master

Distillers Tour, which allows guests to create their own handmade gin.

Further west is the Royal William Yard, a former Royal Navy victualling yard. Stunning early 19th-century buildings designed by Sir John Rennie (1794–1874) are set right on the waterfront here. Abandoned for years, the yard has been beautifully restored and revived, with an array of art galleries, shops, bars, restaurants and luxury apartments, plus a Sunday-morning food market. The most dramatic way to arrive is on one of the hourly ferries that connect the yard with the Barbican.

Ferries also go from the yard to **Mount Edgcumbe Park**. Overlooking the Plymouth Sound, the park is made up of formal gardens, temples and follies, and is home to a herd of fallow deer. Just east of the city is the 18th-century **Saltram House** which has two decadent rooms by Robert Adam and portraits by Reynolds, who was born in nearby Plympton.

The Box
Ⓦ Ⓓ Ⓗ ⌂ Tavistock Pl Ⓞ 10am–5pm Tue–Sun Ⓦ theboxplymouth.com

Royal Citadel
Ⓐ Ⓝ Ⓗ ⌂ The Hoe Ⓞ For tours only, check website Ⓦ english-heritage.org.uk

National Marine Aquarium
Ⓐ Ⓓ Ⓗ ⌂ Rope Walk, Coxside Ⓞ 10am–5pm daily (last adm: 4pm) Ⓦ national-aquarium.co.uk

Mayflower Museum
⌂ 3–5 The Barbican Ⓒ 01752 306330 Ⓞ Apr–Oct: 9am–5pm Mon–Sat, 10am–4pm Sun; Nov–Mar: 9am–5pm Mon–Fri, 10am–4pm Sat

Plymouth Gin Distillery
Ⓔ Ⓗ ⌂ 60 Southside St, Barbican Ⓞ 11am–5:30pm Tue–Sat, 12pm–5:30pm Sun Ⓒ Mon Ⓦ plymouthdistillery.com

Mount Edgcumbe Park
Ⓐ Ⓝ Ⓟ Ⓔ Ⓗ ⌂ Cremyll, Torpoint 🚢 From Torpoint car park Ⓞ House: Apr–Sep: 11am–4:30pm Tue–Thu & Sun Ⓦ mountedgcumbe.gov.uk

Saltram House
Ⓐ Ⓝ Ⓟ Ⓗ Ⓓ Ⓝ ⌂ Devon Expy, Plympton Ⓞ 10am–4pm daily (park closes at dusk) Ⓦ nationaltrust.org.uk

---

⑭ Ⓐ Ⓝ Ⓓ Ⓗ
Morwellham Quay

Ⓐ D5 ⌂ Near Tavistock 🚉 Gunnislake Ⓞ 10am–5pm (Nov–Feb: 10am–4pm) daily Ⓦ morwellham-quay.co.uk

The area of Morwellham Quay was a neglected and over-grown industrial site until 1970, when members of a local trust began restoring the abandoned cottages, school-house, quay and copper mines to their original condition.

Today, Morwellham Quay is a fascinating museum of Victorian life. The staff, who convincingly play the part of villagers, tell the history of this small copper-mining community and give demonstrations. Visitors can lend a hand to the cooper while he builds a barrel, attend a lesson in the schoolroom or dress up in 19th-century hooped skirts, bonnets, top hats or jackets.

→

Historic artifacts on display at Morwellham Quay

EAT

Àclèaf
A memorable fine-dining experience is guaranteed at this lavish hotel restaurant, courtesy of exciting dishes (such as citrus-cured halibut with ceviche and lime) and impeccable service.

Ⓐ D6 ⌂ Boringdon Hall Hotel, Plympton, Plymouth Ⓒ Mon & Tue Ⓦ boringdonhall.co.uk

£ £ £

St Elizabeth's
This top-notch hotel restaurant uses local ingredients and although the emphasis is very much on seafood, the menu offers much more besides, including delicious Sunday roasts.

Ⓐ D6 ⌂ St Elizabeth's House Hotel, Plympton, Plymouth Ⓦ stelizabeths.co.uk

£ £ £

Dusk at the Barbican, on Plymouth's waterfront

⑮ Appledore

🅐D4 🅐Devon 🅘Bideford;
www.appledore.org

Appledore's remote position at the tip of the Torridge Estuary has helped to keep its charms intact. Busy boatyards line the riverside quay, the departure point for fishing trips and ferries to the sandy beaches of Braunton Burrows on the opposite shore. Regency houses line the main street, which runs parallel to the quay, and behind is a network of cobbled lanes with 18th-century fishermen's cottages. Shops retain their original bow windows and sell crafts, antiques and souvenirs.

Uphill from the quay is the **North Devon Maritime Museum**, with an exhibition on the experiences of Devon emigrants to Australia and displays explaining the work of local shipyards. The tiny Victorian Schoolroom, affiliated with the museum, shows documentary videos on local trades.

> ### DEVONSHIRE CREAM TEAS
>
> Devonians claim all other versions of a cream tea are inferior to their own, much to the indignation of the Cornish. The essential ingredient is Devonshire clotted cream, made by heating double cream to evaporate some of the excess liquid, spread thickly on freshly baked scones, with lashings of homemade strawberry jam. Disputes about whether cream (Devon) or jam (Cornwall) should be smeared on first can get very passionate.

North Devon Maritime Museum

🅐🅐 🅐Odun Rd 🅒Apr-Oct: 10:30am–5pm 🅦northdevon maritimemuseum.co.uk

---

⑯ Barnstaple

🅐D4 🅐Devon 🅐🅐
🅘The Square; www.
staynorthdevon.co.uk

Although Barnstaple is an important distribution centre for the whole region, its town centre remains quiet and tranquil due to the exclusion of traffic. The massive glass-roofed **Pannier Market** (1855) has stalls piled high with organic food and produce, much of it from local farms. Nearby stands St Peter's Church, with its twisted spire, said to have been caused by a lightning strike that warped the timbers in 1810.

On the Strand is a wonderful Victorian arcade, now the Heritage Centre, topped with a statue of Queen Anne. The arcade was originally built as an exchange where merchants traded the contents of their cargo boats moored on the River Taw.

Nearby is the 15th-century bridge and the **Museum of Barnstaple and North Devon**, where displays cover the rich history of the town and its surrounding area, including the 700-year- old pottery industry, as well as otters and other local wildlife in the Tarka Room. The 290-km- (180-mile-) long Tarka Trail circuits around Barnstaple and offers lovely views; 56 km (35 miles) of it can be cycled.

Just west of Barnstaple, Braunton "Great Field" covers over 120 ha (300 acres) and is a well-preserved relic of medieval open-field cultiva-tion. Beyond it lies Braunton Burrows, one of the most extensive wild dune reserves in Britain. It is a must for plant

---

← A street lined with colourful cottages in the village of Appledore

and nature enthusiasts, who are likely to spot sea kale, sea holly, sea lavender and horned poppies growing in their natural habitat.

Arlington Court and National Trust Carriage Museum, north of Barnstaple, is packed with treasures. It has a collection of model ships and horse-drawn vehicles, including over 50 carriages; rides are available most days. The museum is set on a grand estate with grounds featuring magnificent perennial borders and a lake.

Pannier Market

🏠 Butchers Row 🕐 9am–4pm Mon–Sat 🌐 barnstaple panniermarket.co.uk

Museum of Barnstaple and North Devon

😐 🏠 The Square 🕐 10am–4pm Mon–Sat (mid-Mar-Oct: to 5pm) 🔒 24 Dec–1 Jan 🌐 devonmuseums.net

Arlington Court and National Trust Carriage Museum

😐😐😐🅝 🏠 Arlington 🕐 Mid-Feb-Oct: 11am–5pm daily; Nov–mid-Dec: 11am–4pm daily 🌐 nationaltrust.org.uk

---

⓱
Bideford

🅐 D4 🏠 Devon 🛈 Burton Art Gallery, Kingsley Rd; www.visitdevon.co.uk

Strung out along the estuary of the west bank of the River Torridge, Bideford is a pretty little town. In the 16th century,

Did You Know?

Westward Ho! is the only place in the British Isles to have an exclamation mark in its name.

↑ The picturesque quayside of Clovelly, a tiny fishing port in North Devon

---

it was Britain's third-largest port, thriving on tobacco imports from the Americas. A few 17th-century merchants' houses survive in Bridgeland Street, including the splendid bay-windowed house at No. 28 (1693). Beyond is Mill Street, leading to the parish church and the fine medieval bridge. The quay stretches from here to a park and a statue of 19th-century social reformer and writer Charles Kingsley (1819–75), famous for his classic novel *The Water Babies* (1863).

To the west of Bideford, the late 19th-century village of Westward Ho!, named after Charles Kingsley's popular novel of the same name, is known for its good surfing and the oldest golf club in England, the Royal North Devon. Also to the west is Hartland Abbey. Built as a monastery in around 1157, it is now a family home. The BBC filmed parts of *Sense and Sensibility* here. There is a museum and garden.

In the Torridge Valley is more of the Tarka Trail. The scenic walking and cycling trail runs along a disused railway line through beautiful, leafy North Devon countryside and past the Royal Horticultural Society's (RHS) **Rosemoor Garden**.

Rosemoor Garden

😐😐😐 🏠 Great Torrington 🕐 10am–5pm daily 🔒 25 Dec 🌐 rhs.org.uk

---

⓲
Clovelly

🅐 C4 🏠 Devon 🌐 clovelly.co.uk

A famous beauty spot since author Charles Kingsley wrote about it in his novel *Westward Ho!*, charming Clovelly village has been privately owned by the same family since 1738, though very little trace remains of the fishing industry to which it owed its birth. Today, it is an idyllic place, with pretty white-washed houses and quaint cobbled streets rising up the cliff from the harbourside. Until as recently as the 1990s, deliveries were still made by donkeys – sledges are now used instead. There are superb views from the lookout points and hillside paths that line the hillsides from the tiny quay.

Hobby Drive is a particularly fine 5-km (3-mile) walk from the village through beautiful woodland that runs right along the coast. The road was constructed in 1811–29 to provide employment at the end of the Napoleonic Wars.

↑ Ascending the Lynton & Lynmouth Cliff Railway, a water-powered railway

19

Lynton and Lynmouth

A D4 **A** Devon **i** Post Office, 26 Lee Rd, Lynton; www.visitlyntonand lynmouth.com

Situated at the point where the East and West Lyn rivers meet the sea, Lynmouth is a picturesque, though rather commercialized, fishing village. The pedestrianized main street, lined with shops selling seaside souvenirs, runs parallel to the Lyn, now a canal with high embankments to protect against flash floods. One flood devastated the town at the height of the holiday season in 1952, fuelled by heavy rain on Exmoor (*p164*). The worst affected area was not rebuilt and is now overgrown with trees in the pretty Glen Lyn Gorge, which leads north out of the village.

Above Lynmouth stands hilltop Lynton, a Victorian town perched on the clifftop at a height of 130 m (427 ft), offering views across the Bristol Channel to the Welsh coast. The two villages are connected by a water-powered funicular railway, called the **Lynton & Lynmouth Cliff Railway**, which since the 19th century has shuttled up the steep bank. The short ride offers impressive views.

Lynton & Lynmouth Cliff Railway

⊕ **A** The Esplanade, Lynmouth **O** Mid-Feb-Oct **w** cliffrailwaylynton.co.uk

---

20

Ilfracombe

A D4 **A** Devon **B** Barnstaple, then bus **Q** **i** Landmark Theatre, Promenade; www.visit ilfracombe.co.uk

Flanked by rugged cliffs, hilly Ilfracombe is a Victorian seaside resort built around a natural harbour. Since 2012 the town has been dominated by *Verity*, a 20-m- (65-ft-) high stainless steel, fibreglass and bronze statue by artist Damien Hirst, who owns a property in the nearby village of Combe Martin. The sculpture features the internal anatomy of a naked pregnant woman with her foetus and womb clearly visible.

Art of a more restrained kind can be found in **The Gallery**. Run by the Ilfracombe Art and Craft Society, it displays some lovely paintings, sculptures, pottery and woodwork, all produced by local artists.

Apart from art, one of Ilfracombe's main attractions is the Tunnels Beaches. This series of natural and man-made tidal swimming pools can be accessed through four tunnels that were carved into the bare rock by Welsh miners in 1823. Today, lively information boards evoke the history of the beaches (originally men and women were segregated for swimming), and there is a lovely café-bar and a children's play hut.

Ilfracombe is surrounded by brilliant beaches. With their sweeping stretches of sand and some of the most challenging waves in the country, Croyde and Woolacombe are popular with both families and surfers. Surf gear can be rented at the shops and stalls above Woolacombe beach, where there are also a handful of cafés and bars. Non-surfers should make for Putsborough at Woolacombe's southern end for a sheltered swim.

Away from the waves, Croyde, a picturesque village of thatched houses in a crescent-shaped bay, is prettier than its neighbour, but the resort of Woolacombe retains some elegant Regency houses among its many bungalows and holiday homes.

The Gallery

⊕ **A** 9–10 The Promenade, Ilfracombe **O** 11am–4pm daily **w** ilfracombeart andcraftsociety.co.uk

21 🍴 ☕ 🏛

Broomhill Sculpture Gardens

🗺 D4 🏠 Muddiford Rd, Barnstaple ⏰ 11am–4pm daily 🚫 Late Dec–mid-Jan 🌐 broomhillart.co.uk

These mesmerizing sculpture gardens lie in the enchanting grounds of a Victorian country house, with paths twisting through rhododendrons and woodland to a pretty river. There are 300 sculptures in all, both abstract and figurative, by over 60 contemporary artists. The pieces have been artfully placed within the woodland by Dutch owners Rinus and Aniet van de Sande. Among the most striking of the sculptures is a giant red stiletto shoe by Greta Berlin, who has been involved with Broomhill since it was founded in 1997.

Every year the gardens host the Broomhill National Sculpture competition, with works by the ten finalists exhibited in the meadow. The house is a hotel, and has a café and restaurant open to non-residents.

---

22 (NT)

Lundy Island

🗺 C4 🏠 Devon 🚉🚌 Barnstaple 🚢 From Bideford or Ilfracombe 🌐 nationaltrust.org.uk

Jointly owned and managed by the National Trust and the Landmark Trust, Lundy Island is a 5-km- (3-mile-) long sliver of granite lying 19 km (12 miles) off the North Devon coast. Once important for its stone quarries and copper mine, it is now abundant in birdlife, including puffins.

Despite its diminutive size, the island has a turbulent history. At one time it was owned by the Knights Templar, at another by pirates, and it's seen its fair share of self-proclaimed kings.

One of the most remote places in England, it can be visited as a day trip from Ilfracombe, but it is also possible to rent holiday houses for a longer stay.

↑ An Atlantic puffin, one of the many birds that live on Lundy Island

---

Did You Know?

Lundy has its own stamps and coins – the stamps are legal, the coins are not.

The **cemetery** is an ancient burial ground with several gravestones dating to the 5th or 6th century AD.

The **Lundy Granite Company**'s abandoned buildings lie along the north coast. The company was founded in 1863 and went into liquidation just six years later.

The **Battery** operated as a fog signal station between 1863 and 1897.

North Lighthouse

Built in 1819, the **Old Light** has the highest base of any lighthouse in the UK. Abandoned in 1897, it can now be rented as a holiday home.

Devil's Slide

→ Lundy Island, a haven for birdlife, especially puffins

From late March to late October, the **MS Oldenburg** brings visitors and supplies to and from the island.

Opened as a village shop for quarrymen in the 1860s, Lundy's sole pub – the **Marisco Tavern** – is decorated with relics of local shipwrecks.

South Lighthouse

CORNWALL

Cornwall occupies the extreme tip of the southwest peninsula, jutting out between the wild Atlantic Ocean and the calmer English Channel. Its remote position has kept the county cut off from the rest of Britain; when dinosaurs roamed the Jurassic Coast, Cornwall was actually an island. Its volcanic past has also left it richer in minerals – including gold, copper and tin – than anywhere else in Britain. Although mining continues, many pits have been abandoned and repurposed – the famous Eden Project was created within a disused clay quarry.

Cornwall remains in many ways a land apart. For centuries, harbours such as Falmouth were part of an international network of ports, safe havens and anchorages, linked more by sea trade (and piracy) than any loyalty to state or Crown. Its isolation and natural beauty have fostered a distinct culture and mythology. King Arthur is said to have been born in Tintagel, while the arrival of Celtic missionaries from Wales, Ireland and Brittany gave rise to a plethora of legends and holy sites where Christian mythology merged with popular ideas of magic, resulting in a folk tradition that remains a vibrant part of contemporary culture.

The region has a long history of attracting non-conformists, artists and exiles from metropolitan life, including the artists whose work forms the core of the renowned Tate St Ives. The area's wild, dramatically rugged landscape and romantic history have also inspired several novels, by authors ranging from Daphne du Maurier to Patrick Gale.

CORNWALL

Must Sees
1. Eden Project
2. St Ives

Experience More
3. Bude
4. Tintagel
5. Boscastle
6. Padstow
7. Newquay
8. Helston
9. The Lizard Peninsula
10. Falmouth
11. St Mawes
12. Truro
13. St Austell
14. Looe
15. Lost Gardens of Heligan
16. Bodmin
17. Fowey
18. Cotehele
19. Penzance
20. St Michael's Mount

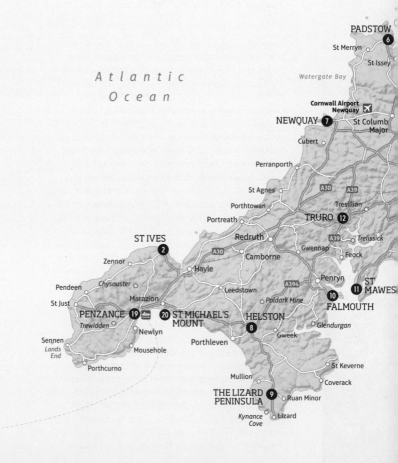

PADSTOW 6
St Merryn
St Issey
Watergate Bay

Atlantic Ocean

Cornwall Airport Newquay ✈
NEWQUAY 7   St Columb Major
Cubert
Perranporth
St Agnes   A30   A39   Tresillian
Porthtowan
Portreath   TRURO 12
Redruth   A39   Trelissick
ST IVES   A30   Camborne   Gwennap   Feock
2   Hayle
Zennor   Penryn   ST MAWES 11
Chysauster   Leedstown   A394   FALMOUTH 10
Pendeen   Poldark Mine
St Just   Marazion   Glendurgan
PENZANCE 19 🚂   20 ST MICHAEL'S   HELSTON
Trewidden   MOUNT   8   Gweek
Newlyn   Porthleven   St Keverne
Sennen   Mousehole   Coverack
Lands End
Porthcurno   Mullion   THE LIZARD   Ruan Minor
PENINSULA 9
Kynance Cove   Lizard

← Scilly Isles

0 kilometres   10

0 miles   10

Hortland
Point

Clovelly   Bideford

Hartland

Deptford   A39

Morewenstow   West
           Putford

Kilkhampton   Stibb Cross   Great Torrington   A377

     Chilsworthy   Bradford   Merton

BUDE 3   Stratton   A388   Hatherleigh   North
             Holsworthy   A386   Exbourne   Tawton

Widemouth   **D E V O N**

Crackington   A388   Ashwater   Okehampton   A30
Haven

St Juliot   **DEVON**   High Willhays
          A39   Canworthy   p158   621 m (2,037 ft)
BOSCASTLE 5   Water

TINTAGEL 4   Davidstow   Chillaton   Dartmoor
       Hallworthy   Launceston   National Park
Delabole   Altarnun   A386   Postbridge
Port   Camelford   Lewannick
Isaac   A388   Tavistock
St Teath   Bodmin   Two
Polzeath   Moor   Bolventor   Bridges
Rock   A30   Linkinhorne   Yelverton
   Wadebridge   Callington   A390   Bere
A39   **C O R N W A L L**   Alston
       Cardinham   **COTEHELE 18**
BODMIN 16   Liskeard   St Mellion   A388
Lanivet   A38   Menheniot   Plymouth
Lanhydrock   A390   Saltash   A38
Roche   Restormel Castle   St Keyne   A374   Ivybridge
A30   A391   Lostwithiel   St Germans   Plymstock   Modbury
St Denis   Lanreath   Pelynt   A387   Torpoint
   EDEN   Cawsand
   1 PROJECT   **14 LOOE**   Bigbury-
ST   **17**   Polperro   Rame   on-Sea
AUSTELL   **13**   **FOWEY**
A390   Charlestown
   LOST GARDENS
15 OF HELIGAN
Tregoney   Mevagissey
Portloe

E n g l i s h   C h a n n e l

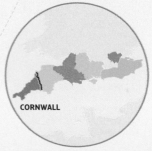

CORNWALL

*Roscoff,
Santander*

1 🗡️ 🍴 💻 🛍️

EDEN PROJECT

🅰️ C6 🏠 Bodelva, St Austell 🚉 St Austell 🚌 Dedicated bus service from St Austell 🕐 9:30am–6pm daily (Jul & Aug: to 6:30pm) 🌐 edenproject.com

A global garden for the 21st century, the spectacular Eden Project is nestled in a huge crater, providing a dramatic setting in which to tell the fascinating story of plants, people and places.

The Eden Project's most iconic feature is its biomes. Hundreds of octagonal and pentagonal plastic cells form the biomes, which mimic the environments of warmer climes. The hot and humid Rainforest Biome houses the largest enclosed rainforest in the world, while the Mediterranean Biome re-creates the warm temperate climate and landscapes of the Mediterranean, South Africa, California and Western Australia. The relationship between humans and nature is interpreted in sculptures throughout the site. The Core education centre hosts exhibitions and workshops. For an aerial view you can ride over the biomes on a 660-m (2,165-ft) zip wire, the longest in England.

Building Eden

Cornwall's declining china clay industry left behind many disused pits which the Eden Project made ingenious use of. After partly infilling a pit, the biomes were constructed using a record 370 km (230 miles) of scaffolding.

The vast Rainforest Biome, a lush jungle of trees and plants ↓

The coffee plant (Coffea arabica) is one of the many plants on display that are used in our everyday lives.

Some plants in the South American area reach enormous proportions.

The West Africa section features the Iboga plant, which is central to the African religion Bwiti.

The titan arum flower in the Malaysia area smells of rotting flesh.

The tropical islands here have many fascinating and rare plants.

The Eden Project's iconic geodesic domes, and *(inset)* the interior of the Mediterranean Biome

Did You Know?

The Eden Project hosts music concerts called the Eden Sessions towards the end of June every year.

Transparent hexagons made of ultra-light high-tech plastic

The entrance to both the Rainforest and Mediterranean biomes is via the Link, where the Eden Bakery is located.

STAY

YHA

The Eden Project's unique on-site youth hostel is housed in recycled shipping containers, blending in with its eco-friendly surroundings. Bedrooms have good en-suite bathrooms. You can even bring your own tent (or hire one) to pitch in the garden in the summer months.

🏠 Eden Project, Bodelva
🌐 yha.org.uk

£ £ £

②

ST IVES

🅰B6 🏠Cornwall 🚌🚐 ℹ️St Ives Library, Gabriel St; www.stives-cornwall.co.uk

With its whitewashed cottages, flower-filled gardens and beautiful sandy beaches, this historic fishing town combines coastal charm with a prestigious artistic heritage. The town is famous for the colony of artists that settled here in the 1920s, and today hosts Tate St Ives along with scores of small galleries and studios.

①

Tate St Ives

🏠Porthmeor Beach
🕙10am–5:20pm daily
🌐tate.org.uk

Perched above Porthmeor Beach with sweeping views of the ocean, this major art gallery showcases works by 20th-century modern British artists linked to St Ives and nearby Newlyn and hosts changing special exhibitions. Housed in a striking white modernist building, on the site of an old gasworks, it opened in 1993 and was the first regional outpost of London's Tate galleries (p71), founded by sugar baron and champion of British art Henry Tate. Within its light-filled galleries is an impressive range of work by St Ives

School artists, including iconic pieces by leading figures such as Barbara Hepworth, Ben Nicholson, Alfred Wallis, Peter Lanyon and Naum Gabo, as well as abstract pieces by associated international artists such as Brancusi, Mark Rothko and Piet Mondrian.

②

Beaches

With one of the mildest climates in Great Britain, St Ives is a beach-lover's paradise. A string of golden beaches stretches along St Ives Bay as far as Godrevy Lighthouse. The smallest beach, Porthgwidden, has soft golden sand and is very sheltered, making it great for children and family trips. Just a stone's throw from the centre of St Ives, Porthmeor is popular with both surfers and swimmers. The star beach, however, is sweeping Porthminster with its crescent of golden sand in a glittering bay of clear water. It also has an 18-hole golf course and a beach café serving great local dishes.

ST IVES ARTISTS

In the 1920s, St Ives, already known among painters for the clarity of its light, became a magnet for aspiring artists. Ben Nicholson and his then wife, Barbara Hepworth, formed the nucleus of a group of artists that made a major contribution to the development of abstract art in Europe. Other prolific artists associated with what became known as the St Ives School include the potter Bernard Leach and the painter Patrick Heron, whose *Coloured Glass Window* dominates the Tate St Ives entrance. Much of the art on display at Tate St Ives is abstract and illustrates new responses to the rugged Cornish landscape, the human figure and the ever-changing patterns of sunlight on sea.

↑ St Ives' sheltered beach basking beneath supremely beautiful skies

EAT

Cellar Bistro
Dine among upcycled and vintage bric-a-brac; the menu is largely gluten-free.

🏠 29–31 Fore St
ⓦ cellar-bistro.co.uk

£ £ £

Porthmeor Beach Café
While away an hour or two on the breezy terrace, tucking into shared small plates.

🏠 Porthmeor Beach
ⓦ porthmeor-beach.co.uk

£ £ £

③ 🏄 🏛

St Ives Museum

🏠 Wheal Dream
🕐 Apr–Oct: 10:30am–4:30pm Mon–Fri, 10:30am–3:30pm Sat ⓦ museumsin cornwall.org.uk

Run entirely by volunteers, this quirky independent museum contains a treasure-trove of artifacts related to local history and life, from the earliest times until the town's modern transformation into a tourist destination. The fascinating collections include mining, boat building, fishing, farming, Victorian clothes, photographs and wartime memorabilia. There is also a studio where films of local interest are shown.

④ 🏄 🏛

Barbara Hepworth Museum and Sculpture Garden

🏠 Barnoon Hill 🕐 10am–5:20pm daily ⓦ tate.org.uk

Run by the Tate, this museum presents the works of one of Britain's most important 20th-century artists in the house and garden (formerly named Trewyn Studio) where she lived and worked from 1949 until 1975. Sculptures in bronze, stone and wood are displayed outdoors and in the house, where there are also paintings and drawings. The garden was designed by Barbara Hepworth in collaboration with a friend, the composer Priaulx Rainier.

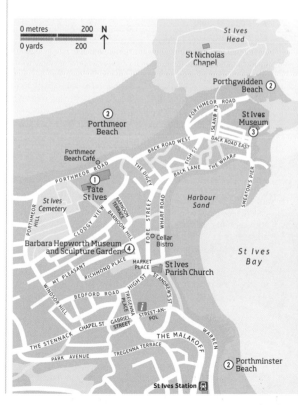

EXPERIENCE MORE

❸ Bude

🏕C5 🏛Cornwall
ℹ️Crescent Car Park;
www.visitbude.info

Once a bustling port, Bude has become a popular resort due to its wonderful clean golden beaches. In the 18th century, lime-rich sand from here was transported along a canal to inland farms, where it was used to neutralize the acidic soil. The canal was abandoned in 1880 but a short stretch survives, providing a haven for birds.

❹ Tintagel

🏕C5 🏛Cornwall 🚌Opp
Visitor Centre ℹ️Bossiney
Rd; www.visitboscastle
andtintagel.com

The romantic ruins of **Tintagel Castle** were built around 1240 by Richard, Earl of Cornwall. He was persuaded to construct the castle in this isolated spot by the popular belief that this was King Arthur's birthplace. The ruins are dramatically

KING ARTHUR

Historians think the legendary figure of King Arthur was inspired by a Romano-British chieftain or warrior who led resistance to the Saxon invasion of the 6th century *(p47)*. Geoffrey of Monmouth's *History of the Kings of Britain* (1139) is the source of many legends connected with him – how he became king by removing the sword Excalibur from a stone, his final battle with Mordred, and the story of the Knights of the Round Table.

perched atop two separate hilltops, which were linked by a landbridge during the Middle Ages. In 2019, a spectacular new footbridge was unveiled which finally relinked the two halves.

Fine Mediterranean pottery from the 5th century has been discovered here, indicating that the site was a trading centre long before the castle was built. A clifftop path leads from the castle to Tintagel's church, which has Norman and Saxon masonry. In the village, the **Old Post Office** is a rare example of a restored 14th-century Cornish manor house.

Tintagel Castle

♿🏛📷 🏛Tintagel Head
🕐Apr–Sep: 10am–6pm daily;
Oct: 10am–5pm daily; Nov–
Feb: 10am–4pm Sat & Sun
🌐english-heritage.org.uk

Old Post Office

⊘⊘ NT 🏠 Fore St ⏰ Apr-Sep: 10:30am-5:30pm Mon-Fri; Mar & Oct: 11am-4pm Mon-Fri 🌐 nationaltrust.org.uk

❺
Boscastle

🅰 C5 📍 Cornwall 🚌 Boscastle Bridge 🌐 visitboscastleandtintagel.com

Squeezed into a narrow natural inlet between the ominously rugged headlands of Willapark and Penally Point, the pretty village of Boscastle was North Cornwall's main commercial port until 1893, when the railway arrived at Camelford. The River Valency runs down the middle of the main street to the fishing harbour, which is sheltered from the sea by high slate cliffs. Access from the harbour to the sea is via a channel cut through the rocks.

The village is home to the **Boscastle Visitor Centre**, which recounts the village's history – including the story of the 2004 flood when the River Valency burst its banks – and the **Museum of Witchcraft and Magic**, which contains the UK's largest

← Looking over the ruins of Tintagel Castle and its striking footbridge

public collection of items related to the occult.

Boscastle Visitor Centre

🏠 The Harbour 📞 01840 250010 ⏰ 10am-4pm daily 🚫 25 & 26 Dec

Museum of Witchcraft and Magic

⊘⊘ 🏠 The Harbour ⏰ Apr-Oct: 10:30am-6pm Mon-Sat, 11:30am-6pm Sun (last adm: 5pm) 🌐 museumofwitchcraftandmagic.co.uk

❻
Padstow

🅰 C5 📍 Cornwall 🚌 🛈 North Quay; www.padstowlive.com

A picturesque little fishing port, chic Padstow is a magnet for foodies. The gastronomic revolution was triggered by celebrity chef Rick Stein, who opened his first restaurant in the village in 1975 and has since devoted much energy to shining the spotlight on Cornish produce. Other chefs have since followed in his wake, making Padstow the undisputed gourmet capital of Cornwall.

The heart and soul of the village is the quayside, where the daily catch is landed. Behind it, the port's labyrinthine cobbled streets are studded with boutiques, art galleries and delicatessens.

The **Padstow Museum** displays a range of artifacts, including archaeological finds and costumes from the annual Obby Oss (Hobby Horse) May Day ritual.

The Elizabethan manor house **Prideaux Place** has been home to the Prideaux-Brune family since 1592. The family's ancestors include famous figures such as William the Conqueror and Jane Austen (p136). The house, with its richly furnished rooms and superb plasterwork, has been used as a location for many films and TV series.

Padstow Museum

🏠 Market Pl ⏰ Apr-Oct: 10:30am-4:30pm Mon-Sat; Nov-Mar: 11am-3pm Mon-Sat 🚫 Jan 🌐 padstowmuseum.co.uk

Prideaux Place

⊘⊘⊘ 🏠 Padstow ⏰ Mid-Apr-Sep: House: 1:30-4pm Sun-Thu; Grounds & Tearoom: 10:30-5pm Sun-Thu 🌐 prideauxplace.co.uk

7

Newquay

⬛B5 🅰Cornwall
✈Newquay 🚗Cliff Rd
🚌Marcus Hill ℹMarcus Hill;
www.visitnewquay.org

Beginning life as an Elizabethan sailing port, Newquay quickly became one of Cornwall's biggest pilchard fisheries. It morphed into the beach resort that we see today after the arrival of the railway in the 1870s. Today, the proximity of the airport has helped maintain its popularity.

Traditionally downmarket, with its huge sandy beaches attracting a budget-conscious crowd of backpackers, surfers, clubbers, pensioners and families, parts of Newquay are now showing signs of gentrification, with a Rick Stein restaurant now in town, along with boutique hotels and two sustainable living projects, sponsored by the Duchy of Cornwall.

8

Helston

⬛B6 🅰Cornwall 🚉 🚌From
Penzance ℹMarket Pl;
www.visithelston.com

The attractive town of Helston is famous for its annual Furry Dance (also called Flora Dance), which welcomes spring with plenty of revelry, including dancing through the streets; the **Museum of Cornish Life** explains the history of this ancient custom, as well as other aspects of local life.

The Georgian houses and inns of Coinagehall Street are a reminder that Helston was once a thriving stannary town, where tin ingots were brought for weighing and stamping before being sold. Until the 13th century, locally mined tin was brought downriver to a

Sunbathing in Kynance Cove, on the Lizard Peninsula ↑

harbour at the bottom of this street, but access to the sea was blocked when a shingle bar formed across the River Loe, creating the freshwater lake Loe Pool. A lovely walk skirts its wooded shores.

In 1880, Helston's trade was taken over by a new harbour created to the east on the River Helford, at Gweek. Today, Gweek is the home of the **Cornish Seal Sanctuary**, where sick seals are nursed back to health before being returned to the sea.

Cornwall's tin-mining industry, from Roman to recent times, is covered at the **Poldark Mine**, named after Winston Graham's books. The mine has underground guided tours, which showcase the difficult working conditions of 18th-century miners.

Museum of Cornish Life
♿🅿 🅰Market Pl 🕙10am-4pm Mon-Fri 🚫Christmas week 🔗museumofcornish life.co.uk

Cornish Seal Sanctuary
♿🥤🅿 🅰Gweek 🕙10am-dusk daily 🚫25 Dec 🔗sealsanctuary.co.uk

SURFING AROUND NEWQUAY

The UK's self-styled surfing capital, Newquay attracts surfers from all over Europe and hosts several competitions. It's also an ideal place for novices. Fistral Beach, with its regular, consistent waves, is a good place to start. Mawgan Porth has similar waves but without the crowds. Don't fancy surfing? Watergate Bay also offers bodyboarding, SUP and kitesurfing.

Poldark Mine

⊘ⓈⒹⒸ 🏠Wendron
🕐10:30am–3pm daily
🌐poldarkmine.org.uk

9

The Lizard Peninsula

🅰B6 🏠Cornwall 🚍🚌🚐
🌐lizard-peninsula.co.uk

The southernmost peninsula on the British mainland, the Lizard Peninsula is an area of extreme and beautiful contrasts, stretching from the quaint villages, dense woodland and labyrinthine route of the River Helford to serpentine cliffs and dramatic sea-sculpted coves.

In the northeast of the peninsula, a circular route runs from the whitewashed village of Helford, which has a picturesque waterside pub, through the oak woodland to Frenchman's Creek, named after the famous novel by Du Maurier, which was later adapted for a film and a TV series. En route is **Kestle Barton**, a cultural centre which stages exhibitions and has a café.

In the centre of the peninsula is a raised plateau known as the Goonhilly Downs. Once home to the largest satellite station in the world, the dishes can still be seen from miles around. The Dry Tree Menhir (standing stone) is found near the satellite station. The downs are a Site of Special Scientific Interest and are home to rare plants, including Cornish Heath – the county's flower.

At the very end of the peninsula (accessible by road or the coastal footpath) is Lizard Point, the most southerly point in Britain, and the **Lizard Lighthouse Heritage Centre**. Built in 1619, the tower was automated in 1998. Today, you can take a tour of this restored building, which includes climbing to the top of the tower. There are also interactive displays describing the workings of a lighthouse.

At Poldhu Cove, to the northwest, the **Marconi Centre** marks the spot where, in 1901, Guglielmo Marconi transmitted the first transatlantic radio signal all the way to Newfoundland on Canada's east coast. The station was commandeered

by the Royal Navy during World War I, before functioning as a research centre.

Kestle Barton

☺ 🏠Manaccan, Helston
🕐Apr-Oct:10:30am–5pm Tue-Sun 🌐kestlebarton.co.uk

Lizard Lighthouse Heritage Centre

⊘ⓈⒹ 🏠3 Lighthouse Rd, Lizard, Helston 🕐Times vary, check website
🌐trinityhouse.co.uk

Marconi Centre

🏠Poldhu Rd, Mullion
🕐Times vary, check website
🌐marconi-centre-poldhu. org.uk

10

Falmouth

⚠ B6 🚉 Cornwall 🚌🚐🚏
Opposite Visitor Centre
ℹ **11 Market Strand; www.
falmouth.co.uk**

A vibrant university town, with a clutch of fine sandy beaches, Falmouth owes its existence to having the third deepest natural harbour in the world after Sydney and Rio de Janeiro. The town stands at the point where seven rivers flow into a long stretch of water called the Carrick Roads. Numerous creeks are ideal for boating excursions to view the varied scenery and birdlife.

The liveliest of Cornwall's towns, Falmouth has a packed calendar of festivals – celebrating everything from sea shanties to oysters – which bring visitors in all year round.

The town is a fine sight, its hilly core stacked with multi-hued Victorian and Georgian cottages and townhouses, and topped by the distinctive tower of a meteorological observatory built in 1868. Falmouth's main street, lined with shops and cafés, follows the river. From the Prince of Wales pier, ferries operate across the river to the villages of Flushing and St Mawes. Towards the town centre is the **Falmouth Art Gallery**, which has rotating exhibitions showcasing its permanent collection and the work of contemporary artists.

On the waterfront, the **National Maritime Museum Cornwall** dominates Discovery Quay, a waterside complex with shops, cafés and apartments. The museum features Britain's finest public collection of historic and contemporary watercraft. Exhibits look at maritime themes and the social impact of the sea on those whose lives have depended on it.

↓ The National Maritime Museum Cornwall's interior and *(inset)* exterior

DRINK

Beerwolf Books
What could be better than books and beer? Combining a freehouse and a bookshop in a novel and quite brilliant concept, this place also hosts frequent live music and other events.

⚠ B6 🏠 3 Bells Court, Falmouth
🌐 beerwolfbooks.com

From Discovery Quay, the South West Coast Path *(p165)* heads uphill to **Pendennis Castle**, a striking circular artillery fort built by King Henry VIII. Displays inside focus on the fort's role during Tudor times and World War II.

From the castle the path continues along the coast to a series of long sandy beaches. The most popular are Gyllyngvase Beach, with a lovely café-restaurant, and

Swanpool, named after the swans on the pool behind it.

To the south are two beautiful gardens: **Trebah** is a subtropical haven, while **Glendurgan** contains a stunning mix of exotic and native plants. Both gardens are set in sheltered valleys leading down to sandy coves on the Helford.

Falmouth Art Gallery

⌂ The Moor ⏰ 10am–4pm Mon–Fri, 10am–1pm Sat
🔒 1 Jan, 25 & 26 Dec
🌐 falmouthartgallery.com

National Maritime Museum Cornwall

🔵🔵🔵 ⌂ Discovery Quay
⏰ 10am–5pm daily 🔒 24–26 Dec 🌐 nmmc.co.uk

Pendennis Castle

🔵🔵🔵🔵🔵 ⌂ The Headland ⏰ Apr–Oct: 10am–5pm daily; Nov–Mar: 10am–4pm Sat & Sun 🔒 1 Jan & 24–26 Dec 🌐 english-heritage.org.uk

Trebah

🔵🔵🔵 ⌂ Mawnan Smith
⏰ 10am–5pm daily 🔒 25 & 26 Dec 🌐 trebahgarden.co.uk

Glendurgan

🔵🔵🔵🔵 ⌂ Mawnan Smith
⏰ Mid-Feb–Oct: 10:30am–5:30pm Tue–Sun & public hols; Aug: 10:30am–5:30pm daily 🌐 nationaltrust.org.uk

---

⑪

St Mawes

🔺 B6 ⌂ Cornwall 🚌
🚢 To Falmouth, Trelissick Gardens, Truro & Place Creek 🛈 Roseland Visitor Centre; The Square; www.stmawesandtheroseland.co.uk

A pretty and idyllic village of whitewashed cottages and townhouses with gleaming slate roofs, St Mawes has been an exclusive holiday retreat since Edwardian times. The village is set on the lush, rolling Roseland Peninsula

↑ Cathedral Lane, a charming, shop-lined alley in the centre of Truro

in a sheltered, south-facing corner of the Fal Estuary. Often described as England's answer to St Tropez, St Mawes may be chic, but it is also the perfect place to enjoy muddy walks along the river.

Much of the area can be explored by ferry and on foot. The tiny Place Ferry connects the village to one of the most beautiful stretches of the South West Coast Path. Walks from here take you out to the St Anthony headland – whose snowy-white lighthouse appeared in the famous 1980s TV series "Fraggle Rock" – and to Portscatho, passing pristine sandy beaches such as Towan. There is also a 1.5-km (1-mile) walk along the river to the church of St Just-in-Roseland, set within lush subtropical gardens and deemed by John Betjeman to be "the loveliest churchyard on earth".

To the west of the village is the distinctive clover-leaf-shaped **St Mawes Castle**, the best preserved of all of Henry VIII's coastal fortresses. Inside are elaborate stone carvings of the Tudor Royal Arms, complete with Latin inscriptions.

St Mawes Castle

🔵🔵🔵🔵 ⌂ Castle Drive
⏰ 10am–4pm Sat & Sun
🌐 english-heritage.org.uk

---

⑫

Truro

🔺 B6 ⌂ Cornwall
🚌 Green St 🚂 Trelissick Gardens, St Mawes and Falmouth 🛈 30 Boscawen St; www.visittruro.org.uk

A historic city and one-time port, Truro is now the administrative capital of Cornwall. Truro's Victorian cathedral of 1876 was the first to be built since St Paul's (p66) in London. With its central tower, lancet windows and spires, it looks more French than English.

The **Royal Cornwall Museum** gives an introduction to the history of the county, with displays on tin mining, Methodism and smuggling.

Royal Cornwall Museum

🔵🔵 ⌂ River St ⏰ 10am–4:45pm Mon–Sat (also Sun in Aug) 🔒 25 Dec & 1 Jan 🌐 royalcornwallmuseum.org.uk.

↑ A sleeping giant in the atmospheric Lost Gardens of Heligan, St Austell

⓭ St Austell

🅰C6 🏛Cornwall 🚌🚆
ℹ️ Behind Texaco Service Station, Southbourne Rd; www.staustellbay.co.uk

The busy industrial town of St Austell is the capital of the local china clay industry, which rose to importance in the 18th century. At the **Wheal Martyn China Clay Museum**, displays evoke the history and human impact of clay and clay quarrying, while nature trails weave through the abandoned clay works.

Wheal Martyn China Clay Museum

🏛🖥🛍 Carthew 🕙10am-4pm daily 🚫24 Dec-mid-Jan
🌐wheal-martyn.com

⓮ Looe

🅰C6 🏛Cornwall 🚆🚌🚢
ℹ️Looe Library, Millpool; www.visitlooe.co.uk

A fishing village and seaside resort, Looe straddles the mouth of its homonymous river, the two sides connected by a seven-arched bridge. In Victorian times, Looe was a popular holiday resort and it continues to attract crowds today, who come for an old-fashioned British seaside

holiday and to pick up the latest catches from the famous daily harbourside fish market.

⓯ Lost Gardens of Heligan

🅰C6 🏛Pentewan, St Austell, Cornwall
🚆🚌 🕙Gardens & Estate: Apr-Sep: 10am-6pm daily; Oct-Mar: 10am-5pm daily
🚫25 Dec 🌐heligan.com

Following the deaths of 16 of the 22 gardeners during World War I, these enchanting gardens lay forgotten until Tim Smit (who went on to develop the Eden Project) rediscovered them in the 1990s. Inspired by the story of the lost gardeners, Smit set about not simply restoring the gardens, but reviving the traditional low-impact farming and cultivation methods that had evolved here over the centuries.

⓰ Bodmin

🅰C5 🏛Cornwall
🚉Bodmin Parkway
🚌Bodmin ℹ️Mount Folly Sq; www.bodminlive.com

Cornwall's ancient county town lies on the sheltered western edge of Bodmin Moor. The history and archaeology of

the town and moor are covered by **Bodmin Town Museum**, while **Bodmin Jail**, built in 1779 by prisoners of war, contains interactive exhibits focusing on life inside the jail.

South of Bodmin is the famous National Trust-owned **Lanhydrock** estate, with its immaculate parkland, formal gardens and lovely Victorian manor house, which dates from the 17th century; only parts of the original structure still exist. Visits give an insight into the life of a country house, covering the kitchens, nurseries and servants' rooms as well as the quarters of the family that lived here – there's even a Victorian schoolroom. Exhibits also examine the impact of World War I on the estate.

The wilderness of Bodmin Moor is noted for its network of prehistoric field boundaries. The main attraction, however, is the 18th-century Jamaica Inn, made famous by Daphne du Maurier's tale of smuggling and romance. Today there is a museum telling the story of smuggling and a room devoted to the author.

Bodmin Town Museum

🕙 🏛Mt Folly Sq 🕒Easter-Oct: Mon-Sat & Good Fri 🚫Public hols 🌐museumsin cornwall.org.uk

---

TOP 3 CORNISH GARDENS

Eden Project
An enormous array of plants in two biomes - one Mediterranean, the other Rainforest (p186).

Trelissick
🌐nationaltrust.org.uk
Renowned for its hydrangeas and Mediterranean species.

Trewidden
🌐trewidden.co.uk
A maze of tree ferns, azaleas, camellias and magnolias.

Bodmin Jail

🎨🍴💻🛍 🅰 Berrycombe Rd
🕐 May–Oct: 9:30am–8:30pm
daily (Nov–Apr: to 6:30pm)
🗓 25 Dec 🆆 bodminjail.org

Lanhydrock

🎨🍴🏠(NT) 🅰 Bodmin
🕐 House: Mar–Oct: 11am–5pm
daily; Gardens: mid-Feb–Oct:
10am–5:30pm daily 🗓 25
Dec 🆆 nationaltrust.org.uk

---

⑰
Fowey

🅰 C6 🅰 Cornwall 🅸 5 South
St; www.fowey.co.uk

The river, creeks and gentle
waters of the Fowey (pro-
nounced Foy) Estuary were
most likely the inspiration for
The Wind in the Willows, whose
author Kenneth Grahame
regularly spent holidays here.
The picturesque charm of the
village is undeniable, with its
tangle of tiny and steep
flower-filled streets, seafood
restaurants and views across
the estuary to Polruan.

The Church of St Fimbarrus
marks the end of the ancient
Saint's Way footpath from
Padstow, a reminder of the
Celtic missionaries who arrived
on the shores of Cornwall to
convert people to Christianity.

Inside, there are some fine
17th-century memorials to the
Rashleigh family, whose seat,
Menabilly, became Daphne
du Maurier's home and
featured as Manderley in
her novel *Rebecca* (1938).

---

⑱ 🎨🍴💻🛍 (NT)
Cotehele

🅰 D5 🅰 St Dominick,
near Saltash 🚉 Saltash
🕐 House: mid-Mar–Oct:
11am–4pm daily, Nov–
Dec: 10:30am–4pm daily;
Grounds: dawn–dusk daily
🆆 nationaltrust.org.uk

Magnificent woodland and
lush river scenery make the
grand estate of Cotehele
(pronounced "Coteal") one of
the most lovely spots on the
River Tamar.

Built mainly between 1489
and 1520, Cotehele is a rare
example of a Tudor manor
house, and is set around three
courtyards with a magnificent
open hall, kitchen, chapel and
a warren of private parlours
and chambers. The romance
of the house is enhanced by
colourful terraced gardens to
the east, leading via a tunnel
into a richly planted valley
garden. The path through this
garden passes a domed medieval dovecote and descends
to Cotehele Quay. The quay is
now home to the Shamrock,
a restored sailing barge. The
estate includes Cotehele Mill,
a working mill producing
wholemeal flour. Visitors can
also explore wheelwright,
saddler and blacksmith
workshops, and there is a
traditional furniture-maker
and a working potter.

↑ Small boats in the
charming harbour of
the village of Fowey

↑ Picturesque Chapel Street, leading to St Mary the Virgin church, Penzance

19 Penzance

🅰 B6 **🏛 Cornwall** 🚆🚌🚢
ℹ Station Approach;
www.lovepenzance.co.uk

Penzance is a bustling resort town and port with a climate so mild that palm trees and subtropical plants grow happily in the lush Morrab Gardens. The town offers fine views of St Michael's Mount and Marazion Beach, a great sweep of golden sands across the bay.

The main road through the town is Market Jew Street, at the top of which stands the magnificent domed Market House (1837), fronted by a statue of Sir Humphrey Davy (1778–1829). Davy invented the miner's safety lamp, which detected lethal gases in mines.

Colourful Chapel Street is lined with curious buildings, like the flamboyant Egyptian House (1835), with its richly painted façade and lotus bud decoration, and Admiral Benbow Inn (1696), which has a pirate perched on the roof looking out to sea.

A short walk south from Chapel Street is **Jubilee Pool**, an iconic Art Deco lido which, in 2020, became the UK's first outdoor pool to be heated by geothermal energy. The popular pool was originally opened in 1935 and was built in an unusual triangular shape to complement the line of the coast and help the walls withstand strong waves.

The **Penlee House Gallery and Museum** has many pictures by the local Newlyn School of artists, founded by Stanhope Forbes. The group painted outdoors, aiming to capture the fleeting impressions of wind, sun and sea. The namesake town of Newlyn, which is Cornwall's largest fishing port, is located just south of Penzance.

North of Penzance, and overlooking the beautiful Cornish coast, is **Chysauster**, a fine example of a Romano-British village. Visitors are able to walk around the fascinating site which has remained almost undisturbed since it was abandoned during the 3rd century AD.

From Penzance, regular boat services depart for the Isles of Scilly, an enchanting archipelago forming part of the same granite mass as Land's End, Bodmin Moor and Dartmoor. Along with tourism, flower-growing is the main source of income on the islands – fields of scented narcissi and pinks only add to the exceptional wild beauty of the islands.

Jubilee Pool

🅐🅑 🏛 Battery Road
🕐 Times vary, check website
🌐 jubileepool.co.uk

Penlee House Gallery and Museum

🅐🅑🅒 🏛 Morrab Rd
🕐 10am–5pm Mon–Sat (Nov–Mar: to 4:30pm)
🌐 penleehouse.org.uk

Chysauster

🅐🅑🅒 🏛 Off B3311 🕐 Apr–Jun & Oct: 10am–5pm daily; Jul & Aug: 10am–6pm daily; Sep, Nov–Mar: 10am–4pm daily
🌐 english-heritage.org.uk

⛰ GREAT VIEW
Tremenheere Sculpture Garden

A short distance from Penzance is the beautifully located Tremenheere Sculpture Garden. Take a tour here to see an array of exotic plants, plus stunning views over the bay and St Michael's Mount.

20 🏛️ 🅜 🍴 🖥️ 🛍️ NT

St Michael's Mount

A B6 **Ⓜ** Marazion **🚌** From Marazion (Mar–Oct) or on foot at low tide **Ⓞ** Castle: mid-Mar–Oct: 10:30am–5pm Sun–Fri; Garden: mid-Apr–Jun: 10:30am–5pm Mon–Fri; Jul–Sep: 10:30am–5:30pm Thu & Fri **W** stmichaels mount.co.uk

This craggy island, which emerges dramatically from the waters of Mounts Bay, has inspired many myths and stories of magic. The most famous local legend tells of a giant, named Cormoran, who once lived here and terrorized the land; he was finally vanquished by a young farmer's son named Jack.

According to many Roman historians, the mount was the island of Ictis, an important centre for the Cornish tin trade during the Iron Age. It is dedicated to the archangel St Michael who is said to have appeared here in AD 495.

CORNISH SMUGGLERS

In the days before income tax, the main form of government income came from tax on luxury goods, such as brandy and perfume, which were imported to England by boat. As a consequence, huge profits were to be made by evading these taxes. With its coves and rivers penetrating deep into the mainland, Cornwall was prime smuggling territory; estimates put the number of people involved at 100,000. Some people resorted to deliberate wrecking, setting up deceptive lights to lure vessels onto the sharp rocks, in the hope of plundering the wreckage.

When the Normans conquered England in 1066, they were struck by the island's resemblance to Mont-St-Michel, whose Benedictine monks were then invited to build an abbey here. The abbey was then absorbed into a fortress during the Dissolution, when Henry VIII set up coastal defences to counter an attack from France. In 1659, the mount was bought by Colonel John St Aubyn, whose descendants turned the historic fortress into a magnificent house. It is now managed by the National Trust.

↑ Playing on the beach, with St Michael's Mount rising in the distance

---

Access to the island is by boat from Marazion or on foot by a cobbled causeway at low tide.

The Armoury displays military trophies brought back by the St Aubyn family from various wars.

The Chevy Chase Room takes its name from a plaster frieze (1641) that depicts hunting scenes.

These rocky slopes are planted with subtropical trees and shrubs.

Rebuilt in the late 14th century, Priory Church is at the summit of the island.

The Blue Drawing Room is decorated in Rococo Gothic style and features paintings by Thomas Gainsborough and Joshua Reynolds.

Castle entrance

The South Terrace forms the roof of the large Victorian wing.

Harbourside village

St Michael's Mount, known in Roman times as the island of Ictis

A DRIVING TOUR
PENWITH

Length 50 km (30 miles) **Stopping-off points** There are pubs and cafés in most villages. Sennen Cove makes a pleasant midway stop.

This driving tour passes through a spectacular, remote Cornish landscape, dotted with relics of the tin-mining industry, picturesque fishing villages and many prehistoric remains. The magnificent coastline varies between gentle rolling moorland in the north and the rugged, windswept cliffs that characterize the dramatic south coast. The beauty of the area, combined with the clarity of light, has attracted artists since the 19th century. Their work can be seen in Newlyn, St Ives and Penzance.

Did You Know?

Cornwall has its own language. It is not widely spoken but is taught in some schools.

Derelict engine-houses clinging to the cliffside at **Botallack Mine** are a vivid reminder of the region's former industry of tin mining.

↑ Engine-houses perched on the edge of cliffs at Botallack

Land's End is England's most westerly point and noted for its dramatic and wild landscape. A local exhibition reveals its history, geology and wildlife.

Morvah
Pendeen
B3306
Trewellard
B3318
FINISH
Botallack Mine
Botallack
St Just
A3071
Bosavern
Kelynack
B3306
A30
Whitesand Bay
A30
Sennen Cove
Sennen
Land's End
B3315
Porthcurno
Treen
Minack Theatre

0 kilometres 3
0 miles 3

N ↑

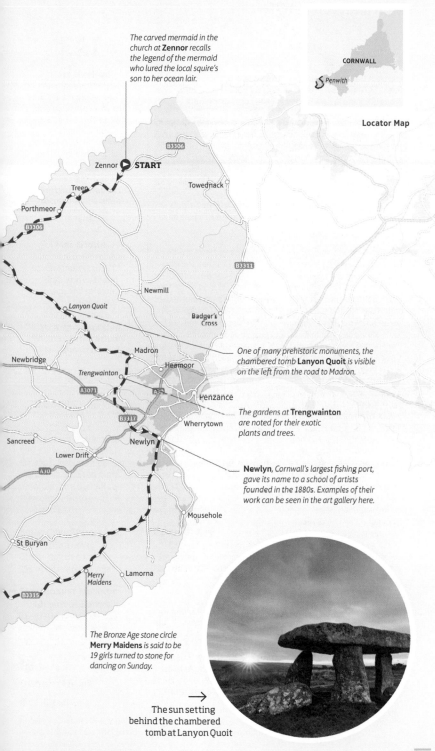

The carved mermaid in the church at **Zennor** recalls the legend of the mermaid who lured the local squire's son to her ocean lair.

CORNWALL

Penwith

Locator Map

B3306

Zennor ○ **START**

Treen

Towednack

Porthmeor

B3306

B3311

Newmill

Lanyon Quoit

Badger's Cross

Madron

One of many prehistoric monuments, the chambered tomb **Lanyon Quoit** is visible on the left from the road to Madron.

Newbridge

Heamoor

Trengwainton

A3071

A30

Penzance

The gardens at **Trengwainton** are noted for their exotic plants and trees.

B3317

Wherrytown

Sancreed

Newlyn

Newlyn, Cornwall's largest fishing port, gave its name to a school of artists founded in the 1880s. Examples of their work can be seen in the art gallery here.

Lower Drift

A30

Mousehole

St Buryan

Lamorna

Merry Maidens

B3315

The Bronze Age stone circle **Merry Maidens** is said to be 19 girls turned to stone for dancing on Sunday.

→
The sun setting behind the chambered tomb at Lanyon Quoit

A DRIVING TOUR
BODMIN MOOR

Bodmin
Moor

CORNWALL

Locator Map

Length 69 km (43 miles) **Stopping-off points** Jamaica Inn and the Blisland Inn are great places to stop for food. To hike to Rough Tor and Brown Willy, park at Rough Tor car park.

Bodmin Moor is a huge expanse of bleak moorland and dramatic granite tors at the heart of Cornwall. This great inland wilderness lies over an outcrop of the granite batholith that runs from Dartmoor through the Cornish peninsula and under the sea to the Scilly Isles and beyond. Covering 207 sq km (80 sq miles), it is a landscape of mystery and legend, with sacred prehistoric sites, a history of smuggling and many associations with King Arthur.

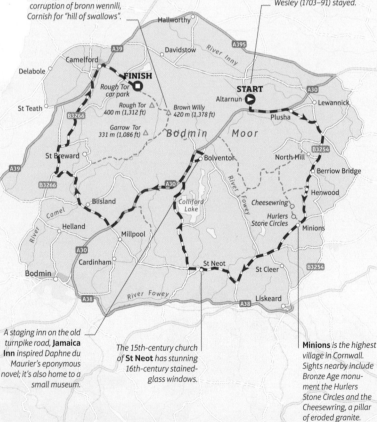

At 420 m (1,378 ft), **Brown Willy** *is the highest point in Cornwall. Its name is a corruption of bronn wennili, Cornish for "hill of swallows".*

Altarnun *village is home to the 15th-century Church of St Nonna, which is known as the Cathedral of the Moor. Nearby at Five Lanes is Wesley's Cottage, where the Methodist preacher John Wesley (1703–91) stayed.*

Hallworthy
Davidstow
River Inny
A395
A39
Camelford
Delabole
FINISH
Rough Tor car park
St Teath
B3266
Rough Tor △ 400 m (1,312 ft)
Garrow Tor △ 331 m (1,086 ft)
Brown Willy △ 420 m (1,378 ft)
START
Altarnun
A30
Lewannick
Plusha
Bodmin Moor
B3254
North Hill
Berriow Bridge
St Breward
B3266
Bolventor
River Fowey
Henwood
A39
A30
Blisland
Colliford Lake
Cheesewring
Hurlers Stone Circles
Minions
Camel River
Helland
Millpool
Cardinham
Bodmin
River Fowey
St Neot
St Cleer
B3254
Liskeard
A38
A38

A staging inn on the old turnpike road, **Jamaica Inn** *inspired Daphne du Maurier's eponymous novel; it's also home to a small museum.*

The 15th-century church of **St Neot** *has stunning 16th-century stained-glass windows.*

Minions *is the highest village in Cornwall. Sights nearby include Bronze Age monument the Hurlers Stone Circles and the Cheesewring, a pillar of eroded granite.*

0 kilometres 5
0 miles 5

N ↑

Remains of old engine-houses, ↑ which were part of Wheal Jenkin mine on Bodmin Moor

NEED TO KNOW

Train on the Greenway Viaduct, Devon

BEFORE
YOU GO

Things change, so plan ahead to make the most of your trip. Be prepared for all eventualities by considering the following points before you travel.

AT A GLANCE

CURRENCY
Pound Sterling (GBP)

AVERAGE DAILY SPEND

SAVE	SPEND	SPLURGE
£70	£125	£200+

BOTTLED WATER	COFFEE	BEER	DINNER FOR TWO
£1	£2.80	£5	£70

CLIMATE

The longest days occur May–Aug, while Oct–Feb sees the shortest daylight hours.

Daytime highs average 22°C (75°F) in summer. Winter can be cold and icy.

The heaviest rainfall is in October and November, but showers occur all year round.

ELECTRICITY SUPPLY

Power sockets are type G, fitting three-pronged plugs. Standard voltage is 230 volts.

Passports and Visas

For entry requirements, including visas, consult your nearest British embassy or check the **UK Government** website. Post-Brexit arrangements for citizens from EEA countries will vary depending on the terms agreed; rights of Irish citizens will not change.
UK Government
🆆 gov.uk/check-uk-visa
🆆 gov.uk/guidance/visiting-the-uk-after-brexit

Government Advice

Now, more than ever, it is important to consult both your and the UK government's advice before travelling. The **UK Foreign and Commonwealth Office**, the **US State Department** and the **Australian Department of Foreign Affairs and Trade** offer the latest information on security, health and regulations.
Australia
🆆 smartraveller.gov.au
UK
🆆 gov.uk/foreign-travel-advice
US
🆆 travel.state.gov

Customs Information

You can find information on the laws relating to goods and currency taken in or out of the UK on the **UK Government** website.
UK Government
🆆 gov.uk/duty-free-goods

Insurance

We recommend that you take out a comprehensive insurance policy covering theft, loss of belongings, medical care, cancellations and delays, and read the small print carefully.

Emergency treatment is usually free from the National Health Service (**NHS**) for UK residents, and there are reciprocal arrangements with Australia, New Zealand and some others (check the NHS website for details). Healthcare arrangements for EEA citizens – covered by the

European Health Insurance Card (**EHIC**) – are likely to change in 2021. Check the NHS website for the most up-to-date information.
EHIC
[w] gov.uk/european-health-insurance-card
NHS
[w] nhs.uk

Vaccinations

No inoculations are needed for the UK.

Money

Major credit and debit cards, plus contactless payments, are widely accepted. Some smaller businesses and markets, however, operate a cash-only policy. Cash machines are located at banks, train stations and main high streets.

Tipping in England is discretionary. In restaurants it's customary to tip 10–12.5 per cent for good service. It is usual to tip taxi drivers 10 per cent, and hotel porters, concierge and housekeeping £1–2 per bag or day.

Booking Accommodation

England offers a variety of accommodation, from family-run B&Bs to budget hostels.

Lodgings can fill up and prices become inflated during the summer, so it is worth booking well in advance. The lists of accommodation maintained by local tourist boards are useful but international booking engines have the best nationwide coverage.

Travellers with Specific Requirements

The best guide for wheelchair users is *Holidays in the British Isles* published by **Disability Rights UK**. Many modern buildings and infrastructure have been designed with wheelchairs in mind, while most trains and buses have been adapted for wheelchair use. Accessibility information for public transport is available from regional public transport websites.

Many major museums and galleries offer audio tours and induction loops for those with impaired sight and hearing. **Action on Hearing Loss** and the **Royal National Institute for the Blind** offer information and advice.

Action on Hearing Loss
[w] actionhearingloss.org.uk
Disability Rights UK
[w] disabilityrightsuk.org
Royal National Institute for the Blind
[w] rnib.org.uk

Language

English is spoken throughout England's southern regions. Accents vary tremendously, however, and can at times be stronger in certain areas.

Opening Hours

> **COVID-19** The pandemic continues to affect England. Some museums, tourist attractions and hospitality venues are operating on reduced or temporary opening hours, and require visitors to make advance bookings for a specific date and time. Always check ahead before visiting.

Mondays Some museums and attractions close.
Sundays Most shops operate limited opening.
Public holidays Some shops and attractions either close or operate shorter hours.

PUBLIC HOLIDAYS	
1 Jan	New Year's Day
2 Apr (2021) 15 Apr (2022)	Good Friday
5 Apr (2021) 18 Apr (2022)	Easter Monday
3 May (2021) 2 May (2022)	Early May Bank Holiday
31 May (2021) 2 & 3 Jun (2022)	Spring Bank Holiday
30 Aug (2021) 29 Aug (2022)	Summer Bank Holiday
25 Dec	Christmas Day
26 Dec	Boxing Day

GETTING AROUND

Whether you're visiting for a short city break or planning a coastal retreat, discover how best to reach your destination and travel like a pro.

AT A GLANCE

PUBLIC TRANSPORT COSTS

SINGLE BUS JOURNEY

£1.50

London zones 1-9
(flat fare)

SINGLE TUBE JOURNEY

£2.40

London zones 1-2
(off peak)

DAILY TRAVELCARD

£13.10

London zones 1-6
(off peak)

SPEED LIMIT

MOTORWAY

70 mph
(110 km/h)

DUAL CARRIAGEWAYS

70 mph
(110 km/h)

SINGLE CARRIAGEWAYS

60 mph
(95 km/h)

URBAN AREAS

30 mph
(50 km/h)

Arriving by Air

The south of England is well served by a number of airports. The largest is Heathrow, west of London. Served by leading airlines and with direct flights to and from most major cities, it is one of the world's busiest international airports and a principal European hub. Gatwick, south of London, plus Stansted and Luton, account for a third of UK air traffic. Outside of London, Bristol and Southampton have regular flights to and from Europe.

Train Travel

International Train Travel

St Pancras International is the London terminus for Eurostar, the high-speed train linking the UK with Europe. Buy tickets and passes for multiple international journeys via **Eurail** or **Interrail**; you may still need to pay an additional reservation fee for certain trains. Always check that your pass is valid on the service on which you wish to travel before boarding.

Eurostar runs a regular service from Paris, Brussels and Amsterdam to London via the Channel Tunnel. **Eurotunnel** operates a drive-on-drive-off train service between Calais and Folkestone, in the south of England.

Eurail
W eurail.com
Eurostar
W eurostar.com
Eurotunnel
W eurotunnel.com
Interrail
W interrail.eu

Domestic Train Travel

The UK's railway system is complicated and can be confusing. Lines are run by several companies, but they are coordinated by **National Rail**, which operates a joint information service. The railway is generally reliable, though it is best to check online before travelling. Always try to book rail tickets in advance. If you have a disability and need assistance, call the train operator in advance.

Travel across the region via train is more than doable, but most journeys will involve changes and possibly travelling via London. London's Paddington, Victoria, Waterloo, St Pancras and London Bridge stations serve the south. There are also over 300 smaller London stations. Each main terminus is the starting point for local and suburban lines that cover the whole of south-east England. For visitors, rail services are most useful for trips to the outskirts of London and areas of the city without nearby Underground connections (especially in south London).

Train tickets can be bought online, by phone and at railway stations. An advance ticket is usually cheaper than one bought on the day. While tickets are available from National Rail, third-party online portals, such as **Trainline**, usually offer discounted fares.

If you plan to travel extensively by train, consider buying a rail pass. **BritRail** offers three passes covering the south, while the **Network Railcard** could save you up to a third on travel.

BritRail
w britrail.com

National Rail
w nationalrail.co.uk
Network Railcard
w network-railcard.co.uk
Trainline
w thetrainline.com

Long-Distance Bus Travel

In England, long-distance buses are usually referred to as "coaches". The biggest operator is **National Express**, which serves several hundred destinations in southern England and offers online discounts. It is advisable to book ahead for the more popular routes.

The **Megabus** is a cheap-and-cheerful alternative to National Express, with tickets to a number of south coast destinations, including Bristol, Plymouth and Exeter, available from as little as £1 (plus a 50p booking fee), providing you book well ahead.

National Express
w nationalexpress.com
Megabus
w uk.megabus.com

RAIL JOURNEY PLANNER

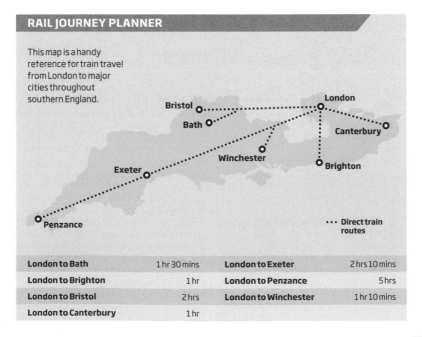

This map is a handy reference for train travel from London to major cities throughout southern England.

London to Bath	1 hr 30 mins	**London to Exeter**	2 hrs 10 mins
London to Brighton	1 hr	**London to Penzance**	5 hrs
London to Bristol	2 hrs	**London to Winchester**	1 hr 10 mins
London to Canterbury	1 hr		

Public Transport

Public transport in the UK is a combination of private-sector and city-operated services. Most cities have only bus systems, though London has a fully integrated public transport system, with underground and light suburban railway networks. Most public transport in London is coordinated by Transport for London (**TFL**). Safety and hygiene measures, timetables, ticket information, transport maps and more can be found on their website.

TFL
Ⓦ tfl.gov.uk

Travelling in London

TFL divides London into six charging zones for Underground, Overground and National Rail services, radiating out from Zone 1 in the centre to Zone 6.

Tickets and travelcards can be bought at stations, but paper tickets are expensive and most people use a contactless debit or credit card, or an Oyster Card (a prepaid electronic card that can be "topped up" for use on all forms of TFL transport). Both contactless and Oyster payments are subject to daily and weekly caps.

When using public transport, you "touch in" with your card on a yellow card reader, and the corresponding amount is deducted. On Underground, DLR and Overground trains, "touch out" where you finish your journey, or you will be charged a maximum fare.

London Underground and DLR

The London Underground (referred to as "the Tube") has 11 lines, all named and colour-coded, which intersect at various stations. The construction of a new line, the Elizabeth line, is underway and will open in late 2021 at the earliest.

Trains run every few minutes 7:30–9:30am and 4–7pm, and every 5–10 minutes at all other times. The Central, Jubilee, Northern, Victoria and Piccadilly lines offer a 24-hour service on selected routes on Fridays and Saturdays. All other lines operate roughly 5am–12:40am Mon–Sat, with reduced hours on Sun.

The Docklands Light Railway (DLR) is a mostly overground network of trains that run from the City to stops in east and southeast London. It operates roughly 5:30–12:30am Mon–Sat, 7am–11:30pm Sun.

Stations with step-free access are marked on Tube maps, which are located on all trains and at every station.

London Overground

Marked on Tube maps by an orange line, the Overground connects with the Underground and main railway stations at points across the city. It operates in much the same way as the Underground, and covers most areas of the city without nearby Underground connections.

London Buses

Slower but cheaper than the Tube, buses are also a good way of seeing the city as you travel. Bus routes are displayed on the TFL website and on maps at bus stops. The destination and route number is indicated on the front of the bus and the stops are announced on board. Buses do not accept cash so a ticket, Oyster card or contactless payment is required.

A single fare costs £1.50, while unlimited bus travel caps out at £4.50 – just use the same card each time you use the bus to reach the daily cap. The hopper fare allows you to make unlimited bus journeys for free within an hour of travel.

Travel is free on buses for under-16s as long as they carry a Zip Oyster photocard. Apply for one on the TFL website at least four weeks before you are due to arrive.

Night buses (indicated by the letter "N" added before the route number) run on many popular routes from 11pm until 6am, though the service is less frequent than during the day.

Regional Buses

Urban bus networks are generally fast, frequent and reliable. In most cities, a single fare applies for all bus travel within city limits. Multiple-trip tickets and one-day travel passes are available in major cities. These can be bought online and stored on your phone. Single-trip tickets can be bought from the driver when boarding your bus but change is not given so you must pay the exact fare in cash.

Public transport in rural areas is less extensive. Timetables are often designed around the needs of local workers and school students, so schedules are less convenient for visitors, with infrequent departures.

Taxis

Britain has two sorts of taxis. Some, such as London's iconic black cabs, can be hailed on the street and are identified by a yellow sign on the roof that's illuminated when the cab is available. The other sorts of taxis are private-hire minicabs, such as **Dial-a-Cab** and **Gett Taxis**; practically every town or city will have its own local service. Private taxis are generally lightly modified regular cars or minibuses, and are usually only bookable online or by phone. All taxis are metered, with fares locally set, but usually starting at around £2.50. Taxi apps such as Uber also operate around England.

Dial-a-Cab
Ⓦ dialacab.co.uk
Gett Taxis
Ⓦ get.com/uk

Driving

For visitors from abroad, driving in England is a challenge simply because you drive on the left. The measurement of distances in miles can add to the confusion, as can narrow roads, the many roundabouts, congestion and scarce parking in most cities. But in rural areas driving can be a pleasure and the key way to get around.

Driving to England

For those driving to southern England, the simplest way is to use the Eurotunnel shuttles between Calais in France and Folkestone, both of which have direct motorway access. From Folkestone it is possible to drive to London in about two hours. To take your own foreign-registered car into and around England, you will need to carry the vehicle's registration and insurance documents, a full and valid driving licence, and valid passport or national ID at all times. EU driving licences issued by any of the EU member states are valid (though this situation may change following the UK's departure from the EU). If visiting from outside the EU, or if your licence is not in English, you may need to apply for an International Driving Permit (IDP). Check with your local automobile association or consult the UK **Driver and Vehicle Licensing Agency** (DVLA) for the latest regulations.
Driver and Vehicle Licensing Agency
🌐 dvlaregistrations.direct.gov.uk

Driving in England

Though often busy, England's roads are generally good, with motorways or dual-carriageway highways connecting all major towns and cities. In rural areas, sealed roads connect almost all communities, though in remote areas these may be a single carriageway, shared with oncoming traffic and using designated passing places.

In the event of a breakdown, contact the **AA**, a British motoring association, for roadside assistance. This may be free if you are a member of a partner organization in your home country.
AA
🌐 theaa.com

Driving in London

Driving in London is not recommended; traffic is heavy and parking scarce, plus there is the added cost of the **Congestion Charge** – a £15 daily charge for driving in central London between 7am and 10pm Monday to Friday.
Congestion Charge
🌐 tfl.gov.uk/modes/driving/congestion-charge

Rules of the Road

Drive on the left. Seat belts must be worn at all times by the driver and all passengers. Children up to 135 cm (4 ft) tall or of the age of 12 or under must travel with the correct child restraint for their weight and size.

Overtake on the outside or right-hand lane. When approaching a roundabout, give priority to traffic approaching from the right, unless indicated otherwise. All vehicles must give way to emergency services vehicles. It is illegal to drive in bus lanes during restricted hours, as posted on roadside signs. Third-party motor insurance is required by law, but fully comprehensive insurance is strongly advised.

The drink-driving limit (p213) is strictly enforced and penalties upon conviction can be severe. Avoid drinking alcohol completely if you plan to drive. Mobile phones may not be used while driving except with a "handsfree" system.

Car Rental

To rent a car you must be 21 years of age or over (or in some cases, 25) and have held a valid driver's licence for at least a year. You will also need a credit card for the rental deposit. Rental cars with automatic transmission are rare, and must be booked in advance. Returning a car to a different location will incur surcharges.

Driving out of central London will take about an hour in any direction, more during rush hours; if you plan to travel to the southern counties it can be easier to take a train to a town or city outside of London and rent a car from there.

Cycling

England's country roads make touring by bicycle a real joy. The National Cycling Network, created by **Sustrans**, provides more than 20,000 km (12,427 miles) of cycle paths across Britain, ranging from off-road routes to gentle traffic-free trails, suitable for families. A bike can be taken on most off-peak trains, but you may have to book a spot for it. Check before you travel.

Cycling is one of the greenest ways of getting around London – though you might need a strong nerve to cope with the city's traffic. **Santander Cycles**, London's self-service cycle hire scheme, has docking stations throughout the centre.

Drink-drive limits also apply to cyclists.
Santander Cycles
🌐 tfl.gov.uk/modes/cycling/santander-cycles
Sustrans
🌐 sustrans.org.uk

Walking

An extensive network of footpaths covers the south of England. The region's main cities, including London and Bristol, are also eminently walkable (in London, you'll be surprised at how short the distance is between places that seem far apart on the Tube), making for a rewarding way to see the sights.

PRACTICAL
INFORMATION

A little local know-how goes a long way. Here you'll find all the essential advice and information you will need during your stay.

AT A GLANCE

EMERGENCY NUMBERS

GENERAL
EMERGENCY

999

TIME ZONE
GMT/BST
British Summer Time
(BST) runs late March
to late October.

TAP WATER
Unless otherwise
stated, tap water
in England is safe
to drink.

APPS

what3words
Dividing the world into 3 m x 3 m squares,
this geocode system pinpoints your exact
location - ideal when exploring England's
expansive countryside.

TFL Oyster and contactless
Top up and manage Oyster payments for
London transport with this app from TFL.

Trainline
Use this app to find the cheapest train
tickets and check journey times.

Visit England
Detailed website with tourist
information, including help with
accommodation.

Personal Security

England is a generally safe country to visit.
Use your common sense and be alert to your
surroundings. If you have anything stolen,
report the crime as soon as possible at the
nearest police station. Get a copy of the crime
report in order to claim on your insurance.
Contact your embassy or consulate immediately
if your passport is stolen, or in the event of a
serious crime or accident.

Be careful around the sea – currents can
change quickly. Never enter the water when a
red warning flag is flying. To locate beaches
supervised by a lifeguard, visit the **Royal
National Lifeboat Institution** (RNLI) website.

The English are generally accepting of all
people, regardless of their race, gender or
sexuality. Homosexuality was legalized in
England in 1967 and the UK recognized the
right to legally change your gender in 2004;
LGBT+ rights here are now considered among
the most progressive in Europe. Many English
cities, particularly London and Brighton, have
vibrant LGBT+ scenes. Despite all the freedoms
that the LGBT+ community enjoys, however,
acceptance is not necessarily a given. If you do
feel unsafe, the **Safe Space Alliance** pinpoints
your nearest place of refuge.

Royal National Lifeboat Institution
w rnli.org
Safe Space Alliance
w safespacealliance.com

Health

The UK has a world-class healthcare system and
emergency medical care is generally free. If you
have an EHIC *(p207)*, and it is still valid, be sure to
present this as soon as possible. Visitors from
abroad may have to pay upfront for medical
treatment and reclaim on insurance at a later
date; check the NHS website *(p207)* for details of
reciprocal agreements in place for treatment
between your home country and the UK.

For minor ailments go to a pharmacy or
chemist. These are plentiful throughout the
region; chains such as Boots and Superdrug

have branches in almost every shopping district. You may need a doctor's prescription to obtain certain pharmaceuticals; the pharmacist can inform you of the closest doctor's surgery or medical centre where you can be seen by a GP (general practitioner).

If you have an accident or medical problem requiring non-urgent medical attention, find details of your nearest non emergency medical service on the NHS website. Alternatively, contact **NHS 111** (the NHS emergency care service) at any hour online or by phone. If things are serious, call 999 or go to your nearest Accident and Emergency (A&E) department.

England has no special health issues, but hikers might pick up ticks, which can carry Lyme disease; if you see a tick on your body, contact a doctor or pharmacist promptly.

NHS 111
w 111.nhs.uk

Smoking, Alcohol and Drugs

Smoking and "vaping" are banned in all public spaces. However, many bars and restaurants have outdoor areas where smoking is permitted.

Alcohol may not be sold to or bought for anyone under 18. The UK legal limit for drivers is 80 mg of alcohol per 100 ml of blood, or 0.08 per cent BAC (blood alcohol content). This is roughly equivalent to one small glass of wine or a pint of regular-strength lager; however, it is best to avoid drinking altogether if you plan to drive.

Possession of all recreational drugs is an offence and could result in a prison sentence.

ID

There is no requirement for visitors to carry ID, but in the case of a routine check you may be asked to show your passport and visa documentation. Anyone who looks under 18 (and in some cases, under 25) may be asked for photo ID to prove their age when buying alcohol.

Responsible Tourism

Be sure to familiarize yourself with England's **Countryside Code** before you set off. This sets out the responsibilities of visitors to the countryside and includes such things as taking away your litter, keeping dogs under effective control, and leaving gates and property as you found them.

Countryside Code
w gov.uk/government/publications/the-countryside-code

Mobile Phones and Wi-Fi

Free Wi-Fi hotspots are widely available in city centres. Cafés and restaurants may give you their Wi-Fi password, providing you make a purchase. Visitors from outside the UK should check whether they are affected by data roaming charges.

Post

Post office branches and counters, plus England's distinctive red post boxes, are found in most cities and towns throughout the region. They generally open 9am–5:30pm Monday–Friday and until 12:30pm Saturday. Stamps – 1st class, 2nd class and international – are available in post offices, shops and supermarkets.

Taxes and Refunds

Value Added Tax (VAT) is charged at 20 per cent and almost always included in the marked price. Stores offering tax-free shopping display a distinctive sign and will provide a VAT 407 form to validate when you leave the country. EU residents should check www.gov.uk for the lastest advice.

Discount Cards

Most attractions offer concessionary rates for children, seniors and students. If you are a student, the **International Student Identity Card** (ISIC) is recommended. Some city tourist offices offer passes and discount cards (such as the **London City Pass**). These are usually worth purchasing if you're in a city for more than a couple of days. If you intend to visit several castles, historic homes and gardens, an annual **National Trust** membership may be worthwhile.

International Student Identity Card
w isic.org
London City Pass
w londonpass.com
National Trust
w nationaltrust.org.uk

INDEX

Page numbers in **bold** refer to main entries

ACKNOWLEDGMENTS

DK would like to thank the following for their contribution to the previous edition: Edward Aves, Ros Belford, Leonie Glass, Matthew Hancock, Philip Lee, Nick Rider, Joe Staines, Amanda Tomlin

The publisher would like to thank the following for their kind permission to reproduce their photographs:

Key: a-above; b-below/bottom; c-centre; f-far; l-left; r-right; t-top

123RF.com: colindamckie 24t; flik47 65c; Serhii Kamshylin 46t.

4Corners: Pietro Canali 188–9t; Nicolò Miana 4; Arcangelo Piai 13cr; Maurizio Rellini 12cl; Maurizio Rellini 24br.

Alamy Stock Photo: Arcaid Images / Nigel Corrie 23tr; Archivart 47bc; Art Collection 2 48tl; Jonathan Ayres 181cra; Martin Bache 156bl; Adrian Baker 126tr, 148cla; Peter Barritt 114bl; Anna Bednarkiewicz 148t; Chris Beer 11br; Kevin Britland 26bl; Michael Brooks 198t; Anthony Brown 34bl; Rick Buettner 138bl; Adam Burton 27crb, 163crb, 164–4t, 176–7; CBCK-Christine 89cra; Denis Chapman 117tl; Chronicle 47tr, 60bc, 61bl; Classic Image 67cr; Colin Cadle Photography 32–3b; Gary Cook 26–7tc; Craig Joiner Photography 203; Peter Cripps 8clb; Ian Dagnall 23tl, 68c, 92–3tc, 94bl, 170–71b, 195tr, Ian G Dagnall 38–9t, 143tl; David Pimborough 24cl; Jon Davison 96–7b; dbphots 150–51; Helen Dixon 201br; Stephen Dorey 47cla; dpa picture alliance archive 61br; Everett Collection 50br / CSU Archives 168bc; eye35.pix 31tr, 134b; Malcolm Fairman 64–5b; Farlap 27bl; Stephen French 95t;

Tim Gainey 45bl; Jeff Gilbert 37tr, 187cra; GL Archive 174bl, 190tr; Dimitar Glavinov 142–3b; Elly Godfroy 39cl; Manfred Gottschalk 163c; Tim Graham 96tl; Granger Historical Picture Archive 50cr; Greg Balfour Evans 11crb; Chris Harris 41c; guy harrop 43c; Clare Havill 44bl; hemis.fr / Gerault Gregory 10clb; Heritage Image Partnership Ltd 94cr; Heritage Images / Ashmolean Museum of Art and Archaeology 46clb / London Metropolitan Archives (City of London) 61bc,/ Werner Forman Archive / Dorset Nat. Hist. & Arch. Soc 46bc; Marc Hill 13t; Jim Holden 105; Sue Holness 125b; Robert Hughes 20bl; Chris Hutty 45c; Ianni Dimitrov Pictures 58–9bc; Image Professionals GmbH / Franz Marc Frei 121tr; Imagebroker / Arco / J. Kruse 147t,/ Helmut Meyer zur Capellen 68bc / Martin Siepmann 162cl; incamerastock / ICP 28tl, 32–3tc, 47cb, 121tl; J Marshall – Tribaleye Images 106bl; graham jepson 39b; Alun John 175br; John Chard St.ives Cornwall 34–5t; John Peter Photography 122b; Bjanka Kadic 68cl; R Kawka 36tl; Alan King 152bl; Oliver Kite 41br; Elitsa Lambova 63tl; Lebrecht Music & Arts 67crb; Loop Images / Mark Bauer 129; De Luan 60br; M.Sobreira 115cra; Luke MacGregor 30–31b; Neil McAllister 146br; Natrow Images 124tl; Kirill Nikitin 45br; Dru Norris 162–3b; James Osmond 164bl; parkerphotography 100–1b; Paul Riddle-VIEW 137cl; Derek Payne 107tr; Roy Perring 174tr; Neil Phillips 43br; Photononstop / Philippe Turpin 149crb; Pictorial Press Ltd 50–51tc, 197tc; PjrTravel 67cra; Prisma by Dukas Presseagentur GmbH 63tr; Lana Rastro 90br; Realimage 10–11bc, 12–13bc; Simon Reddy 13br, 178cra; robertharding 197b / Rob Cousins 136t / Michael Nolan 196tl; Marcin Rogozinski 140bl; Maurice Savage 99tl; Gordon Scammell 35cr, 192bl;

Cover images:
Front: **Shutterstock.com:** Helen Hotson.
Back: **Alamy Stock Photo:** Jeff Gilbert cl;
Getty Images: DigitalVision / Philip Kramer
c, Westend61 tr; **Shutterstock.com:**
Helen Hotson b.
Spine: **Shutterstock.com:** Helen Hotson t.

Illustrators: Peter Bull Art Studio,
Arun Pottirayil

For further information see: www.
dkimages.com

Penguin Random House

This edition updated by
Contributors Rebecca Flynn, Lucy Sara-Kelly,
Hollie Teague, Danielle Watt
Senior Editor Alison McGill
Senior Designers Laura O'Brien,
Stuti Tiwari Bhatia, VInita Venugopal
Project Art Editor Ben Hinks
Editors Rebecca Flynn, Rachel Laidler,
Lucy Sara-Kelly, Danielle Watt
Proofreader Kathryn Glendenning
Indexer Helen Peters
Senior Picture Researcher Sumita Khatwani
Jacket Coordinator Bella Talbot
Jacket Designer Laura O'Brien
Senior Cartographic Editor Casper Morris
Cartography Manager Suresh Kumar
DTP Designers Rohit Rojal, Tanveer Zaidi
Senior Production Editor Jason Little
Production Controller Kariss Ainsworth
Managing Editors Hollie Teague
Deputy Editorial Manager Beverly Smart
Managing Art Editors Bess Daly,
Priyanka Thakur
Art Director Maxine Pedliham
Publishing Director Georgina Dee

First edition 2017

Published in Great Britain by Dorling Kindersley Limited,
One Embassy Gardens, 8 Viaduct Gardens, London SW11 7BW

Published in the United States by DK Publishing,
1450 Broadway, Suite 801, New York, NY 10018

Copyright © 2017, 2021 Dorling Kindersley Limited
A Penguin Random House Company
21 22 23 24 10 9 8 7 6 5 4 3 2 1

The publishers cannot accept responsibility for any consequences
arising from the use of this book, nor for any material on third
party websites, and cannot guarantee that any website address
in this book will be a suitable source of travel information.

A CIP catalog record for this book
is available from the British Library.

A catalog record for this book is available
from the Library of Congress.

ISSN: 1542 1554
ISBN: 978 0 2414 6204 1

Printed and bound in China.

www.dk.com

MIX
Paper from
responsible sources
FSC www.fsc.org **FSC™ C018179**

This book was made with Forest
Stewardship Council ™ certified
paper – one small step in DK's
commitment to a sustainable
future.
For more information go to
www.dk.com/our-green-pledge

A NOTE FROM DK EYEWITNESS

The rapid rate at which the world is changing is
constantly keeping the DK Eyewitness team on our
toes. While we've worked hard to ensure that this
edition of England's South Coast is accurate and
up-to-date, we know that opening hours alter,
standards shift, prices fluctuate, places close and
new ones pop up in their stead. So, if you notice
we've got something wrong or left something out,
we want to hear about it. Please get in touch at
travelguides@dk.com